Praise For *Davonte's Inferno: Ten Years in the New York Public School Gulag*

A devastating look at the experience of teaching in a high-poverty school in the years of the Bloomberg mayoralty. *Davonte's Inferno* is the angriest teacher memoir I have ever read, and perhaps the best written.
Dr. Mark Naison
Chairperson,
Department of African and
African American Studies,
Fordham University

This eye-opening tell-all had me gasping with outrage: what teachers endure these days is beyond abuse. Considering America needs two million new teachers in the next decade, who on earth will sign up for this torture?
Priscilla Sanstead
Co-Founder,
Badass Teachers Association

A brutally honest, gripping tale of life in the trenches of a high-poverty school, in the framework of today's corporate assault on teachers, unions and public education. A must read!
Marla Kilfoyle
Parent Advocate and Educator,
Long Island Opt-Out of Testing,
Parents and Teachers Against Common Core

Laurel M. Sturt contextualizes the nightmare that No Child Left Behind, Race to the Top and the Common Core have brought to public schools, offering readers a first row seat to the experience of teaching under such ill-conceived policies. Rarely is there this level of candor in a discussion about education, and it's a damn good read, to boot.
Catherine Ionata
Veteran Teacher,
Charter School Administrator

DAVONTE'S INFERNO

TEN YEARS IN THE NEW YORK PUBLIC SCHOOL GULAG

LAUREL M. STURT

WRITTEN WARRIOR PRESS
NEW YORK

WW
PRESS

Published by Written Warrior Press, New York
writtenwarriorpress@gmail.com

Library of Congress Control Number: 2013921140
ISBN-13: 978-0-9912051-0-3 (paperback)
ISBN-10: 978-0-9912051-1-0 (e-book)

For questions about public speaking, personal appearances and other considerations, please go to: laurelmsturt.com

Connect on Facebook at: facebook.com/laurel.sturt, facebook.com/davontesinferno.

*This book is dedicated with love to
all those in the trenches, the heroic teachers
of America's urban public schools.
And, of course, to Dad.*

1

"Shut the fuck up!" screamed the math teacher at the top of her lungs, standing on the table glaring down at the eight-year-olds. After being tortured for months, she'd lost it and now had leapt Ninja-style on top of the table of some very impressed, very quiet kids. That is what all of us *want* to do—she had the cojones to actually do it. *Shut the fuck up.* Most schools would have initiated termination proceedings against her. Lisa only got a reprimand with a warning she might not get a satisfactory rating at the end of the year. She did not last that long. A couple weeks later, my friend quit. Another casualty, another statistic among the seventy percent of Teaching Fellows who were leaving within the first three years. Another score for the little infidels.

But they were still just a gleam in my eye. Besides, as I emerged from the train station, I had bigger fish to fry: the armies of muggers I expected to meet in the next six blocks. Hyper-vigilant, scanning the street ahead and off to the sides, I soon realized I had better give the sidewalk equal attention: I had just stepped on a molten blob of chewing gum. It immediately took up residence on the sole of my shoe, stringing determinedly as I walked, branding me with the neighborhood. From now on, I could no longer dismiss this place at the top of the subway map, one I would never in a million years visit. It was useless to try and scrape the gum off on the crumbling curb—continued walking and a steady application of layers of grit would pound it down to the point where it was part of my shoe, and me.

I parsed my way through the dog shit, garbage-strewn minefield that was the sidewalk, stepping over a milky used condom and detouring around a splayed, fecally-festooned disposable diaper. There was the corpse of a rat, inert yet alive with a scrum of maggots. Gaudy wrappers of cheap, high fructose corn syrup snacks from non-unionized Southern companies and discarded twenty-five cent plastic "juice" (scary blue fructosed water) bottles cluttered the path, testimony to this ground zero of the obesity and diabetes epidemics.

Up ahead I saw two teenage boys coming toward me—I crossed the street nonchalantly. Phew. I made my way past the old twenties apartment buildings, once the pride of working and middle class immigrants. Those scrubbed, shiny new citizens had long ago removed to the suburbs. Now the cheesy Art Deco motifs of the Manhattan wannabe architecture did nothing to mitigate their sense of barred fortification, NYC Police warning stickers, "No loitering in the hallways" marking them as public housing. Many of these buildings had been slashed with vandalism, the ersatz glamour of the American Dream rendered malevolent with the scorn of graffiti. Now the dream had been twisted, tortured, recast as the American Nightmare.

There on the corner, I noticed a recognizable and strangely comforting reminder of civilization, a Korean dry cleaning store, though it had entrained with the neighborhood with a diagonal scar across the smashed, duct-taped front window. On the side wall loomed a lurid mural of a young Dominican, Tito, birth and death dates inscribed underneath—a memorial to a life taken by Crips, Bloods or maybe DDPs—Dominicans Don't Play. I heard laughter behind me, seizing up with terror as three young men who'd come out of a store passed in front of me. Phew again. Though this was a densely populated urban area, a rooster inexplicably crowed from an open window on the other side of the street.

The lilting notes of Bachata from a passing car lent a further tropical incongruity to the aggressively unromantic scene, bringing to mind crystalline water, swaying palms, the clammy grasp of a sweating tropical drink with an all-inclusive umbrella. But this was, after all, the poorest urban congressional district in the nation. If the peeling Metro station and ancient, pocked sidewalks and potholes passing for streets did not signal it, then the burned-out, boarded windows of insurance fires were there to testify. Yet this was no *Bonfire of the Vanities*; twenty years on, things were looking up. Sporadic eruptions of dignity, modest two-family brick houses, though barred like Sing Sing against those less mobile, had well-swept driveways with parked cars behind gates. Gardens behind chain-link fences teemed with trellises, statues and hanging tchotchkas.

I found myself contemplating, were I suddenly to need a weapon, the lethal capabilities of a garden gnome. Despite my conviction of impending doom, though, nobody who crossed my path, Hispanic or African American, gave me a second glance: the elaborate Charles Bronson scenario I had conjured was ridiculous. My first, right-off-the-bat presumption had been busted—others would rupture in time.

I was born on the day Rosa Parks refused to give up her seat on a Montgomery bus, a fitting debut for a lifelong activist. The division of the world into Haves, Have-Nots and "Have-Mores" as George W. Bush called his base—always execrable but emphatically worsened by Clintonian deregulation, with tax cuts and the diversion of trillions into nonsensical wars soon to come—had become impossible to bear. My frustration had reached critical mass; no longer would the palliation of protesting and volunteering suffice. At forty-six I was giving up fashion for more fulfillment than designing a dress could provide, flipping the equation to make social justice my full time job.

Once I had made the decision, the opportunity came within a week, in the perfect Jungian synchronicity of the words, "No One Remembers a Middle Manager," an ad on the R train for New York City Teaching Fellows. That was it—I could make my contribution through education, the great social equalizer, the meritocratic ticket out of poverty available to all. What could be more effective than influencing children, the very future of the planet? I had always loved kids, so I applied for a position at the elementary level; one out of nine of us was selected in a rigorous competition. In return for the city paying for a master's degree in education, we would commit two years to a "high needs" school in the slums, a school where nobody wanted to teach. Along with a brief couple months of education classes, hands-on experience would be gained assisting a teacher during summer school.

Built in 1927, four loft-like stories of white brick, constructed when high ceilings were not a luxury, rise behind a patch of crabgrass and an iron fence. The groove in the middle of the main stairs testifies to the ascent of generations of students and teachers, their sagging appearance a marble monument to a downtrodden public school system serving, yes, the downtrodden. Surviving details of the *Little Rascals* era abound: polished oak transoms, room-length wooden closets with barely functional sliding doors, auditorium chairs with embossed metal sides, the ancient hand-lettered "Principal" on the office door.

But the decor is mostly the infelicitous result of brief budget windfalls and lengthier droughts. Green linoleum evoking a late fifties rec room—cracked and pitted—vies with stained, pilling armchairs from the seventies in the library and office. The once glorious burgundy auditorium curtains evoke a Tennessee Williams heroine, faded fitfully to a melancholic rose, bordered at the bottom with an eighty-year-old crust of grey filth.

The walls are uneven, patched and plastered repeatedly over decades, and covered every August in a fresh coat of cheap paint for the new school year. The floors of the hallways glisten, too, at the beginning of the year, with their new gloss of cobalt blue or whatever industrial color is on hand. The hallway clocks (which anyone middle-aged will recognize from the sixties), frozen at different times throughout the building, reflect the dysfunction and stagnation, not to mention *Alice in Wonderland* quality of the system itself. It is not in the custodian's contract to set them, nor anyone's, so they exist as decor: a bureaucratically persistent *Persistence of Memory*.

The general effect is that of a third world institution—you might be in the backwaters of Southeast Asia—with a handful of embellishments as economic boom times have allowed. Indeed, the only areas of the school in sync with the "richest nation in the world" are the library, renovated with a donation from Starbucks (a vast improvement, despite the tasteful but blatantly propagandistic murals with coffee cup motifs) and the computer room, replete with rows of Dells, again the result of a grant. For years, this was the only air conditioned classroom, technology demanding more respect from the Department of Education (DOE) than hapless humans. Ultimately, thanks to arm-twisting by the teachers union during a particularly brutal July, a handful of classrooms became air conditioned, though only those which are used for summer school.

In sultry May and June, it is hard to reconcile the staggering national GDP or the formidable economic heft of Wall Street with the extreme discomfort of a soupy torpor more appropriate to the Mekong monsoon. Moreover, during these periods physical education classes continue in the steaming gymnasium with its sealed windows, while students and teachers crawl up the steep stairways, there being no modern extravagance such as an elevator (the *dernier cri* one hundred forty years ago). It is not just physically miserable for all of us, it feels like an endless, vicious diss from the powers that be (be sitting in air conditioned comfort, that is). Children do not donate to PACs. Nor do the parents of these children, typically, vote.

As I entered the building, I peered into the cafeteria. Some kids were engaged in their first carb-loading of the day of cheap agribusiness, government-issue Frankenfood, complete with subsidized, genetically modified frosted corn; hormone and antibiotic-laden milk, and if federal largesse so provided that morning, a desultory nod to "health" in the form of a waxen piece of fruit refulgent with pesticide. Though free meals are on offer to nearly all of the kids (the formula for establishing the school's eligibility for federal poverty funding), other students breakfast on snack cakes or chips from the bodegas that litter the neighborhood, chasing the diabetic time bombs with the ubiquitous glowing blue "juice," a cocktail surely as destructive as any Molotov, just slower to kill (and to take down the health care system in twenty years).

Once ingested, the wrappers and bottles are summarily tossed on the sidewalk, thanks to the dearth of parental instruction and that greatest of parenting techniques, example. The situation is abetted by the infrequency of garbage cans (people light fires in them), however, where those are placed the trash is disturbingly just as prevalent. The city lets the containers overflow, while down on Madison Avenue they are regularly and meticulously maintained.

Most of the kids (ranging from the recent seven hundred fifty to nearly one thousand my first year), around sixty-five percent, are from the Dominican Republic. About twenty-five percent are African Americans, with the next biggest group Latinos mostly from Mexico but also from Central America. In each class there are a couple of Bangladeshis. A smattering of West Indians, three Greek siblings, two Chinese (parents own the neighborhood take-out) and one Serbian complete the mix. A majority of the students are ELLs (English Language Learners). Within this number the condition of poverty ranges, disease-like, from mild and temporary to chronic and severe.

At the extreme end of the spectrum are the shelter kids. Two homeless shelters disgorge legions of kids daily in time to breakfast at Chez Federal. These are among the most impoverished, the most neglected, with the greatest number of issues. Many have not been taught nor provided rudimentary hygiene; they often come to school with unwashed clothes, mouthes teeming with stinking bacteria (I once thought there was an open sewer nearby, but it was just the kid next to me breathing through his mouth) and in winter and allergy season, green stalactites of mucous depending from their nostrils. Disheveled and abandoned, these sad, violent children act out, create drama and generally wreck the chances of teachers to teach and students (including themselves) to learn. Knowing only negativity and turmoil at home, they bring this deep resonance with chaos to school, where they recreate it everyday.

Many kids like this actually live in a home of their own but with countless siblings spawned typically by several fathers, not one of whom deigned to stay and make the requisite sacrifice of parenting.

These are the children who know all about prison, for there is a father, an uncle, an older brother doing time.

After school you see the mothers of these kids hanging out on the street corner together, gossiping, admonishing their kids to "get the fuck over here!" with that gratuitous, damaging verbiage that characterizes truly unconscious parenting. Considering violence is born of powerlessness, many of these poorest, most desperate parents have an ax to grind, frustrations which often get vented on their kids. Though unfortunate, their destructive behavior is logical, in fact, given the double whammy of abandonment they themselves have sustained—the one they likely experienced as children, followed by society's adult smackdown version.

Once, one of these parents came in at dismissal time and discovered that her first grade child had been pushed by another child at recess. She bellowed, echoing through the hallway, "I'm gonna fuck her up the ass!" and keep in mind, though this came from a woman, nobody doubted what might be between her legs. Like other scenes played out in front of hundreds of children and parents, this was unfathomable. Looking at the first grader, I shuddered to imagine her life at home. Later on my way to the train, I passed the woman weaving out of a bodega, drinking from a paper bag, holding the child's hand. The little girl, six going on forty, looked up at me with a resigned expression—I have seen that so many times.

My heart aches for the innocents involved. Coming through the gate one morning, I passed two of my students, brother and sister. Their mother was bidding them a good day with, "... and don't you be fuckin' cursin' today—I don't wanna hear nuthin' 'bout that shit from the teacher when I picks you up!" Even if the mother did not, the kids knew she was being inappropriate, and they cast embarrassed looks in my direction.

Another time I watched, dumbstruck, as a teenage mother roughly encouraged her thirteen-month-old, barely-walking child out the school door *with her foot,* garnishing her physical abuse with the unfortunate, "Move yo' fuckin' ass!" It would not take Dr. Spock to predict who that kid will become: four years later, she will be in our kindergarten, traumatized and learning-disabled, disrupting the class with her need for the same negative attention—the beginning of a lifetime of self-destruction and recreation of the abuse she has suffered. Just like Mommy.

The abusive behavior, I would discover, was merely a classic symptom of "toxic stress," poverty's plague of disadvantages born of disenfranchisement. Despite my shock and dismay at their treatment of their kids, given the cards stacked against these parents, my heart went out to them. Yet as much as I wanted to understand and empathize, my solidarity with them could only extend so far. After all, I was, in fact, a spoiled, transitory tourist in their permanent horror, one who could escape at any moment.

A lot of students live with their grandmothers (though they are just middle-aged), exhausted saints who signed up for another round of parenting, resignedly filling in for daughters incapable or gone. There are also many children in foster care—babies born addicted to drugs or victims of family violence—with biological parents in prison, on drugs, in rehab or just plain disappeared. Foster parenting is a popular past time in the neighborhood, whether from the goodness of their hearts or the mercenary reason: the position is, after all, a way to get government money.

On the other end of the spectrum are the kids from Bangladesh, most of whom live in tidy clapboard houses, electronically wired and barred to the hilt, around the school. The fathers, many who vend fruit or drive taxis downtown, have engineering degrees back home, their striving echoed in these children, the high-performers of the school. Friendly but culturally isolated from their neighbors, the mothers wear their native dress and seldom speak English, and on Fridays the fathers attend the modest store-front mosque a couple blocks over. The Asian cultural imperative of not only present but exemplary fathers, stay-at-home mothers, structure, and discipline in a stable family, yields a predictably well-adjusted group of children.

Similarly, the students from Mexico and Central America exhibit the same happy security, the parents' adherence to the Catholic and cultural paradigm of family values obviously critical to the children's success. These happy, cherished kids come to school with combed hair and spotless white shirts, their pregnant little mother holding an infant, a toddler's stroller and a sibling's hand as she marches dutifully through the gate.

In between, in terms of behavior and academic success (invariably linked) are the Dominican immigrants, many just off the boat. This generation's Puerto Ricans, they may be at any place in the spectrum depending on their socioeconomic status (SES—a statistical tool combining parents' income, education and profession). Often there is an absent father and the child has a different last name than the mother. For some, the parents are here to take advantage of the system—at the check-out line they have benefit cards, even healthy young adults—yet others work hard at minimum wage jobs babysitting rich kids or aiding elderly people downtown, many sacrificing parenting time at home to required moonlighting.

Some of these parents go to school part-time, striving for a better life, and though many are single and struggle with child rearing, it is gratifying to teach students living with such an example. But in this population, too, there are many with disturbed home environments, with family members in jail, teenage mothers on drugs and relatives lending a hand. Naturally, these kids act out.

When I walked up the steps to the school office to clock in that morning, this was what I was taking on; a lifetime steeped in Hollywood's hackneyed idolatry of saintly educators had warned me of the stakes. Indeed, I was naive enough to believe it would be different for me. But Glenn Ford and Sidney Poitier had been chalk-full of positivity as well; when I took those steps that first time, I knew I could well end *Up the Down Staircase*.

Summer school was a poor stand-in for the regular school year, and my first clue that something was wrong with this picture. First, because it was as laid-back and languid as the weather outside. The half-day class was improbably, blissfully small, made up of heretofore unmotivated students who suddenly had an impetus to learn the material—scripted, facile lessons provided by a publisher with city contacts and million dollar contracts. As they had neither passed the state tests in math and reading nor their portfolios (accrued school work), they would be held back if they failed to perform now.

Yet not only was summer school curriculum notoriously watered down, but all summer students had to do was attend a certain percentage of the time and they were automatically promoted. Then that child would be handed up to the next teacher in September, unprepared for the next grade.

This farce would play out again and again until the child would graduate among a record group to finish high school; nobody mentioned the easy state tests, the absurdly elementary Regents exams nor the endless unearned promotions that got the kid to that point. A teacher who'd left our school three years before because she was sick of babysitting the "behaviors" (the kids who act out) tried her hand at high school but was soon back looking for work.

"There," she lamented, "they're in twelfth grade and they read and write like they're in third grade. At least here I'll teach eight-year-old third graders."

My first day in training I had planned to have all the kids call me by my first name. Ms. Graham, the seasoned teacher whose class I assisted in, quickly disabused me of this idea: formality fostered a sense of structure and decorum. Uh oh. Graham marveled repeatedly that I had signed up for such a challenge.

"You're crazy," she said, "anything's better than this."

Having floated in on my bubble of idealism, I just smiled quizzically at her comments. "But here you're doing something important," I offered. Duh.

The classroom was unlike any elementary one I had ever seen, though it was typical of the school. Joy, enthusiasm, optimism even, were as conspicuously absent as the whimsy and cheerful colors usually associated with kids; the principal had banned the usual uplifting commercial decor, and none of the teachers were motivated to create their own. The resultant drab gulag impression was enhanced by such ornamentation as there was, charts and posters scrawled with vapid dictums and desiccated state standards (brand-new education policy, these statements delineated learning goals for each subject) written in arcane education industry lingo.

Like a witch doctor's sonorous incantations, the schoolwide repetition of slogans and canned bromides seemed intended to

16

exorcise failure from the school. The effect was not simply dismal but outlandish: the notion that the kids would give the sea of posters a second glance was already delusional—there were so many, they merely merged into ugly background noise. The carpet bomb of paper became still weirder when one considered the children were incapable of reading that language, let alone understanding it.

The Soviet leitmotif—pervasive throughout the school—was thanks to the recently arrived No Child Left Behind (NCLB) law, educational reform President Bush had foisted upon the nation, buttressed by its vigorous stewardship by the hard-ass principal of this failing school.[1] This was my first indication that I was an actor on an elaborate set in which props were as central to the show as the plot itself, even at times standing in for the story. As I watched Graham teach—scripted cookie cutter summer school lessons—and then worked with students individually, I could not help noticing the flat surroundings reflected the uninspired information being force-fed the students, who were equally dull and dispirited. Fifth graders in danger of not making it to middle school, their reading and writing levels were years behind what you would expect. Essays were shockingly unintelligible, full of every possible error.

Given the circumstances I had not expected competence, though certainly nothing a judicious dose of red ink could not remedy. As it was, the work was so appalling that discriminate revisions were impossible; my impulse was to recycle them as paper airplanes and have the kids start all over.

Interestingly, when I asked the kids to read them aloud to me, not only did they not notice their writing made no sense, but they passed right over the mistakes, reading what they *thought* they had written. Rushing to get over. Later, I would find that same expediency to be most of the kids' standard approach to doing any work. Despite some tiny gains in math understanding, little could be changed in writing that had incredibly made it from one grade to the next, unchecked.

As writing depended on reading skill, naturally this ability was in the basement as well. The immediate frustration this engendered in me was just the first in numerous like sensations to follow in the next ten years. Because exhorting the kids to read at home as much as possible, the obvious antidote to their handicap, fell on deaf ears. In the face of this lazy indifference I would have to rely on parents to enforce my enjoinder, but obviously they had not turned off the television or video games before, so why would they now?

Despite their dim skills and prognosis all the kids—save one whose mother deemed a vacation in the Dominican Republic more important than her child's future (an attitude I would see repeatedly the next few years)—passed summer school successfully, on their fraudulent march towards a meaningless New York City high school diploma.

Summer school was an introduction to a culture of distinctive names; for many parents naming is a creative sport. Though many Hispanics have classic names mercifully easy to remember, the contingent named Angel, Christian, Messiah and especially Jesus would ironically be among the most depraved of delinquents. All in all, it would prove challenging to pronounce and remember hundreds of names, especially the unusual ones. My first time in one fourth grade class I faux pas-ed when referring to a kid in braids as "she," then pronounced her name "Devon" like the cream. I was corrected on both counts: Devon was a boy.

In the meantime, graduate school proceeded at City College, where all of the Teaching Fellows in SURR schools had been placed to get our master's degrees. The "School Under Supervisory Review" designation was given to schools which had a history of failing. This stigma came with a bonus of additional federal funds and city money for extra professional development (teacher training sessions) as well as an extended school day and year. Though we new teachers could have used far more classroom preparation, instead our initial graduate school curriculum consisted of classes on the history of education (female teachers were not allowed to marry!), types of pedagogy and crusty retirees summarizing dos and don'ts for the beginning teacher. The most salient: don't ever get used to an instructional program—it will be replaced within five years by something else, whether because of new research or hooked-up educational publishers.

Yet the new reform law that had been passed earlier that year seemed more than the usual housecleaning; our professors warned us to expect a chaotic ride as the new mandates kicked in. Many of them were so relieved not to be a part of it, you could almost see them crossing themselves, even the Jewish ones. What had I gotten myself into?

NCLB not only represented a sea change in the way public education was conducted in the nation, but at its very foundation it was, in fact, illegal. According to the Tenth Amendment of the Constitution, education is the purview of state and local, not federal, government. Nevertheless, similar to other rushed, shortsighted and destructive Bush initiatives which would end in debacles, NCLB had been hustled into law in January 2002. At its very inception the law predicted a disturbing trend in educational policy-making at the federal, state and local levels: teachers would not be part of educational reform policy, but politicians and business people who had never taught themselves.

Typical of these was one of the authors of NCLB, Margaret Spellings, a Bush acolyte going back to his first campaign for governor of Texas; though she lacked any educational background, in 2004 she was rewarded with the position of secretary of education. Spellings' equally politically-connected husband had even been a lobbyist for school vouchers at one point, as anti-public school as you can get. But as Bush's two terms moved forward, these unsavory links would prove characteristic of dozens of appointments based on patronage rather than merit.

On the surface of it, NCLB sounded pretty good. Providing support to traditionally under-served students with disabilities (special education kids, in other words), those living in poverty, and English Language Learners (ELLs), the law was designed to narrow the achievement gap between those with lower and higher SES by setting high standards and measurable goals. Stricter qualification standards for teachers resulted in increased credentials requirements mandating master's degrees and the passing of written and performance tests. Schools would receive federal aid in return for demonstrating "accountability" as shown in test scores from yearly standardized math and reading tests; in the beginning these measures were administered by individual states in fourth and eighth grades, plus one high school grade.

The "high-stakes testing" meant that schools with Title I funding, federal aid to disadvantaged kids, would have to show yearly improvement in test scores: Adequate Yearly Progress (AYP). Schools who failed to make the grade two years in a row would be subject to punishment: budget cuts and increasingly draconian measures, including the firing of staff, bringing in outside management and even closing the school. The concept of "choice" was included, allowing parents to track a school's data and transfer their child out of a failing school; the formation of publicly-funded, privately-run charter schools—serving a hand-picked, specialized population a specific curriculum—as an alternative was encouraged. By 2014 all students, even ELLs and those with disabilities, were required to be "proficient," performing at grade level, in reading and math.

The *Zeitgeist*, a bipartisan frenzy for educational reform, plus the purported success of legislation Bush had pushed in Texas, with standardized testing the primary measure for accountability, enabled NCLB to be handily rammed through Congress. Indeed, in 2000 Bush had been elected partly based on his pledge to be the "Education President," a claim resting on the stunning gains—in test scores and graduation rates—his state had achieved while he had been governor. So impressive a feat was the "Texas Miracle," Bush subsequently named the superintendent of Houston's schools, Rod Paige, his first secretary of education.

But NCLB was not the only shake-up to the system: Michael Bloomberg, the new mayor of New York, had won the right from the state to dissolve the old Board of Education and wrest control of the schools for himself. Under the previous system the ossified, byzantine institution—riddled with incompetence, corruption and redundancy—seemed like a Rube Goldbergian fantasy of an education factory spitting out barely educated students. The entangled structure of the bureaucracy itself—the thirty-two school boards with their thirty-two community school superintendents, the board of education, the schools chancellor and the mayor—encouraged a blatant lack of accountability.

That July while I was doing my teacher training Bloomberg, touting himself as the "Education Mayor" whose legacy will be the reformation and improvement of the city's public schools, took charge of the system. As the CEO of Bloomberg L.P., a financial services and information firm, he had enjoyed unchallenged, centralized authority, a complete power he would now wield over the city's schools. Promising accountability from himself, not some irresponsible, impersonal entity like a board of education, Bloomberg declared there was no need for checks and balances since his approach would slash through bureaucracy to get things done. In charge of all decisions, then, Bloomberg chose leaders for the Department of Education (DOE) including the chancellor of schools. The old school board would be replaced by a Panel for Educational Policy with the chancellor and thirteen members, a majority of whom Bloomberg appointed, while the others were posted by borough presidents.

Sweetening the United Federation of Teachers (UFT—the New York City union) approval for the reforms, Bloomberg granted a wage hike to teachers. He telegraphed his interest in administrating education like a business by appointing Joel Klein, a lawyer and former head of the antitrust division of the Justice Department, as schools chancellor of the biggest school system—over one million kids—in the nation. Since he had barely a *soupcon* of educational experience (he had taught math briefly), Klein did not have the requisite three years of educational experience required by the state, necessitating a waiver from a panel of experts.

Anyway, businessman Bloomberg had chosen Klein specifically for his corporate outlook and management acumen. Klein's heritage as a trust buster was expected to be useful in breaking up the entrenched Board of Education bureaucracy, but it also portended the wrestling matches to come with the UFT. A hierarchy of command extended from the mayor at the top, down through the chancellor, the district and school administrators. Principals were given unprecedented autonomy, with complete discretion over budget and instructional considerations.

At City College we discussed the new developments with trepidation, the professors putting a positive spin on it to cheer us rookies on. Anyway, we were just focused on getting through the first terrifying week: we needed tips. Addressing practical matters in the classroom, among other nuggets of wisdom a couple old timers advised us, "Do not smile until December!" which we thought hilariously misguided. How could we, who became teachers because we loved kids, not smile at the cute little people? No, that rule could not apply to *us*. With two weeks to go till school opening, we adjourned for vacation.

All the Teaching Fellows were invited to Madison Square Garden to be welcomed by the newly appointed chancellor. In his post Klein would be implementing management theory: running the schools on a top-down, business model, with a slew of new directives, gleaned from Wall Street, for administrators and teachers. The chancellor's speech was disarmingly charming and eloquent; in very little time he would become our fiercest detractor and despised adversary. Eventually, I would meet him personally.

Then I got the call: the Teaching Fellows office suddenly said I had no job for the school year—I would have to find one on my own. This was at odds with the offer the principal at school had made me of a second grade teaching position. Given no help save the addresses of two job fairs to attend, I was left to my own devices with less than a week to go. My head swimming at the lack of professionalism, I went to the job fairs, but also walked through East Harlem, since only schools in poor communities would accept a Teaching Fellow. From school to school I went, leaving my resume and trying to catch an interview with a principal, many of whom were on vacation, on the spot.

Strange things happened. I was offered the chance to teach gym, then there might be an opening in science—though I had no background in those, no problem. In the parking lot of one school, two guys who had heard me in the school office yelled across at me, "Do you want to teach middle school English?" I could not because my license was for elementary school. It struck me as outrageous that children would be put in the care of teachers recruited this way; I was starting to get a feel for the slapdash, by-the-seat-of-its-pants nature of the public school system. The contrast with my own education was extreme.

I had attended good public schools in a university town in Michigan until high school, when I switched to private prep school. Girls only, in rolling Virginia horse country, The Madeira School included students so entitled their last names were commercial and political dynastic brands. Classes were a dozen students or less, conducted with great rigor and greater expectations by teachers of the highest caliber. (After I graduated the headmistress, Jean Harris, conferred a notoriety by association on the school when she murdered her lover Dr. Tarnower in a jealous rage.) At Vassar I continued this elite education in similar circumstances, with many small classes and seminars, the best curriculum and world-class faculty, as well as demanding coursework. Considering my privileged background, I was a connoisseur of education. My own experience only served to cast the shoddy urban public system into greater relief.

Four days before school was to start, I still had no idea what I would do. The phone rang. It was Graham, the teacher I had worked with in summer school.

"Where've you been?" she asked, "We've been waiting for you to come in for the week of professional development before school starts, why did you disappear?"

I told her the Teaching Fellows had said I had no job there. She said that was ridiculous, the principal wanted to talk to me, and by the way—she was calling from a shopping mall and had just seen the principal in Old Navy.

"Wait a minute," she said and hustled the phone over to that store.

Dumbfounded at this latest twist, I listened to the principal's offer. She had given a second grade to someone else when I didn't show up (she had not bothered to call me first). Now she said I could take my pick: be a "cluster" teacher (going from class to class) in Social Studies, Science or English Language Arts. I told her I would gladly take the latter, not entirely sure of what it was, but certainly it involved reading and writing. I knew from summer school the train wreck that was the kids' writing; that was a place for a meaningful contribution. I was on my way.

2

The first day of school we were there early in the "yard," a paved, fenced-in recess area, to welcome and organize the students by class. Yawning kids freshly alarmed by their clocks but still on summer time ambled towards their new teachers, while moms clutched tearful kindergarteners to their breast. Many of the little ones clung to their mothers, too, or required dragging like recalcitrant dogs on a leash to the dreaded new teacher's line. The really loud screamers and cryers (at least two every year) would end up torturing their kindergarten teachers for weeks till they finally got acclimated.

For the previous three days I had been trying to speak to the principal: what was my job teaching English Language Arts, exactly? She had never been available. Nobody else knew as it was a new position. Now, at last, with my first class scheduled in forty minutes, I *had* to find out. Practically tackling her as she rushed into the building, besieged by parents, I asked my question. "Just do a read-aloud and have them respond to it with writing" she said, waving dismissively as she hurried off.

And so, it was very much every man for himself. I had no classroom, so there was nowhere to hang my coat or put my stuff. Not a locker nor a closet. I tied my leather jacket around my waist, using a backpack to haul my books from class to class. In the winter I chose to freeze on the subway platform rather than drag a heavy coat around. Between the stifling humidity of late spring, and the man-made sauna courtesy of the wheezing, popping and clanging radiators in the winter (the ancient boiler has no automatic temperature regulation, so windows are raised to let the hot air, and tax payers' dollars, escape), cold temperatures were welcome anyway.

Later I would make classroom teacher friends and beg a small space from them, as they barely had enough to themselves, or join the rabid competition for a closet left by a retired teacher, or just take a chance and leave my stuff in the antediluvian teachers lounge. There was an unmistakable Darwinian charge to the atmosphere; one was required and expected to fend for one's self in the absence of normal infrastructure which, in any other profession, would be taken for granted. The appearance of furniture, supplies or space summoned primal emotions more appropriate to a Filene's Basement bridal brawl.

We had been over it again and again in graduate school: the first week is about creating classroom rules and expectations, establishing a foundation, a structure to support the year. Best to have the students come up with the rules—empowerment—though you guide them to it invisibly. When it is all done, a handful of aphorisms suffice: respect ourselves, respect each other; keep our hands and feet to ourselves; when others are speaking, we are listening, etc. Normal enough in the Miss Manners domain, however many of these children have not gotten the memo.

Social assumptions one never questions, such as queuing up, taking turns, even saying "please" and "thank you," here are foreign concepts that need to be taught. It is me, me, and me some more—when supplies are handed out many grab and snatch, oblivious to the destruction of the materials. Respect for personal property, even the teacher's, does not stand a chance either when it comes to two little egos battling over a proffered book (pulled apart at the binding), bag of clay (destroyed), my labor-intensive art exemplar (torn in half), the flexible wooden body model for life drawing (*dismembered*).

Of course, cherished material like a special book, after being passed around one too many times, may well come back with scrawled embellishments of that perennial boyhood favorite—a dick and balls—as well as the salutary proclamation "bitch." Here, as once etched on the door of the principal's car in a vandalous burst of literary inspiration, the word was spelled "bicth," clearly implicating one of our typical students in the heinous (not least for its spelling) act.

In that first week, as a new teacher, kids initially viewed me quietly, with curiosity, which I mistakenly took as a normal sign of respect for the teacher. After all, that was how we treated a teacher when I was growing up. However, after a few minutes of me talking or reading aloud, the disruption that was to characterize the rest of the year began. I was able to enthrall most of the kindergartners, first graders and second graders (the "lower grades") with read-alouds and discussions, brought to life with my hammy acting and voices. That is, except for the "hardcores:" kids so screwed up they will do anything for attention.

They talked, they fidgeted, they poked and kicked. They crawled and somersaulted. They screamed and ran in circles around the room. Whether disabled, abandoned, abused or just plain needy, every class had one of this ilk, and more often than not, the room contained several. These kids were hellish to deal with on their own, but even worse was the fact that their misbehavior then pulled the "marginals," frequently as much as half of the class, over to their anarchic cause. The result: bedlam.

But I quickly established my preference for them over the "upper grades," third through fifth, where interest in my new face barely lasted a couple minutes before the sharks started to circle. With each higher grade level the precipitous lack of respect dropped proportionately. Though I was addressing the class, conversations at normal decibels started, abetted by the absurd placement of the students at tables of four, astonishingly grouped, in any other venue, to play cards. This outlandish arrangement had struck me as counterproductive from the get-go, but it turned out to be a mandated component of "cooperative learning," the philosophy du jour that was, and is still, tyrannizing teachers over the past decade. Despite what my retiree professor stated at City College, though I have indeed seen other ideas come and go, this special brand of stupidity is enjoying a long run.

The asinine seating plan begs the obvious question: what is the point in grouping uncooperative children to work cooperatively? Of course, there is none. This would be just another instance of preposterous pretense in a school system more at home in the land of *The Emperor's New Clothes* than New York City.

The older kids, grouped specifically to socialize as opposed to listen, seized the opportunity to create their own entertainment. Having been a kid myself, I knew the parameters expanded when an unknown sub was in class, and I was as guilty as anyone for pushing the behavior boundaries. But that would have been limited to whispering in the back, or the random snide comment. Here, by contrast, the kids in the front, just a couple feet from me, were holding boisterous conversations—in my face.

When I asked a fifth grade table of girls to stop being rude and disturbing everyone else's learning, all that came of it was an eye-rolled "whatevuh," then they would recommence. I would get one table quiet only to have another erupt. I pictured Lucy frantic with the chocolates on the conveyor belt in the candy factory, never able to catch up—I was getting nowhere, and the effort was intense. As I lost the battle to quiet them my strained voice grew ever louder but soon I could not be heard over them.

I realized I was not a teacher, but a screaming, just short of hysterical, babysitter. My exasperation level was off the charts: I sensed my adrenals throbbing, blood pressure spiking and my hair turning grey. I seemed to be aging, shriveling on the spot. All that would be left of me, like the Wicked Witch of the West, would be curled up shoes, though mine would be Teacher Sensible. Truly, years were actually, actuarily vanishing from my fated allotment. The great lesson I had planned, the discussion, the follow-up, was for nothing; I felt a lump in my flayed throat as I fought the urge to cry. But I knew if I established that precedent, these kids would surely feast on my exposed viscera for the remainder of the year.

Barely sentient as I walked down the hall, I recalled a research study involving babies who pushed buttons which activated pleasant noises or pictures. Through learning, the babies had come to expect a certain predictable effect from their actions. Then the scientists

LAUREL M. STURT

changed it up, making some of the buttons nonfunctional. As the babies pushed the button over and over without result, with each unsuccessful effort their frustration levels mounted, to the point where their physiology was affected. Blood pressure skyrocketed and the stress plunged their immune systems.

Studies of adults in Britain similarly demonstrated those on the lower end of the power spectrum are haunted by depression and frequent illness; the higher the position of power, the healthier and happier an individual becomes. A sense of power—in other words, of independence and control—is essential to our emotional and physical well-being.[1] Now I was one of those powerless babies, and aging fast.

When lunch time came, I fled outside, shell-shocked, to chain-smoke in the shabby thirties WPA-built "park" which was nothing more than a few peeling benches on lumpy asphalt, surrounded by young trees and garbage. I was traumatized. So many issues were coming together: frustration with the glazed look of so many of the students; their lack of respect, interest or capacity; the constant babysitting and disciplining; the sneering insensitivity of the older kids; the overwhelming assaultiveness of the day. On the bench I cried at last, not just because I was wounded, but out of heartfelt disappointment: so much for my idealism. I was not going to change their world, they would not let me. I now had a real taste of that same powerlessness that was driving the parents to the brink of violence and despair.

To make it worse, as a single parent working in my first full-time job since his birth, I was feeling tremendous separation pains from my kid downtown, from whom I felt galaxies away. It was a nightmare to get someone at dawn to just watch him an hour and take him to school: if I finally got someone, they would not stay. In fact, my whole relationship with Manhattan had changed: it was now an oasis of civility.

From the top floor of the school I would sneak wistful glances out the windows that looked on Manhattan far away. It rose up Oz-like in the distance, with just as much allure. The Empire State Building, the Chrysler Building (the World Trade Center had been destroyed the year before in view of the fifth grade teachers), beckoned me back to the world of, well, normalcy. "Reality," as I now thought of it. After school, the problems with child care continued as I sped across town to Harlem to the master's program at City College.

Though I struggled with parenting, sweating through the stressful day job and going to school at night, getting together with the other Teaching Fellows in those graduate classes was heavenly therapy. We were, to a person, going through the same exact torment at our schools, all equally stunned by the low level of the kids and the skewed nature of the classroom, with students bullying the teacher, something we could not fathom given our own childhood experiences. That vision—where neat kids sat in neater rows, raised their hands, listened, learned—spooled now only on Disney celluloid. The educational experience we had exists only as a fantastical Hollywood conceit, at least in the slums.

I would learn there was a pecking order among teachers, though the students were doing the pecking: classroom teachers got the most respect (home territory, stable, familiar, structured routine, eight-five percent of a child's instructional time); substitutes, according to the age-old tenets of academe, received the least respect (unknown, ephemeral, structureless).

Cluster teachers like myself, who visited classes once a week, fell in the middle (somewhat familiar, permanently temporary, with a structure, albeit once per week—just three percent of instructional time—so one less fortified) and would, at best, be accorded only a modicum of respect. In other words, the degree and permanence of structure determined the tenor of a class. While my cluster status would always be a factor in the kids' behavior, later the situation would improve somewhat for me as time passed and I became closer to students through the grades.

It also helped that I mastered the withering look; the affronted, Margaret Dumont-like "How dare you!;" the clenched growl "Shut your mouth!" and the vicious, shrill "Get in your seat!" I learned these tonal weapons from the scary teachers who command through intimidation, frankly, the most successful approach. Though it does not feel right to speak to children this way (a guilt which dilutes my delivery), that seems to be all that many understand. Eventually I realized that when these admonitions are aimed at a kindergarten audience, by the time they are in fifth grade Pavlov can assist me when the hormones launch and the eyes start rolling.

But ultimately, I could never expect the degree of control of the classroom teachers, especially the authoritarian Hispanic and black ones, not only because I was not with the students as much, but because of the way I look and behave. There is a pronounced difference in the kids' attitudes toward most of the white teachers (unless those teachers have learned from experience the value of classroom martial law), maybe because the teachers of color remind them of their own authority figures, their mothers or grandmothers. For whatever reason, with us, they automatically think they can get away with stuff, as if they have gotten a cultural message that we are not threatening, it is not in our DNA.

Indeed, one of the veteran white teachers told me the principal herself had drawn attention to the elephant in the room with a stunningly honest observation: when the teacher was unsuccessful at controlling a chaotic line of students going down to lunch the Hispanic principal whispered, "If you were black or Latina they'd behave better."

Little did I comprehend that the kids were actually on their best behavior that first week, and the few to follow; by Thanksgiving they had started their descent into the abyss. If they had pecked me before, well, now I was Tippi Hedren. It was like being in a war— every day was a battle, and every class a skirmish. I read aloud wonderful books, Dr. Seuss and other great authors, and for those who were listening, they were well-received. After, depending on their age, they had to respond to the work through writing or art—a state English Language Arts standard.

A friend of mine in publishing rescued me when she sent me some books including *Shaq and the Beanstalk* by Shaquille O'Neal. It was a collection of fairytales re-written to star Shaq as a child in the central role. Shaq made his way in and out of tales like "Little Red Riding Shaq" and "Shaq and the Three Bears" in an over-all story that riveted the younger kids. Two factors, a black basketball hero and popular fairy tales, conspired to save my lime green ass. All at once, the kids sat in rapt attention. It did not hurt that I did my crowd-pleasing voices for all the characters, from Granny to the Big Bad Wolf to the Troll under the bridge, plus over-acting worthy of Joan Collins. For once, I was enjoying myself. I was not stopping every ninety seconds to yell, "Stop that!" or, "Shhhh!" or "Sit down!"

But I still could not do anything with the upper graders who, even though they ran the gamut from innocent preteen of my generation to the contemporary worldly, surly adolescent, still were not interested in doing anything but talking. They were also fond of being out of their seats and strolling around the room at will. As time went on I came to dread that the most, because from that, arguments and virtually guaranteed disputes ensued. Fights were frequent, as many as one or two a day, an understandable phenomenon given the fact that some parents taught their kids to always hit back (parents should be forced to come to school to deal with the consequences of *that* command).

Typically, two boys who had exchanged insults jumped up and pressed against each other, chests puffed out and heaving with cartoonish aggression. Then a stature contest commenced, each stretching as tall as possible to dominate, no matter what their height difference—the little guys had chops, too. By this point you half expected them to pound their chests like gorillas, but they either backed off the posturing or began punching. But unlike the Sunday evening PBS test drive of testosterone it evoked, this primal *pas de deux* was no flat-screened pixellation: the recurring ritual prompted whoops and exclamations as expectations of entertainment rose, in tandem with my blood pressure.

One memorable girl-on-girl between Jatzerie and Shontiqua resulted in tufts of hair all over the floor. According to rules, we were not supposed to touch fighting students—if we were hurt breaking up a fight we would not be covered by disability insurance. This was all forgotten, however, when Datrease and Mekhai were beating the shit out of each other. Though some of the fifth graders were huge, I tried to pull them apart, standing between them, doing

LAUREL M. STURT

anything to get them to stop, while the rest of the class stood in a circle chanting, "Fight, fight, fight!"

It was terrifying, especially since there was nobody to help. There was one jaded guidance counselor we could call, Mr. Stockman, (for whom the fourth floor men's bathroom was informally named, as he spent a lot of time in there reading the newspaper) but not only was he phoning it in, but the ratio of him to students was one to nine hundred fifty. If Stockman even showed up to take them out of the room, it was a rare gift.

My worst days were my frequent subbing assignments. The lack of morale among the teaching staff resulted in high absenteeism, plus no regular subs would come to our school after experiencing it once. Over and over, my already shaky sense of control was demolished as I arrived at school and instead of my planned, prepared-for schedule, was given a class for the whole day. This happened most often in the winter, but also when it rained, some teachers could not face coming in.

The kids were sure to behave badly, too, when the weather was inclement, not just as a curious phenomenon, but because they were cooped up inside at lunch in the stifling auditorium, ostensibly to watch old Pixar videos but actually talking and fighting. During the course of the day, depending on the horror level of the class, there might be two or three fights, plus one at lunch and one in gym. I longed for the simple expedient of putting a kid out in the hall, yet even that was against the rules and there would be (more) hell to pay, for me, if I did it. Stockman was always told to support me and anyone else subbing a particularly notorious class, however, even when I saw him passing in the hall and leapt out to beg him to help, he hissed, "Handle it yourself!"

During a, for all intents and purposes, third grade riot, I called the assistant principal (AP) Ms. Dubrow. She came in, mad as hell, declaring, "Call me only if there's blood!" and left immediately. There were two security guards downstairs but they would only come if they were not busy, and then, just remove the offenders only to bring them back, because they were not required to hold them.

It was obvious that the culture of violence was so entrenched because there were no consequences. The principal wanted nothing to do with it, she just sat in her office most of the day, emerging only, as I would find out myself, to attack teachers. So it was not like the old days when you could send the rascals to the principal's office. Even if you had, the students would not have cared: many were known to have cursed at the principal, too.

The worst that could happen was that the guilty *might* get suspended for a pleasant day or two, doing their class work in a little SAVE room (from the Safe Schools Against Violence in Education law) with a benign veteran teacher who was ready to retire.[2] Rarely there would be an out-of-school suspension at another school for something particularly bad.

Such paltry repercussions hardly deterred the headstrong, impulsive kids, chronically defensive and programmed to fight at the slightest real or imagined provocation: "He said something about my mother!" (it was nothing)...."She kicked me!" (barely brushed the person, clearly accidental)...."He took my pencil!" (you have not had one in days)...and endless injustices ad nauseum. After the brawl, the off-the-charts stress of which only accelerated my progress towards a premature demise, student witnesses and I were required to write up statements regarding what had transpired. But suspensions, though merited in the dozens, were rarely given: suspensions had to be recorded, and the principal did not want to look bad to her superintendent.

Though nothing could be further from the truth, maintaining the fiction of running a tight ship was paramount to her reputation. This disingenuous, ego-driven stance took precedence over school welfare and safety, subjecting teachers and students alike to frequent violence, stress, and the disruption of learning. To prevent student lawsuits over injuries, we had to protect the DOE from litigious parents (opportunists abound) by filling out a multi-formed "Accident Report" which took most of my lunch period to do, a time when I very much needed to cry, chain-smoke or stare catatonically into space.

I did catch a break in one class I was given on a snowy day, the most dreaded fifth grade room, host to several professional tough guys. Teaching was hopeless because they started conversing as soon as I walked in, and they would soon be fighting once they finished copying the assignment off the board I had given them. A girl, Brittany, found out I speak French. Brittany was one of the worst behaviors in the grade, never allowing any learning to take place, her need for attention trumping any other consideration. (Later this violent child would gift the neighborhood with three babies by the age of eighteen.) She begged me to teach her, and I could not believe my good fortune: I actually held the cards for a moment.

I yelled as loudly as I could to be heard over the tumult, "Would anyone like to learn French?" They thundered their approval, screaming and pounding their desks. I was thankful for something to do that would enlighten them, distract them from fighting and not least, make them shut the fuck up.

Anyway, in Brittany's class that day, those budding Francophiles were fascinated, and soon engaging in French niceties while pretending to be *du haute monde* with cinematic gestures. I had a brief measure of relief, if only for a moment; in fact, in a fifth grade, for a change, I was killing it! I would have taught French again but given my assigned subject area I could not. Besides, once the difficulty of learning the language would pass from easy to more involved, requiring extensive memorization, they would naturally revolt. Anything necessitating actual work was dismissed by most of them with a moan. Just learning by rote, which I had found in graduate school to be the lowest of the six levels of learning, was too demanding for them. Even elementary memorization such as that required to learn the multiplication times tables was too much to ask; as late as fifth grade most had not learned them.

What they did excel at was copying from the board. This involved the most minimal amount of thought, and they always did it robotically, without complaint; I could tell they had been doing it for years. If I were especially upset by an unruly, dangerous class, I would write on the board the long beginning of an essay, for example, that they would have to finish creatively, and have them copy it. This could, depending on the degree of delinquency of the students, calm them down a bit, however, the fact that my back was necessarily to them while I wrote meant that all manner of crimes were taking place. No fool, having been a kid myself, I knew to whirl around periodically; however that did not halt the breeze from spitballs whizzing behind me. I chose to ignore them—there were so many other battles to pick.

From its palest expression as rudeness, to vile, obscene cursing, hence to its most vivid, cardinal expression in full-on fist fighting, the ever-present threat of violence stalked my every working moment. Emotionally and physically, I was a wreck. My immune system was shot; I had no less than ten sinus infections that first year. Louise Hay, the spiritual healer who describes emotional causes for physical ailments, cites these infections as arising from being "irritated" with someone close to you. That word would only constitute a euphemism for what I was feeling for those little Visigoths. I dreaded going to work every day. Getting up in the dark was of course horrible already, and taking the train uptown was to endure an unwelcomely colorful thirty-minute indignity twice a day.

I still saw the beauty in them, particularly the young ones, but so many, especially a few older kids, challenged me as never before in my life to draw deep into my capacity for love, just to sheerly tolerate them. On an intellectual level I could understand and even rationalize their behavior, considering their socioeconomic roots. But at my core I was traumatized by the endless assault I was enduring in the name of doing some good in the world. I felt like I was being flayed alive—I was absolutely raw. As I entered some classes, sometimes, was that actually a hint of sulphur in the air?

In one third grade, Zuleika, a literally insane girl of ten, danced and cackled maniacally on the tables with her friend Stefan, during the entire class. I was powerless to stop them, so as time went on it became a knee-jerk behavior for them when they saw me: I became reduced to a cue to salsa. (Zuleika's little brother was no better, caught taking a dump under the playground slide during dismissal.) In another, Justin, a huge, serially held-back linebacker, when displeased picked up tables and threw them—if it was a good day, down the hall—if not, at us. Enraged Alitecia, a tiny third grader with a classic history of abuse and now in foster care, wrenched the room's heavy mahogany door off its hinges.

After trudging up and down the steep school stairs all day, those at the elevated subway and finally the ones in the Manhattan station, I would emerge, barely alive, it seemed, in the Shangri-la that Midtown had suddenly come to represent. Aaah, I exhaled as I stepped onto the familiar streets of civilization, now, for a few hours, I would be here, in Reality, Normal Land...and then back to *It*, up there. But I didn't need to think of that now. I was just so relieved to be back where the environment was either neutral or downright pleasant, where I was not afraid for my safety, my psyche or my sanity. Sometimes, at home, during the evening I would shudder involuntarily at the thought of *It* and that I was going back to face *It* again in a few short hours; I was stranded in a fifties B movie.

Nevertheless, I went back, day after day. I had a contract to do this for two years, and my master's program was contingent upon staying in the school. I believed ethically that I should keep my promise to the Teaching Fellows, but I also wanted to accomplish the master's degree. Anyway, I was optimistic that things would get better; however negative so much of it, I was getting close to many wonderful kids and that fleeting enjoyment might multiply, I figured, with greater experience. More than anything, though, I did not want to give up.

After all, I had sought out to do something meaningful: the challenging nature of the work was part and parcel of its significance. That sense of responsibility I had always had, of feeling obligated to do something, was, now that I was in the belly of the beast, even more exigent. To walk away would mean not only defeat but worse, guilt. Given my nature, at least I could look in the mirror satisfied that I was fulfilling my highest potential as a human being, even if my reflection was starting to resemble W. H. Auden in his later years.

Despite my tenacity, however, daily affronts conspired to vex my outlook. Along with the recalcitrant kids, there were other depressing factors, most notably the antiquated hierarchical system, so at odds with modern, team-oriented organization and its concomitant *esprit de corps*. Odious, too, were the often unprofessional, unqualified administrators and the galling litany of trivial rules. When grappling with the bureaucratic minutiae, "Paging Franz Kafka" kept recurring in my head. For example, no matter what, the day before or after a holiday could not be taken off for any reason: to do so would invite an investigation, and punishment! Once a teacher dared to have the flu before vacation, an act of subversion sufficient to summon Torquemada; the administration delighted in enforcing every petty decree.

The principal, who I nicknamed Cruella in homage to her evil character, was a Hispanic veteran educator with a visage so reptilian that the slits which passed for eyes summoned Voldemort to mind. Capable of both capricious, unhinged behavior as well as methodical acts of sadism, "She Who Must Not Be Named" tyrannized the teachers staff to her heart's, or likely a more bilious organ's, content. Cruella stayed in her office a great deal of the time, schmoozing on the phone with the superintendent to whom she ostensibly owed her crony position, emerging occasionally to stoke her plasma with the essence of some hapless victim, preferably one of the newest, brightest and most promising teachers.

It was rare for Cruella to hit and run; instead, her *modus operandi* was a systematic campaign of serial attacks. In the seven years before I had arrived, she had already driven several teachers not only out of the school or the system, but out of the profession of teaching altogether. As if the students were not already tribulation enough, Cruella's brutalization created a pervasive atmosphere of low morale and for her chosen targets, one of outright terrorism.

My personal encounter with the harridan came one snowy January morning when I was so sick I barely made it to school. By the time I got there I had determined I had better stay home the next day, but for now I was there, and I would have to get through it. I grimaced as I saw my name listed next to a class—several teachers were absent, as usual. I would be subbing in a fourth grade class all day, once again. Cringe.

At the time there was a lucrative city contract for a reading program for failing schools called, Politburo-style, "Success For All." Kenny G music came over the loudspeaker at nine thirty, and students would exit their classes, walking in an orderly and, given the music, etherial, lobotomized way (was that Nurse Ratched announcing pill time?) to other classes where they would be taught reading in a group of peers, regardless of their age or grade. The daily ritual dramatized the choked conditions in the jam-packed school, groups convening even in the hallways, corners of the gym or like my regular SFA gig, the right wing of the auditorium stage. Now, since I was subbing, the SFA group assigned to my classroom came in for the period.

As the dreamy mood dissipated with the fading strains of Kenny, the kids, faced with an unfamiliar teacher, began to unravel. It did not help that nobody could agree on what part of the book they had stopped the day before. As they devolved into chaos, walking around the room, hitting each other, I noticed the book had a short play that could be performed. They had never done this and were suddenly enthusiastic, though they set about arguing over the roles. First, I would have to take attendance, which I sat in the back at the teacher's table to do.

In SFA every part of the session—reading, vocabulary, written questions—was timed in a strangely rushed and impossible way, just another facet of what seemed to be a conspiracy to beleaguer teachers, as well as cheat children of true learning. Segments would have to be completed at breakneck speed, whether the students had absorbed the material or not. A clock was always needed as a timer.

Maria volunteered to get the class alarm clock, which was plugged in at the front of the room. Febreze (air fresheners make fine names, too), unbidden, ran and snatched it away. Predictably, they started fighting over it, and the clock dropped and broke. They started punching each other. From the back, over the heads of the students chanting, "Fight, fight, fight!" I stood up to see the fracas, yelling at them to stop and about to go break it up. I was so hot I certainly had a fever, and now my heart was pounding from the stress.

Then I saw the viper face of Cruella peering in the door window, gargoyle-like. I blanched. My adrenals leapt into overdrive. The door swung open.

"Sit down!" she thundered. The students took their seats. "What's going on here?" she demanded.

Sick as I was I gathered my wits, replying that the kids were doing a play from the book, that a clock had been broken ... the slits were not buying it, they seemed to gleam red at this point. She grunted and spun on her heel, but I did not think I had heard the end of it. That afternoon, I got called to the office to sign a letter stating that I would have a meeting with her and my union representative in a couple days regarding my "failure to teach SFA."

When one received a letter like that, the result could be the dreaded "Letter to File" occurring, meaning that it could result in a recorded reprimand, establishing a paper trail in the event that repeat offenses might follow. Those, or just a host of different infractions, provided evidence to "terminate" a teacher. "Letters" were a much whispered-about means of intimidation and an excellent way of keeping the power hierarchy robust. In the school grapevine, the news that someone had gotten a letter traveled fast, warning luckier teachers not only not to do what had engendered the rebuke, but that Cruella was on the warpath and to watch their backs.

Considering the gravity the staff imparted to these letters, I was full of trepidation. I stayed home the next day, sweating the fever or my impending encounter with the principal, I could not be sure which. When the meeting finally happened, it was very formal. The principal, the union representative, Graham, and I all signed our names to a special form designed just for the occasion. Then Cruella proceeded to describe what she had witnessed the morning I "failed" to teach SFA: the class was out of control while I was in the back *applying makeup*. With that pronouncement the slits narrowed, if that were possible.

Dumbfounded at the bizarre lie, my hard drive frantically ran an application of possible retorts, not coming up with even one that passed muster. Clearly, I was dealing with an egomaniacal, one-celled organism, like a cop in a third world country, drunk with power. As she had shown herself to be a lusty predator, I had to reconcile the necessity to make a stand or be preyed upon the rest of the year, with the delicate task of not hurting her ego, the offense of which would *also* invite future depredations. It certainly seemed prudent to show contrition, though I did not feel the need for any. I had not told the kids to break the clock and fight, and I certainly had not given any face time to Estee Lauder, either.

Graham, who though the union rep was a buddy of Cruella's (major conflict of interest), began defending me, quietly, gingerly, as if talking a bull out of charging, or a gun out of the hands of a retarded psychopath. Graham said I was a first year teacher and she knew I would get better fast, I just needed a second chance. Carefully balancing some dignity with the requisite humility I hoped would placate the tyrant, I explained the situation. The class was out of control, I should have been in the front (in reality that would not have made any difference, given those girls). Despite what she thought she saw, I was not putting on makeup.

Cruella wrote a paragraph stating what we had discussed, that I was to demonstrate better class control in the future, and we all signed it.

"Phew!" said Graham when we got out to the hall, "That was close! But you did not get a letter!"

I thanked her for her help. It was obvious to me that I was spared because I had trained in Graham's class in the summer, and she and Cruella were friends outside of school; their cozy relationship had embraced me too, at least momentarily.

As the weeks went on and I met more teachers, the picture of Cruella's monstrosity was vividly drawn. There were many tales of abuse, unmerited letters, and stories of her castigating teachers among colleagues, or even worse, in front of students, were legion.

In high-needs schools the hallway bulletin boards—completely fraudulent displays of the students' academic prowess solely for the benefit of visiting hot shots—were an indicator of the quality of a school, and therefore Cruella's self-serving obsession. Among her many stipulations regarding their construction, she only liked certain colors for backing.

One legendary incident involved her slithering down the hall in a particularly nasty mood when she saw a bulletin board with a yellow paper background. Cruella tore the despised color down with gusto—ferally, even—ripping the paper and the kids' work into a frenzy of shredded strips; if she could have, she would have accomplished this with her teeth. The demolition complete, she sauntered away, the pile of villainous yellow shards left to the clean-up efforts of the flabbergasted teacher.

Another incident involved a veteran kindergarten teacher in her last years to whom Cruella, for no apparent reason, had taken a gratuitous dislike. Though she could find nothing wrong with her, the bully visited her classroom every day in a Robespierrian campaign of terror, harassing, threatening, wearing down the teacher until the *coup de grace* at a meeting in her office, one promising a "U" ("Unsatisfactory") rating for the year. The ill-fated, diabetic teacher inadvertently flattered Cruella's twisted omnipotence by collapsing from stress-induced low blood sugar, right there in her office. An ambulance was called amid snorts of disbelief, yet, at the same time, solemn credence from the darkly amused staff. The teacher never returned, electing retirement over death.

In another case, the frequent sick days of a teacher ostensibly being treated with chemotherapy for breast cancer aroused Cruella's suspicion and predatory predilection. According to the legend, she recruited a minion to run up to the victim and pull her wig off. As it turned out the teacher was indeed as bald as an eight ball sans the Eva Gabor road kill that was her coiffure.

Anyway, I managed to avoid another ugly encounter. Like all the other teachers, as the year went on, when I saw Cruella coming down the hall, I ducked into a room. To be off her radar was the best way to escape torment.

In a Martin Luther King Day speech in Harlem, Bloomberg portrayed his effort to improve the schools as a "civil rights" battle, calling the initiative "Children First."[3] The chancellor's office would be dictating the curriculum and pedagogical approaches, while in a continuation of the precepts of NCLB, Bloomberg threw his weight behind school choice, competition and incentives (merit pay) in education. Klein joined him, shortly establishing his support for charter schools and rewarding effective teachers. Klein took an aggressive stance against the teachers union, opposing work rules like provisions for seniority and those which purportedly safeguarded the jobs of incompetent teachers (they do not, they merely assure due process).

Though other professions would never be held accountable to "customers" (parents) for the failing outcomes of their "products," as Bloomberg's business model referred to students, we were now in an absurd climate in which teachers were assigned total responsibility for the low academic performance of kids.[4]

Seen as a model for national reform, Bloomberg's market-style innovations got support from the media and the business community, receiving funds for planning and new schools from the Gates Foundation and the Eli Broad Foundation, two educational philanthropies. In the coming years, Wall Street hedgefunders would jump on the bandwagon, too. The media loved each news-making soundbite, especially the right wing rags owned by Rupert Murdoch.

Most of us had been educated in "teacher directed" environments in which teachers taught at the front of the room while students facing forward watched and listened. By contrast, in progressive education, a theory which has been advocated under different names: constructivism, discovery learning or inquiry-based learning, over the last half century, students are given partial guidance while being expected to work together and construct their own learning. Klein was being heavily influenced by constructivist zealots loyal to this progressive idea, one which had its roots in the Romantic era when the philosopher Rousseau asserted that children learn everything, including reading, naturally through hands-on, constructivist activities in child-centered environments.

But no matter how exciting the concept of kids discovering knowledge appears, there was no research supporting it: instead, research over the past fifty years has proven direct instructional guidance from a teacher to be more effective and efficient. Nevertheless, using these sexy, progressive ideas Klein had a view to impose a single instructional approach systemwide for teaching math, reading and writing.

Still, systematic, explicit modes of teacher-directed education, like using phonics to learn to read, not only had the research backing NCLB required, but were traditionally deemed best to educate disadvantaged children. But Klein could not be bothered with facts; his choice of Diane Lam in August 2002 as deputy chancellor for teaching and learning (the only educator in Klein's posse of business and think tank refugees) signaled his card-carrying fealty to the progressive approach.

A brash boor of an administrator who had left a trail of blood across four cities, most recently as schools chancellor in Rhode Island, Lam had forced her progressive agenda of "balanced literacy" and "fuzzy math" programs on a system of fifty-five schools, fifty-four of which were low performing. After her three-year tenure, only one had moved up a notch.

Yet Klein wholeheartedly embraced Lam's expertise and espousal of progressive teaching, relying on her to oversee curriculum and pedagogy decisions. Hundreds of thousands of students would be taught reading through "balanced literacy," with its faint nod to phonics instruction the only proven, valid component of the program. Though experts reviled it and the unsound literacy program did not qualify for federal funding of thirty four million dollars per year, the Bloomberg administration did not change course.[5]

Instead, the famous Columbia University Teachers College theorist Lucy Calkins marshalled the signatures of one hundred education school professors—some not even connected with teaching reading—to keep balanced literacy in the schools (she was later rewarded with millions of dollars in contracts).[7] Klein installed an actual phonics program in forty-nine schools just to get the federal money, my school was one of them.

At lunch I continued to flee to the spot in the park, something which the other teachers considered very brave. They only left the building to walk to the bodega on the corner, then straight back. I had to be outside: it was the only way I could be alone to recover from the morning's barrage of over-stimulation and underachievement. The classroom teachers could hang in their rooms during lunch, and even some of the clusters had their own rooms. For gypsies like me the sole place to go was the decrepit teacher's lounge, which offered only inane conversation or the ever-popular, addictive whinefest that was our primary communication every day.

Anyway, outside it was a relief to be out of the creepy institutional fluorescent lights. With their ghoulish glare making sure no pore was left unexplored, one could hardly resist the urge to perform surgery. I could not wait to get into natural light and the soothing balm of silence.

Just one time I was accosted not far from the school gates as I was walking back: two boys were strolling behind me, teen dropouts, and one yelled at me, "Hey there, white bitch!" (I wondered if he pictured it, "bicth".) The other boy shushed him, embarrassed. I turned around and declared, "That was not a very nice thing to say!" and kept on walking. "That wasn't a very nice thing to say!" mocked the smartass with a sing-song voice.

Once, when three of us Teaching Fellows were walking from the train in the early morning, a guy suddenly yelled at my friend, "Hey, you bumped me—you spilled my coffee!" "I'm sorry," she said, though he had actually careened into her. Furious, he then tossed the coffee on the front of her (white!) coat. We knew better than to say anything—that would have resulted in escalation. In the Bronx there are plenty of weapons more threatening than the feeble bodega coffee—though hidden, guns, knives, and even machetes, are ubiquitous.

In time, I discovered at lunch I could walk fast to a main thoroughfare and make it back in time to teach my next class. I could do errands as if I were in Manhattan; for me that was a welcome dose of normality. There was a McDonald's, Rite Aid, Staples and Blockbuster, etc., all denizens of Reality, whose generic corporate assurance, impersonal and distasteful under regular circumstances, here bolstered me for the afternoon onslaught of Crazy.

There was a time when I was truly apprehensive, and that was Halloween. The lead-up to the holiday was suspenseful as talk of the dangers crescendoed among the older teachers as well as the kids.

Apparently, the neighborhood was no place for children to celebrate, as adolescents would temporarily commandeer the streets, throwing frozen eggs, attacking trick-or-treaters and probably, since everything was on the table, inserting the fabled razor blades into apples (that healthful scourge of treat bags which nobody ever ate anyway). Children were planning to wear costumes, but trick-or-treating would be done right after school, in daylight, or better yet in another neighborhood, or a party would stand in for going door to door.

As the talk increased, my imagination started working overtime: I became worried about getting home safely. At lunch, instead of going to my spot on the bench across the street, I sat on the school's steps, becoming increasingly alarmed as parents came in to take their children home early. By the time school was out I was on orange alert, the color warning Bush was using at the time to deftly hype anxiety levels just prior to invading someone else's country.

As I walked down the street I felt like Rambo, giving everything a three hundred sixty degree once-over, indeed spying some guys on the rooftops. It was like Beirut, 1975. But they left me alone, maybe because I started walking backwards, watching them, like the nervous wreck I had become. When I got to the main street to the train, lined with businesses and lots of people, I thought well, that is done—it must be safe here, there are so many people around.

That is when it hit me, right in the abdomen, with a thud. "I got frozen egged!" I thought, amazed that I was a statistic, after all.

I looked ahead of me. There, a teen in a gray sweatshirt a half block away was waiting for me to make him, reveling in his success. I still had the whole street to get down to the train. I thought if I did not do something, he could continue to egg me all the way. But I could not be aggressive, that would *assure* it. So just to take a stand I ended up wagging my finger at him, schoolmarm-like. I knew it was lame, but both to do nothing, or do too much, would be to invite more. He seemed amused by my gesture and turned away, walking ahead of me. Still vigilant, I made it to the metro station and up the steps to the train, unscathed.

Kids on the elevated platform were spitting on people below, but they did that everyday, not just on Halloween. While I waited, I readjusted the leather jacket that was tied around my waist. As I did I felt a hard lump and pulled it out: I had not been egged, I had been potatoed! I got on the train, but what I had taken for a haven turned out to be anything but. At every stop in the Bronx, as the doors opened, teens threw stuff—garbage, eggs, blobs of shaving cream—inside the car, then as the doors closed ran off down the platform. The next day walking the streets near school, the usual potpourri of urban detritus was glazed with a slick of Halloween carnage.

The school's curriculum was generously augmented with frequent preparation and drilling for the state math and reading tests. The results of these mandated exams, given at the time in our fourth grade, were the ultimate focus of the academic thrust as they supposedly demonstrated the all-important, trendy concept cherished by NCLB, "accountability." The statistics could make or break a school, indeed failing scores had landed the school on the dreaded Chancellor's List. One of the buttresses that came with that assignation was "Extended Time," an additional period at the end of regular classes used for test prep.

I was assigned to an unruly fourth grade class taught by a Canadian teacher with two years of teaching experience in Taiwan as an imported ESL (English as a Second Language) instructor, informal, inadequate training at best. In the early aughts Canada, unable to employ all of its teachers, supplied a steady stream of fresh victims to the difficult urban schools of the United States. Later, as the Teaching Fellows and other programs were popularized for American teachers, the Canadians were phased out.

At the end of the grueling school day, nothing was less appealing to drained students and the even more zombie-fied teachers than engaging in mind-numbing math story problems. The alternative was to prep for the other state test, the ELA (English Language Arts), by reading soporific texts for comprehension with accompanying multiple choice or short answer questions. Amazingly, this was just an extra daily dose of the stultifying test prep that was already consuming so much of regular classroom time.

The late afternoon's glucose levels did nothing to mitigate the stupefying enterprise. We did not need to practice the strategies outlined in the reading comprehension booklets (once again, materials sourced from test prep publishers with gargantuan contracts, a national industry worth billions since the inception of NCLB), to put us to sleep: every cell in our beings cried out for repose.

So we all, teachers and students, dragged through it daily, though many kids stared blankly into space at frequent intervals, if not the entire time. Some chose to ignore the work altogether, strolling around the room looking for a fight. If an ongoing drama were still simmering from say, lunch, there might be some chaos to enliven the torpor. All in all, very little learning took place. There were three teachers in the room, the primary classroom one as well as two of us clusters assigned just for that period.

A few months into the year the AP, Dubrow, called a faculty meeting to address school behavior issues. She highlighted the outrage of a particularly heinous event, a fourth grade boy throwing textbooks out the window at people below entering the school. Dubrow pointed out that this happened with three teachers in the room, a situation I found unbelievable. Later I was mortified to discover that Textbookgate happened in *my* extended day classroom: I was one of those three ditzy teachers! Like the other two, my head had been bowed, attention directed to the work of a student. In future, then, less teaching—far less—and much more babysitting, appeared to be in order.

The curriculum's focus on test prep struck me not only as an inauthentic education, but a means of obliterating, for many kids, any interest in school. The irony of further boring, already alienated, disinterested children, was breathtaking. If a program were intentionally designed to foster high levels of absenteeism and dropping out, then this would be highly effective. Moreover, the deathly ennui of the work could only encourage restlessness and acting out.

Thus, along with the authoritarian Success For All reading program, the day's learning consisted of a prescribed curriculum and the all-important test prep, all served up according to a rigid schedule posted on the classroom wall. Small wonder that the veteran teachers spoke nostalgically of the days when a teacher closed the door and actually was able to teach according to talent, experience and individual personality. Those were pleasant, positive times, when there was a sense of community; teachers looked forward to teaching every day, even having the energy to play volleyball after school.

Now the lack of freedom, and the patronizing control of what was taught and how, contributed to a omnipresent atmosphere of disrespect. Curiously, you were required to get a master's degree in education to get the job (indeed the city paid for mine), yet all that you had learned during that graduate work was now not to be used. Instead, outside companies were filling their coffers by peddling their pedi-greed programs to shaking principals terrified of low test scores and losing their place in the food chain.

Few aspects of human relations are as destructive as a lack of trust, and the oppressive micromanagement and extermination of spontaneity and inspiration, all for the pretense of "education" based on test scores, is obscene. Both teachers and students are victims of this skewed system: kids carry the stigmata into circumscribed futures of intellectual and career limitation, while demoralized teachers endure their bleak existence in a pension-focused endurance test presided over by an insecure, predatory hierarchy. It is a totalitarian system with all the trappings of a repressive, sclerotic police state.

The teachers, at the bottom of the pyramid, are persecuted by assistant principals (henchmen of the principal) over countless trivial mandates. Bulletin boards, for example, are deemed so important that every month all other class work is dropped just to complete them, even if something is just quickly assigned for the sake of fulfilling the pointless obligation; in other words, an officially mandated waste of time. Moreover, creating the bulletin boards according to the strict edicts governing their construction involves elaborate, time-consuming details, so valuable time and energy is taken away from actual instruction and lesson planning.

But worst of all, perhaps, *nobody looks at the bulletin boards*—neither students nor teachers, and they simply become wildly expensive, in terms of educational and human cost, sacrificial background decor. Only administrators view them once in their asinine monthly inspection of the "boards," scratching check marks on their clipboards in a ridiculous tally of the requisite details, an act of intimidation which degrades the tormented teachers that much more.

There are many other fatuous rules irrelevant to instruction yet in place, unquestioned and unchallenged, for years. At any given moment, teachers have to be teaching the subject stated for that time in the "Flow of the Day" wall chart: to change the order, even when it is totally necessary, is to court discovery via drive-by administrative ambush. When teaching that subject, the teacher has to take time to write the objective on the blackboard, i.e., "Students will be able to multiply two digit numbers by one digit numbers." Sometimes these objectives are very lengthy, but nevertheless, always required, regardless of the fact that yep, *nobody looks at them.*

That is, unless an administrator suddenly launches a surprise attack, in which case, the lack of an objective can cause a reprimand. A couple of these heinous mistakes are sufficient for the principal to form a certain idea of a teacher, which subsequently morphs into a negative viewpoint. With sufficient evidence, then, collected through constant harassment, that opinion finally gels into downright bias, then hatred and an all-consuming drive to fire the teacher.

Further up the chain are the literacy and math coaches, former teachers usually owing their premier positions (they do not have classrooms and the attendant responsibilities and stress) to unctuous cultivation of the principal, or worse, as would be the case in my school.

The assistant principals, once teachers themselves, are bureaucrats who have decided more money is preferable to the direct contact with kids that keeps true teachers, regardless of less income, in the classroom. In that sense these administrators possess a mercenary streak, one that well serves the principal's primary pursuit, which is complete hegemony. They grovel to the principal, who kowtows, in turn, to the superintendent.

That politically adept, pencil-pushing functionary, at a remove from the unglamorous drudgery of educating, brown noses the chancellor, who sucks up to the mayor. The system would collapse without its most important foundational layer, the teachers; yet as those lowest on the totem pole they receive the brunt of the work as well as the blame; credit, and money, goes to those at the top.

The predatory, hierarchical construct, based on intimidation and not the easy flow of talent and ideas, is antithetical to modern horizontal notions of collaboration. Moreover, its intrinsic disenfranchisement of those most valuable can only result in dysfunction. The appearance in the schools of the creepy bromide "Together We Achieve More," apparently lifted from a May Day banner on a Chinese tank, could not mask the abject fear and disunity pervading the system.

At the master's program at City College, all the other Teaching Fellows complained of similar politics and anxiety in their assigned schools. Though I had assumed—having never before been exposed to such savagery in a boss—Cruella to be an anomaly, it turned out the ferocious unprofessionalism of my principal was typical of theirs as well. One, a very competent former journalist, had been attacked unfairly by her principal for incorrectly teaching SFA, a program for which she had been given no training whatsoever. Instead of supplying the requisite training and waiting until the end of the year, the principal invented other charges to deep-six her immediately.

The union, usually helpful in these situations, could neither disprove the claims nor protect her because she did not have tenure. Unemployed, but committed to teaching, she borrowed money to stay in the master's program. The final insult came a couple years later after she finished the degree work: not only would New York City not hire her because she had been fired, but the termination on her teaching record nixed the likelihood of any other district hiring her. The principal got away with unjustifiably wrecking someone's life; the numberless children who missed having a rigorously-vetted, dedicated teacher is arguably the bigger crime.

I knew the schools we had been appointed to were not typical, if only because my son was attending a good one in our Manhattan neighborhood with its socioeconomic mix and throngs of involved parents. Kids there were not failing and teachers did not appear to be clawing for survival. The atmosphere was so positive and equanimous the teachers dared to go by their first names—intimacy did not threaten a sense of respect, in fact, it may have enhanced it.

Knowing how much time was wasted in robotic test prep throughout the system, I got my son into a Talented and Gifted class, an excellent program offered by the city in certain schools. The TAG curriculum was targeted at such a high performing group, test prep was only administered the week before the state tests, as opposed to all year long.

Despite the presence of kids from housing projects, less than half, the rest of the students were socioeconomically upscale enough to be from educated households where books were a natural part of life, whether through bedtime stories or parents modeling reading for entertainment. The presence of books also decreased the influence of television and video games, two less than desirable influences when it comes to scholastic accomplishment. These factors were among those predictive of student achievement all the way to college.[8]

Another advantage of the better-off children was the rate of participation of their parents in the PTA; up in the Bronx at my school, parent involvement was consistently so low that the PA (Parent Association) members could be counted on one hand.[9] Indeed, in most years there was only one member besides the president; at those times there were over seven hundred fifty students in the school.

When I visited my son's school, I was overwhelmed by the contrasts with my own. The place exuded warmth and cheer, of the teachers and students both. The staff was a community, a team, not the traumatized victims that taught at my school. Classes had assistants, Columbia Teachers College students completing the necessary in-class hours requisite for their licenses. In my school where we needed assistants far more, there were none: no student teachers ever applied because of the neighborhood.

In one lower grade class I had to observe for my master's work, I was amused when the teacher became angry with a boy squirming on the rug, while she taught the kids new words. In my school his behavior was so common, not to mention innocuous, it would not have made the radar—we had bigger, more violent fish to fry, and a whole lot of them.

Also, in the higher-functioning school there was no dissimulation: hallway bulletin boards were not monthly mandated, complex productions, there as a tool of tyranny or to impress the occasional official: they simply displayed student work with a hand-written title, cropping up naturally when there was work worthy of display. Teachers and students were not spending hours on them—there was teaching and learning to be done. The commitment to authentic education was a refreshing rational change from the pretense of learning that consumed so much of our day in the threatened and threatening Bronx school.

Considering the picayune educational regulations, the perpetual harassment by the administration and the difficult students, of course most staff discourse involved complaining. Morale was so decimated, in the company of these energy vampires, *chi* just seeped away. I must confess I became somewhat of a Deatheater myself. Grumbling was usually expressed in hushed murmurs, accompanied by darting, ferret-like glances to make sure administrators or eavesdropping spies were not around. This was especially true of the timorous veterans.

Indeed, as in any authoritarian scenario, there was a contingent of resident Stasi—bootlickers looking to protect themselves as well as advance. Some were known to be treacherous; others' duplicity was unproven but suspected. Intrigue smoldered constantly among the Dress Barn Machiavellis.

Between the directives of NCLB and those of the new Bloomberg administration, the workload had escalated but the pay had increased, too. Now, New York City was starting teachers at a salary that mid-career teachers made elsewhere. With the new regime the old timers, more than most, had been reduced to quaking jellies, at all times panicked over losing their jobs and thus eminently manipulable.

They were in a rut so profound that they had come to view teaching, and teaching specifically at this school, as the only job in the world.

Despite the raise, the exhausted veterans groused continuously in whispering cabals, disgruntled but impotent to confront the situation. Indeed many were so terrified of Cruella, they would transform into unabashed toadies whenever she was around. The most committed invertebrates openly ingratiated themselves to her, sycophantically insuring themselves against the ever-present threat of collapse in her office.

As a place of predominantly women, there was never a lack of communication, and the second favorite pastime after griping was naturally gossip—even the few male teachers could be counted on to dish the clods of dirt flung around school. Always to be dreaded were the compulsive talkers who rewarded the wretched sucker who said "Good Morning" with a cascade of endless drivel. When assaulted by their blitzkrieg of blather I headed, as politely as I could, for the hills.

The school was full of nice teachers, mostly Hispanic and African American; the ones I vibed best with tended to be Teaching Fellows who had recently come aboard with intelligence and passion. Still, I found few kindred spirits to lighten up the gloom with the *bon mots* which were my stock in trade: there was no Round Table in the teacher's lounge. Where I connected with everyone was my desire to help the kids. I had never been around so many people who loved children as much as I did.

Though I was sick half the time I kept soldiering on, enduring eighteen-hour days ending when I returned home from City College and my master's degree work. If it were not for the mercy of Sudafed and a day-long I.V. drip of caffeine, I never would have made it.

The unrelenting stress, demoralization, illness and fatigue reached a nadir shortly after the confrontation with the principal over the SFA class debacle. Holding on by a thread, I scraped together enough energy to write Randi Weingarten, the president of the UFT, a letter unburdening myself. I talked about the terrible administration, the lack of support, the absurdity of the city paying for our master's degrees when the abusive system encouraged us to leave teaching as soon as possible. I hoped to express the disappointment I knew other crushed rookie teachers were experiencing as well, working in an indescribably brutal situation.

I did not expect any resolution, of course. Still, I felt compelled to give Randi a heads-up, knowing others were too tired or beaten down to communicate what we all were feeling. Not daring to use my name—published in the union newspaper the letter could get back to a vindictive Cruella—I signed it "Hope Springs Eternal."

Including points I had made, Randi referred to me and other new teachers in her next newspaper editorial, urging us to stand firm against the tyranny of the principals and not to quit. Randi was obviously well aware of their douchebaggery: our union contract, already full of hard-fought safeguards against presumptuous administrators, constituted a literal indictment of their overreach and zeal for excessive control. Yet we still had far to go in winning a normal atmosphere of equality and respect, particularly now that Bloomberg had taken over, and with his new structure, delegated more power than ever to principals.

As the year progressed, at least, I received inspiration for lessons so compelling they averted much of the usual classroom disruption. If they were spot-on, they included learning as well as work craftily served up as entertainment. Many of these were triggered by my activities outside school, especially during our precious time off. On the merciful vacations, I rewarded my weeks of struggle with my passion, trips abroad.

Christmas was spent on the Nile, resulting in an enthralling lesson about Egyptian culture with an assignment to draw their own pyramid and fill it with items their *Ka* needs in the after life, then write about why they had included those elements. Amusingly, many kids assumed the Egyptians played the contemporary card game Yu-Gi-Oh, since the tomb decorations included their symbols and gods.

In February I went to the Ice Hotel in the Swedish Arctic, sleeping under reindeer skins in a resplendent ice-sculptured room, dining on reindeer stew and plunging into heart-stopping depths after sweating in a birch-fed sauna. The kids were awestruck as I recounted the stories, including lassoing (well, attempting to) reindeer, my son narrowly escaping frostbite from the dogsledding, and hot tubbing in zero temperatures under the blazing aurora borealis. The task which came out of this experience was to cooperatively design a hotel with a desired theme, drawing a labeled elevation along with a travel brochure. Of the entire year, this was the kids' favorite assignment. Enthusiastically, they rolled up their sleeves and got busy. I could not believe the creativity: there were chocolate hotels, baseball hotels, underwater hotels, Barbie hotels, flying hotels, rollercoaster hotels. Too many wonderful concepts to mention here—Ian Schrager might be reading.

In Costa Rica in April, an unanticipated nocturnal boom of the Arenal volcano, complete with red neon flowing lava, sent me out of my outdoor cafe seat and jumping for joy (my son shriveled with embarrassment). Since children are universally fascinated by extremes of nature, I seized on this attraction to dodge the ever-present threat of a *classroom* cataclysmic eruption. The Costa Rica tales, adventures like ziplining through the rain forest and a tarantula crawling up my arm, fascinated the kids and led to an assignment: imagine you are living in the town of Arenal in 1961, when the big eruption took place: write a story. The kids used books on volcanos for ideas and illustrations, succeeding better than usual at writing a truly communicative piece, despite the dependably dismal grammar and spelling.

For me, these creative explorations, arising from serendipitous events in my personal life, seeded the conviction that my teaching success would utterly depend on entertainment. After all, the majority of kids join their parents in hours of daily screen time via television, computer and video gaming. I had a feeling, in fact, that this diet of fast-paced entertainment was exacerbating their already fleeting attention spans, propensity for instant gratification, and impulsive behavior. (This hunch would later be validated by 2011 research on kids watching *Sponge Bob Square Pants* and their subsequent inability to focus on tasks later.)[10]

Moreover, the passive, spoon-fed nature of their enjoyment, whichever screen was delivering it, was slowly extinguishing their imaginations. I was often depressed with their general lack of ideas—normally about half wanted to copy mine instead of come up with an original. What a bleak future awaits these kids unable to adventure, to envision, to create. Indeed, artists may become an endangered species within this screen-tranced population.

The lack of creative time extended to school: due to the obsession with test scores, not even a nod was accorded the right brain—as such, there was no art, music, dance or theatre class. Now that I had a clearer vision of what would hold their attention, I had the goal of liberating their creativity and releasing it into the wild. My heart soared to see their imaginations combust; watching them working joyfully blew my mind. My success depended on surviving the typical initial battle to capture their attention, then cajoling them to listen throughout my presentation.

I started out the lesson, screaming my lungs out over the deafening din in a class I had just entered, "Over vacation I stayed in a hotel made of ice!" After a couple more of these declarations the noise had switched to a barrage of questions. Then as I stood there saying nothing, the smarter kids would start to yell at the others, impatiently, "She's waiting for you to stop talking!" It only took a couple minutes for everyone to be silent. During my narrative there were still interruptions of enthusiasm or side commentary, but my audience was so enrapt I would stop, say nothing and fix a scornful eyeball on the offending party until the disruption was brought to an end by furious peers.

Afterward, I passed around photos and brochures from the hotel. The highlights for the kids were the dogsled huskies as well as the crowd-pleasing, safely PG side view of a naked man, fresh from the sauna, jumping into the hole in the frozen lake, the most popular picture of all. They practically ripped the brochure to shreds fighting over who could see it next.

During the most absorbing of these classes based on my trips, heavy-duty behavior issues dropped to zero, though there *was* a great deal of noise from the sheer enthusiasm. I still had to keep up my guard, of course, since the powder keg potential for drama was always lurking in the wings.

The precious moments of connection, unfortunately, were not typical. There were still so many hardcore intractables that one third of my classes were merely difficult, while two thirds were downright cringe-worthy. Outside of these I would cross myself before I went in. Other cluster teachers in the hallway gave a knowing nod: Linda Blair was waiting inside. Keeping the lid on my rage and frustration as well as that of the students in these classes required strenuous, debilitating effort.

Well I understood how a second year Teaching Fellow had lost it when vainly attempting to get through to her obstreperous SFA group: suddenly she had thrown an eraser at a kid who would not shut up (rankly amateur compared to the panoply of medieval tortures peppering my fantasies). She just snapped, her lapse of control like any act of violence (notwithstanding the harmless projectile) born of powerlessness, since there was no way to get the disruptive child to cooperate or failing that, remove him from the class. Without recourse to school discipline we had been reduced to well-meaning, impotent saps who showed up every day for another round of victimization at the hands of those who not only emotionally tormented us, but did so with impunity.

Since the teacher's action constituted a serious violation, Cruella dispatched her to the fabled Rubber Room, the DOE holding pens throughout the city where teachers accused of criminal offenses, abuse or incompetence enjoyed an all-expenses-paid rot while their cases dragged on à la Jarndyce and Jarndyce, a farcical limbo of litigation which offered equal opportunity plundering to city and union lawyers alike. It ended up working out well for the Teaching Fellow: a few months later when I saw her at City College she had gotten sprung to teach math at another school. She gushed happily over her new life far from the cult of Cruella.

The state ELA and math tests arrived and all the school mobilized in hushed lock-down for the most anticipated events of the year. Along with other out-of-classroom teachers I had to proctor in a classroom. Pacing the floor, required to always be standing and moving around, I looked over the shoulders of students at answers which ranged from correct to nonsensical, at least half the latter. The tests themselves were not very challenging, often downright moronic. Some questions were misleading, and others were impossible for ELL students with little understanding of American language or culture, not to mention socioeconomically insensitive: for example, one could only be answered right if the student knew a golf club is used in a type of sport, hardly a ghetto pursuit. Tricky, moreover, because "club" has two meanings.

May and June came and with them the sirocco of sweat swept the hallways. In the auditorium giant oscillating fans from the thirties impotently circulated the oppressive air, creating far more noise than relief. Their loud whirring motors brought to mind the runway ending of *Casablanca,* and a strange desire for, if not a nap, then Letters of Transit. Once the tests had been administered, anyway, the kids had sensed it was Miller time and gotten more rambunctious. Now, with the heat, they were thirsty and martial. Lunch fights increased, the residue of resentment carrying through the afternoon in disputes and outright brawls. Though I was looking at a summer of graduate classes, like everyone, I could not wait to get out.

My English Language Arts cluster position was being eliminated for the next year. An official paper was circulated to be filled out with three grade teaching preferences. Usually requests were honored unless circumstances—or a marauding principal—prevented that accommodation. My three choices were kindergarten, first grade and second grade. Even though teaching those grades had been far from easy, it was the little ones' magnetic tug at my heart strings that pulled me most readily back to school day after day. Though many were, after all, simply miniature versions of ruffians to come, I could not have made it through the year without their spectacularly delightful company, the purest, most ingenuous human beings ever.

The kindergartners, still fresh to the planet with wide-eyed wonder, are just babies in inflated bodies. Pint-sized potentates, these little egomaniacs constantly compete for attention and approval: when you complement one, anyone within earshot insistently demands equal flattery. When helping one child, another will often jump up to shove their work three inches from your face, aggressively forcing your acknowledgement. But in the most beautiful, even spiritual manner this same profound narcissism melts graciously away in the face of another child's suffering. When a peer is crying, whether in physical or emotional pain, others rush over to minister and comfort.

In terms of learning, for the most part they are a pleasure to teach because their curiosity is on fire. They have no history of failure so anything is possible, plus they live in the "now." This quality of enthusiasm—which will never reach such a high level again for those who start falling behind—mitigates the shocking lack of socialization which characterizes so much of their behavior. Rarely parents are teaching the kids rudimentary civilization like saying "please" and "thank you," and those who have not been to preschool, the majority, need constant reinforcement to share, take turns and line up.

But admittedly that same quality of wild abandon is the unbridled exuberance I love in them. Once, I enlisted their help to tear construction paper into pieces for the upper grades' collages, a furtive ploy to improve their motor skills for writing, disguised as a fun assignment. They plunged into the activity with great commitment and had a splendid time. As I was watching the colored piles grow gleefully in the middle of their tables, I remembered—too late—my own October thrill when little, of jumping anarchically into piles of dried leaves. A split second after my predictive recollection they were scooping their hands deep into the piles and upward, raining the paper in a contagion of confetti that immediately swept the classroom.

When I finally subdued them, the psychedelic carnage necessitated a monumental clean-up, a new locus for their ebullience since it required crawling under the tables and the giggly hidden hijinx *that* encouraged. All told, the Mardi Gras Massacre, as I subsequently thought of it, gave me a valuable lesson as a new teacher: to anticipate *any* eventuality in a lesson. Yet as difficult as the class had become, in my heart of hearts I did not regret a minute of it: their elation carried me through the day.

Their peccadillos, however—fascinatingly consistent across their age group—can quickly reach saturation point. Despite the kindergartners' tremendous charm, certain stock annoyances seem wired into their current brain development. For instance, when one asks to go to the bathroom, they *all* clamor to receive equal dispensation: a wildfire epidemic of demands for the bathroom races through the class, often accompanied with what I call the "pee dance," the crotch held tight with the hand while hopping back and forth with an anguished, or more likely pseudo-agonized expression. If this theatre fails to convince then they resort to whiny pleas of, "It's an *emergency!*" since they have seen this phrase work (teachers, at wits end over the number of bathroom supplicants, often query whether it is an emergency). Trying to judiciously sort it out is challenging, since though most of them are definitely faking, you are screwed if you deny one and they pee in their pants.

Another thing many commonly do is shoot their hand up to answer a question only to have nothing to say. They behave as if this is perfectly normal, and when asked why they do this, once again there is no answer. There is also a thriving business in self-righteously fingering who is doing something wrong, and especially ratting out evil-doers. But any irritation they provoke pales in comparison with their overwhelming beauty, a loveliness arising from their exquisite vulnerability. I was seated reading aloud a story to a class sitting on the rug around me when, oddly, a tiny girl stood up and made her way from the middle to where I was, usually a definite rule-breaker. Her expression was so concerned I did not admonish her, but leaned forward to give her my attention.

At eye level, she put her hands on my knees and lamented, whispering, "She said she does not want to be my friend" as a tear trickled down her cheek.

"I am so sorry," I whispered. "You are such a nice friend. There are other nice friends and you can be friends with them instead."

She nodded and, placated, went back to her place on the rug. Over the next ten years that surefire response would be required repeatedly, as far up as third grade.

I enjoyed the gung ho first graders, too, bringing their happy attitudes and Jack O' Lantern smiles (the exodus of front teeth was ongoing) to bear on mastering the reading skills essential to a lifetime of learning. My favorite age group, the second graders, combine the *joie de vivre* of the two lower classes with practiced social skills and burgeoning sophistication. Neither babyish nor jaded, they are simply a pleasure to teach, sweet children in what I consider the sweet spot of elementary education. Still inquisitive but capable of more nuanced understanding, these qualities inspire marvelous discussions and a pervasive atmosphere of learning as fun. The icing on this developmental cake is they are still young enough to respect authority and seek approval, "sticker-able," so I can expend energy on teaching rather than discipline.

The beatific innocence of these radiant young kids—best symbolized by their effortless comprehension of Santa Claus, the Easter Bunny and the Tooth Fairy into quotidian reality—was my reason for favoring the lower grades. (In time rumors questioning Santa would begin, the debate settled definitively by third grade.) This magical interlude of childhood, a rapturous bubble doomed to burst some time after their seventh birthday, becomes that much more miraculous given the grim deterrents in the lives of these kids. Though he comes down the fire escape and through the window, Santa, I have been told many times by those in foster care or with dads in prison, still delivers.

The staff's overwhelming hatred of Cruella rendered the atmosphere holy with prayers that she would leave at last. There had been some rumors that after eight years, she might. Though the professional tremblers contended the known evil was better than the unknown, I did not agree—I felt we could not possibly get anyone worse. Then one day she called the staff to the library to make an announcement: the chancellor was dissolving districts effective the next year, and instead the city would be divided into regions, with regional supervisors. A new position had been created in each of the regions: an "instructional supervisor" would oversee academic initiatives for a group of a few schools.

Thanks to Cruella's connections she had been promoted to one of these positions (a far easier and extremely lucrative job). With dazzling irony, the swath of damage the principal had wreaked on the careers of teachers and the educations of students had resulted in more power, prestige and profit. We just shook our heads: it was just another ludicrous travesty in an institution already riddled with incongruity. A couple weeks later her replacement appeared to tour the school: a short, impossibly young-looking man.

The last week of school the list of teachers' assignments for the next year appeared. My heart sank: I had been given the worst possible position, the dreaded fifth grade. Third grade, a class with increasing social interaction (read constant, annoying chitchat) where struggling kids lapse into chronic laggards, was preferable. Even fourth grade, the year kids switch from learning to read to reading to learn—its emphasis on test prep and test scores promoting a depressed, synapse-extinguishing apathy—was superior.

But to be sentenced to fifth grade meant a ceaseless, quixotic battle with the enraging hormones of surly pre-, or not so pre-adolescents, resolutely opposed to listening or learning. Up to half of each class—the undiagnosed candidates for special ed—gave the impression they were biding time till they could legally drop out. I would be facing off with girls who had discovered they hated their mothers and subconsciously transferring that resentment, me. I would be confronting held-back boys with sketchy moustaches and sketchier reading skills. Try as I did to make my peace with my fate, I was unable. Inside I was as hysterical as a North Korean mourner, except this was no performance art, this was my reality show.

The last day we were given our ratings and I left with my "S" for "Satisfactory" paper tucked in my bag. What a feeling it was, like being a kid again, just floating blissfully home with two months of summer ahead of me. My fifth grade assignment was so far off, after all, and somehow it would work out, like my first year had. Whether denial or optimism, a character trait requisite to my life-long resilience in the face of adversity, the euphoria gently obscured the year's loss of health and sanity.

By the end of the summer, though, I was bobbing in my parents' California pool doing anything but chilling—I was freaking out. The future was bleak, and despite my snorkel and mask, "plastics" was not in it. The prospect of going back and facing those little barbarians and now, an unknown principal, was raising cortisol and trepidation.

3

Our first day back I dragged up the steps, already passive-aggressively too late to clock in; there was a faculty meeting in the auditorium. As I walked down the aisle, two Teaching Fellow friends leapt up and beckoned me.

"Congratulations!" one cried.

"What are you talking about?" I asked.

"You're the art teacher now!" said the other.

They had to be messing with me. I did not actually believe it until I went upstairs and looked at the "organization chart." Yep, the universe had rescued me from certain annihilation: I would indeed be teaching art. A new Teaching Fellow was given the fifth grade I was supposed to get, and she experienced a year from hell. I was spared a turn on that cross.

The gratifying *deus ex machina* actually made perfect sense: not only did I have a bachelor's in art history as well as a degree in design and illustration, at that point I had twenty-two years of professional experience in those two fields. I was elated, convinced that the subject—which did not involve reading, writing or math—would entertain the kids and their behavior would no longer be an issue.

The new principal who addressed us that morning was just thirty years old, with connections at the DOE evidently far weightier than the experience-lite he brought as an educator. Incredibly, he had been appointed a principal after only a handful of years teaching. A short, homely Guido, his forced, dignified demeanor seemed that of an impostor: though he strained to do so, in no way did he give off an executive vibe. At the faculty meeting he gave me an appreciative, ogling look I had rarely received in recent years. That was disconcerting and just plain weird, considering my age as well as the circumstances. Later, when the cluster teachers had a meeting with him, he professed his love of the arts—the reason we now had music and art teachers.

Afterwards, he and I discussed the lack of space for an art room, and I showed him a room I figured could work as one. On the way there and back he kept walking behind me. All at once it hit me that he already knew about the room and simply wanted my ass in front of him. I pretended not to notice his pervy perfidy, though his wholesale creepiness certainly boded ill. For now, better just to take a shower and avoid the new principal as much as possible.

Klein had circulated a CD video to the schools as a primer on how to teach according to the constructivist theory. Using the unresearched tenets of Australian education professor Brian Cambourne, the film promulgated the now-familiar notion that children's learning flourishes with a minimum of adult involvement, just enough to "facilitate" learning. The video featured a checklist of "Conditions for Learning" with an authoritative map; classrooms were to be arranged according to the prescribed diagram.[1]

Every inch of available space had been assigned a value to the constructivist cause, from the positioning of furniture to the allocation of wall space to the display of student work; there were also to be "centers" for student learning activities. Rows of desks facing the chalk board at the front of the room, poised traditionally for a teacher-centered lecture, were strictly forbidden; the dreaded "cooperative" grouping of our kids at tables would continue. Absurdly, the classroom was student-centered to the point teachers were deemed extraneous: there was no teacher's desk on the plan. When our teachers painstakingly rearranged their classrooms to comply, the pesky nuisances had to improvise a work space, such as an unused student desk, as their own.

To give students the cozy feeling of being read aloud to by a parent (a research-backed practice known to result in later reading success) all classrooms were given large rugs for students to sit on, listening.[2] Eventually we got a shipment of rocking chairs (as well as directives on exactly where in the classroom to position them) that completed the faked effect of snuggling up for a bedtime read. Later the large, expensive chairs were thrown out over time, their hazard as well as monopolization of space trumping the pretense of old-fashioned charm. The DOE had not thought to provide for the upkeep of the rugs, so the next year thousands of vacuum cleaners were rushed into the schools; once they died they were never replaced.

Yet the room plan was the least of an oppressive micromanagement that pervaded every aspect of our day. As conveyed in tablets sent down to us from Mt. DOE, the tyranny continued with strict pedagogical directives; every facet of instruction was dictated, teachers commanded to use the "workshop" model, a specific program advanced by Lucy Calkins at Columbia University Teachers College (TC) Reading and Writing Project, considered the paragon of literacy research and theory.[3]

Like the cooperative learning notion of students grouped at a table, TC's concept was never questioned relative to the population we were teaching. Nevertheless, in the same blanket fashion, we were required to use the TC workshop model to teach anything: first the teacher "models" the new material, then there is "guided practice" during which students try their hands at it, still in the large group. Then students disperse and go back to their tables for "independent practice," in which students are expected to work individually and teach each other. At the end students are trained to "reflect" on what they have learned as a means of reviewing and further embedding the new information.

No deviance was permitted from the one-size-fits-all process, made even worse by its timed components; teaching directly for more than ten minutes was strictly *verboten*. Not only did the city buy Columbia's expensive program for the schools (the first no-bid three-year, five and a half million dollar contract was just the beginning), but teachers were sent there for exorbitantly-billed professional development (twelve hundred dollars per day, per teacher). The constructivist instructional practices were further inculcated in weekly school professional development, even though the value to staff of the professional development sessions, costing in the millions, had never been studied. Positions were inaugurated for reading and math coaches specifically to train, and most importantly, *police* us in the use of the pedagogy and curriculum.

Notwithstanding their intellect, credentials, experience, track record, or individual instructional style, teachers were forced into lockstep with the commanded directives. With NCLB's focus on credentials, we all had or were getting our master's degrees in education, not to mention our personal teaching styles; dictating our every move impugned our professionalism as well as stymied the natural joy and creativity we brought to teaching. Obviously most teachers were furious at being told what to do, not to mention dumbfounded at the ridiculous prospect of our population of kids, teaching each other. The motivation, cognitive and social skills necessary to behave themselves in a group, let alone construct their own learning, simply were not there. Using direct teaching we had only been able to get through to a few of them, after all. But the corporate non-educator managers at the DOE remained resolutely deaf to these protests.

The first day of school I found myself thrilled to see the kids, pleasantly clobbered with the astonishing realization that I had missed them over the summer. That did not apply as much, of course, to the ones who had made my life a living hell: just seeing them again inspired a gut wrench of stored panic in my reptilian brain. Now that I was in my second year I had been through the baptism by fire, so that was definitely an improvement. I knew most of the kids from before, and familiarity with the routine was a further advantage. Plus, since I was teaching art I was much happier in a subject where I excelled, gratified, for my own sake and that of the kids, to be using my expertise.

But my romantic vision, which played the second I was given the art position, of tranquil tableaus of kids bathed in golden light, laboring in hushed reverence over their creations, was summarily dashed with the first day. The atmosphere, it turned out, was to be more chiaroscuro than glowing enlightenment.

Yes, the respite from math and literacy brought behavior issues down a notch or two, but only the best artists, a smattering per grade, were invested enough to concentrate in silence. For the rest my arrival, like that of the other out-of-classroom teachers, signaled the same old prompt to kick back and talk, and for those in the darker parts of the composition, play around, fight and satiate the need for drama that seemed at the very nucleus of their DNA. Disappointingly, despite my increased sophistication, the hardcores were just as challenging to manage, though art pulled at least a few of them away from mischief and into the learning orbit, if only sporadically. I discovered children who act out often turn out to be talented at art, an activity that offers a healthy outlet for their anger and also benefits their self-esteem: a win-win for all of us.

An interesting, albeit depressing phenomenon I noticed right away, was the divergence in the attitude towards art between the younger and older kids. Though in each age group there was still a disturbing contingent who wanted to copy me, in general the lower grade kids approached an assignment with vigor. Diving into drawing, for example, they would plumb their fecund imaginations, energetically filling their papers with abandon. By third grade, though, parallel to their emergence from magical thinking and the onslaught of doubt in their abilities, a task engendered a chorus of "I can't do that!"

Whether due to low self-regard, or because now they were comparing themselves to other kids, or both—that greatest saboteur of creativity: self-criticism—had set in. Considering few words incense me more than "can't," I had my work cut out for me. My job took on the quality of a mission: one by one I exhorted them onward, encouraging, flattering, even begging them just to let go and make art. Over and over I preached my gospel of freedom and fun, no matter what the outcome; we could always try again. There were always those who pleaded for me to do it for them, a kind of helpless default mode I found no less destructive. I had to use my own experience to make them understand. "When I was your age," I would say, "I thought to myself, 'I wonder if I can make that?' and I tried. After a few times I did it." Maybe the deeper issue was, actually, there was no cheerleader like me at home.

The summer before, I had read a profile of Howard Dean, running for the Democratic presidential nomination, in a national news magazine. After graduating from Yale he taught public school in inner city New Haven, but he had only lasted a year. He left because there were "too many kids with too many needs."[4]

I almost gasped with sheer resonance, so gratifying was the glaring truth of his words, brilliant in their succinct summation of the obstacles I was facing. Dean's economical analysis so mirrored my experience, I exulted in the solidarity as well as reveled in the prospect we might get a president who would bring that understanding, that humility, to Washington. But Dean's pronouncement had still more significance. For him a lifetime of extraordinary accomplishments was feasible: an Ivy League degree; getting through medical school; practicing medicine; governing a state, and now, the august position of president loomed simply as another viable opportunity. But teaching in an inner city school: too hard.

Now, Howard Dean's words continued to capture my day-to-day reality: the work was overwhelming. Soon I was once again bone-tired, dreading the job as much as before, rising in the black void before dawn, my head frequently pounding with a respiratory infection, then dragging home after my graduate classes to crawl under my comforter into fetal position before getting up and doing it all over again.

The new principal proved to be the most impeccable version of a satyr this side of a Hellenistic frieze. His Friday night partying ritual, one he had initiated during the previous summer school session, had begun the first week of school. The new batch of Teaching Fellows, most just out of college, went drinking with him in a bar in the Bronx, a few regular teachers accompanying them. Despite his position and his marriage, he stayed out late carousing with his "bitches" as he referred to them to bartenders, along with his buddy Jack Daniels, getting shitfaced. Teachers who attended these debauches talked of his flagrantly unprofessional behavior, as well as that of his sycophantic entourage.

A typical outing was rumored to rely on the philosophy that things go better with coke, while prodigious amounts of alcohol enlivened the proceedings with an occasional episode of projectile vomiting; the principal feeling up the looser (or loser, take your pick) teachers while dancing with them; and a disgraceful *denouement* of banging on car hoods as he weaved to his car, which he then drove to his distant home, blind drunk.

At school the principal continued the cozy relationship with his designated homies, while for the rest of us he preferred the role of swaggering martinet. He basked in his new power, especially in this realm of mainly women, ordering the staff around with bravado. The obsequious ones, PTSD-ed from the abusive Cruella years, jockeyed to secure their position in his good graces. Two of the bar buddies aggressively threw themselves at him; the hussies were the talk of the school.

According to the grapevine, one would slowly cross her legs à la *Basic Instinct* every time he was in the room; the other became his "secret" lover, a fact known to everyone with a pulse. I wondered where in the school they hooked up after we went home. Maybe the booty call took place in the cafeteria, for example, where they lustily feasted *Tom Jones*-style on DOE microwaved mystery nuggets, then ravished each other on the seventies formica table.

The principal put his paramour into administrative training along with another crony; the other flirt, with only the scantest of teaching experience, was subsequently awarded "Lead Teacher," an easier out-of-classroom position with a big raise (a job supposed to be open to all staff through application, a protocol he ignored). The girlfriend was naturally promoted, too, to a coach position. Through it all, the principal reveled in being surrounded with a phalanx of cronies. Not only had he created newly minted versions of these standard-issue school parasites, he had brought with him others from his former school. Since Bloomberg had given principals unrivaled autonomy, overseeing hiring choices as well as multi-million dollar budgets, he took full advantage of the mayor's over-confident, reckless policy.

As a supporter of the arts in a time of flush school budgets, the new principal obtained whatever we needed to teach, so that was helpful. Also, he made improvements, for example, organizing the place more efficiently, creating better means of staff communication and to give him his due, was the only principal to get the hallway clocks running and on-time (by getting on a ladder and setting them himself). He was more hands-on than we had ever experienced, possessing tremendous, even suspicious, energy, clicking crisply down the hall, arms swinging, in his apparently steel-tapped Florsheim's.

His ill-fitting, one-size-too-large suits—refugees from the racks of Sears—and his short stature gave him the look of a child dressing up in Dad's clothes. As the year progressed there was still the sense of a *poseur*: he seemed not so much a principal as playing one on TV. Moreover, because his less-than-intimidating baby face thwarted efforts to dominate and impress, he could be scary in his attempt to compensate. The imperial demeanor he assumed was clearly a front for insecurity and a sense of inadequacy which made him insufferably controlling.

With no justification other than a bad mood (or probably a hangover), the principal rudely yelled at me in a group meeting, intent on humiliation. Another time, in front of the kids, he screamed, "See me in my office after class!" when he walked in on a fifth grade class that was out of control, something they all did, no matter what age, at that time of day, last period. The problem was with my lame lesson, he said, it was not interesting enough to them. But that was not the real reason I was there: sitting across from him, it did not matter what I had done or what he was saying: his gaping black hole of need required a serving of life force, and mine was clearly the mojo du jour.

Besides his control issues, the principal was pathetic, even ridiculous. Once when I saw part of a tattoo under his open shirt collar I asked him about it. Unbidden, he unbuttoned his shirt and showed a huge design on his chest to me, then suddenly registered the inappropriateness and blushing, turned on his heel. True, he was a champion of the arts and brought some good to the school in other, organizational, ways. But ultimately his contemptible need to dominate, cultivation of cronyism and grotesque, immature conduct reached a critical mass of repugnance for me: I abhorred the diminutive lech, and I christened him Guido Bonerparte.

Every so often Guido's *clickety click click* echoed from far away down the hall. It was a warning everything had better be in order or there will be blood. He specialized in the drive-by ambush, but only with teachers he did not like. His chums, well, they could be hosting an orgy in their rooms, no problem, because he never bothered them. Entering dramatically, he would puff out his chest importantly and penguin-like, survey the scene. If everything were okay you would look up and poof! he would be gone, the clickety clicks fading off down the hallway to his next strike. Since I had my lessons in order he could not find any reason to browbeat me.

Though uniforms could not be legally mandated, at least outside of charter schools, Guido launched an effort encouraging the students to wear a navy blue and white ensemble he had chosen from styles available at nearby stores. Brochures were sent home to parents detailing the clothes and where to find them; many availed themselves of the opportunity to save money and time getting their kids ready for school every day. But the administration's agenda was far from altruistic or even aesthetic, for that matter. Though the crisp, together look of the outfits telegraphed a grown-up seriousness of purpose (the boys' version even included a clip-on tie) the fashion statement belied the true intent: the symbolic consistency of the sober, rigid look was meant to carry over into student behavior.

In this way the uniform, for all intents and purposes a psychic straitjacket, constituted a nuanced nudge to stay in line, just like the visually restrained clothing. Moreover, with the fixed appearance not only repressing the individual personality and dulling the spirit, the sense of group uniformity was enhanced and the job of keeping order eased. The uniform was a perfect metaphor for NCLB's drive to produce cookie cutter ranks of test-taking automatons, soulless and malleable as future cogs in the wheel of society.

Admittedly, the sartorial ploy to extract more temperate behavior did yield results, though they were uneven, at best moderate and usually immediate and temporary. Unfortunately, the ones who would have most benefited from the psychological confines were rarely provided the uniform, as parents of these tended to be neglectful and generally failed to look at papers sent home, among them the store brochure. Occasionally a child with a recent history of particularly bad behavior would appear suddenly clad in navy and white, evidently a concerned parent's idea. The child, quite aware of the clothing's purpose, invariably behaved better for a week or so, and then it was back to Facebook monster status.

Despite the new male principal, the bantam hellions were in fine fettle, a threat served long past its expiration date in my fed-up opinion. The discipline problem, ever the bane of my teaching existence, caused me to ruminate at length on methods to resolve it. The astounding prevalence of students with undiagnosed ADD and ADHD was the genesis of my favorite solution: piping clouds of Ritalin through the school, an enterprise which would remain a fantasy for a more Orwellian time.

In a cluster meeting discussing the ongoing challenge, I suggested that we dispense tickets for good behavior, to be redeemed for prizes every Friday by school aides or the elusive parent volunteer. The idea, one I would bring up virtually every year for the next eight, was met with approval, though the logistics were seen to be prohibitive. For now, absent a new approach, the *agents provocateurs* in all grades continued to ply their crazy issues with more or less impunity, considering the consequence remained spending a day in suspension with the benign veteran teacher gliding towards retirement at the end of the year.

Halloween landed mercifully on a weekend so getting home alive, or at least without getting molested by a root vegetable, was not a problem. Nevertheless, during our Halloween art projects several objections from Pentecostal and Jehovah's Witness students surfaced regarding the celebration of "the Devil's Birthday." Though I had cheerfully given them something else to do (while inwardly gnashing my teeth), I couldn't stop myself from summarizing the Celtic history of Halloween I had already presented during the lesson; their blinders were preventing them from seeing the truth of an ancient cultural celebration. I tried to bolster Halloween's intrinsic wholesomeness, employing the Day of the Dead defense, pointing out that stalwart Mexican Catholics—fans of Jesus, for Christ's sake—partake in that annually. But the parents had branded their narrow views on their kids, denying them the late night satisfaction of sorting Butterfingers from Reese's into piles (after hurling the razor-ridden apples).

Along with the boycott of the innocent, costumed insulin spike that was Halloween, the zealots insisted on burdening their children with the gloomy premise that the end of the world was coming at any moment, a fact tiny children solemnly declared. Other churches had normal names like the Bronx Baptist or the Community Presbyterian; the one we had to pass everyday screamed in neon "EL FIN SE ACERCA." If only the end *were* coming, in fact, to parents brazenly traumatizing their children with their morbid pronouncements. After all, guzzling the Kool-Aid (flavor: Strawberry Doom) was the *parents'* choice, not a beverage any *kid* would choose to imbibe. Child abuse comes in many forms, but even forcing them to learn a string instrument is a lot less sadistic than the terrorism of imminent death.

Meanwhile, the fad for new-fangled progressive math had secured a foothold in New York City, Joel Klein choosing a constructivist program called Everyday Math. Developed by the University of Chicago, the idea was to encourage "higher order thinking" in math, therefore eliminating instruction in the old-fashioned basics. The traditional foundation for numeracy was discarded for an array of alternatives, even an ancient Egyptian formula for multiplication. Cooperative learning (again, yikes!) was accessorized by a heavy reliance on calculators, even kindergartners trained to use them.

Not surprisingly, prominent mathematicians and scientists, including Nobel Prize winners, had rejected the curriculum as unsound. Constructivist math had been so destructive to California test scores, the state had jettisoned the curriculum in favor of traditional math, yet now Everyday Math swept the nation's school districts as reformers drove their agenda with reform arithmetic. According to the research universities who backed the constructivist approach, the low math scores on state tests were due to some other vague cause.[5]

Obsessed with molding principals according to their rigid views, Bloomberg and Klein launched the nonprofit Leadership Academy to train them, an effort geared to turning around failing schools. Philanthropic contributions paid the salaries of ninety principals in a fourteen month crash course designed, once again invoking the business model, with the input of former CEO of General Electric Jack Welch, a figure on whom Klein relied for expertise in management. Three hundred new principals were needed every year; unbelievably, all you needed to apply were a master's degree and a mere three years of teaching experience.

Winter came and with it clumsy little Michelin men trundling through snow drifts to school, showing up in blizzards which closed all school districts except New York City's: Bloomberg's special brand of sadism. This meant that while the far-flung teachers, many living upstate, did not make the trip, most of the neighborhood children, being close by, did. Consequently, the school was vastly understaffed and classes were combined into huge groups, while every teacher who struggled in was turned into a sub. By now the state of the snow removal in the Bronx was beginning to get to me. The discrimination evident from this missing urban service was striking: nobody of import lived here, and there were never complaints, so the neighborhood was ignored.

While Manhattan was already plowed as I walked to the train, when I arrived uptown it was still a scene from *Dr. Zhivago*, and it would be for days. The snow would just get tamped down into icy slicks, melting a bit and refreezing every night into treacherous swathes of slippery gray crud. Walking to school from the train was a tedious, precarious exercise in balance. The garbage which always covered the sidewalks was frozen underneath, ghetto under glass. The snow drifts, pristine on the first morning, were gradually studded with a slalom course of dog shit, and mottled yellow in homage to Frank Zappa.

One icy morning, the day of the all-important state fourth grade ELA test, I arrived to find I would be subbing a first grade special ed class while we waited for the teacher, who was coming in late due to the roads. Even though it was usually a tough class full of violent boys, I counted on the para to help me. Anyway, I had a good art project the kids would like so I felt okay about it. As it turned out, the para, however, was also going to be late. Nevertheless, all the students showed up and scarily, it was just them and me, a situation which was actually illegal, since I had neither a special education teaching license nor a para, who was required by the state to be in the room at all times.

I took attendance and taught my lesson—so far so good. The kids were interested in doing the art and dug right in. An hour went by and unbelievably neither teacher nor para had shown up. The kids had finished their first project and now I was winging another, but they were getting antsy and starting to snipe at each other. I had them do stretches and a game I invented my first year, "Freeze Sillies," which I used to get the squirms and wiggles out of kids who had been sitting too long.

I would count to three and we would all move around, dancing and doing goofy gestures, then I would suddenly yell "Freeze!" The kids loved this but a couple boys took the opportunity to start pushing and punching each other instead of having fun, so we had to stop. Sitting down again, we got back into the second project and it took all the vigilance I could muster to keep those two boys off of each other.

By now, I had been in the room two hours and still the cavalry did not come; I was at my wits end. The situation was deteriorating rapidly, as I desperately tried to maintain order and keep them quiet, since the fourth graders were taking the test and the whole school was reverentially hushed. All of a sudden Joelis, a kid who had been taken out forty-five minutes before for speech therapy, burst into the room. Rashawn, the boy I had put next to me because he had been pounding another kid, saw Joelis and yelled an insult at him. Joelis, who I had known from the year before as an agitator, rushed towards Rashawn and me—I was in between the two. I put out my arm straight to block Joelis's attack and he stepped back dramatically exclaiming, "You pushed me!" I told him I was preventing a fight and he should sit down across the table and join us in making some art. The next hour of refereeing seemed to stretch into infinity, along with my blood pressure. By the time the teacher came, I had jumped through every hoop possible to entertain the kids and keep them from killing each other. It had been three hours; I had been told I would be there for a few minutes.

Two days later Guido said to me, "You're in serious trouble" and warned me I was going to have a meeting with him. I racked my brain: I could not imagine what he was talking about. The next day I got a letter to see the principal with my union representative: I had been accused of "corporal punishment" by another union member. This was extremely rare. Usually, teachers would go to each other before ratting someone out to the administration.

In the meeting they enlightened me of my crime: I had "shoved" Joelis that icy morning I was stranded in the special ed class, and the teacher from across the hall had espied my transgression from the door window when she came over to investigate the noise. I remembered she had come to the door two times before, complaining that the ELA was being taken upstairs and my class was too loud. Not only had the teacher not helped me (she could have taken Joelis into her class for awhile) but she had the nerve to inform on me; all I had done was to stop another fight from happening, in a class I was illegally supervising. I found her slimy behavior not only shockingly belligerent but especially mystifying because we had had a friendly relationship. I had been through so much that morning, indeed, I felt like I should be thanked profusely for my hours of crucifixion on the special ed cross. Instead, here I was, vilified.

The union tried to protect me from the allegation, backing my claim that I was protecting another student by preventing a fight. But that assertion did not stand a chance given the devious, opportunistic Joelis, eight going on fifty, who had been interviewed and over-dramatized my gesture, getting attention as well as a teacher in trouble. Still worse, the fact that another union member had witnessed the event doomed my efforts to fight the accusation.

So I received the terrible, storied "Letter to File," which, according to the city rules, would remain on my record for three years, at which point I could have it removed. Using my union rights I filed a grievance, but it was to no avail. After that, I did not speak to the informer for three years until I absolutely had to, having been assigned to teach her class. She looked uncomfortable around me—I wondered if she regretted what she had done, yet she never apologized. I moved on.

This disheartening development left me determined to get out of that school. I had noticed that I liked teaching, that was not the problem. It was teaching such a high percentage of difficult kids, in an unsupportive, sabotaging atmosphere, that I could not stand. Since I was in my second year, I would soon be finishing my commitment to the Teaching Fellows. From now on, at the end of every year I would be looking at transfer opportunities within the city.

Traditionally, the city schools' promotion rate had been from ninety to ninety-five percent, yet fewer than half the students were able to read or do math at the next grade level. Test scores, classwork and attendance had been the official factors used in determining promotion, but the unwritten policy for principals was to hold a child back no more than once in elementary school and once in middle school. By the time students reached high school, twenty-five percent of them were older than they were supposed to be. Moreover, less than one in ten Hispanic and black high school students were even graduating with a Regents diploma.

Now, in a move that mollified conservative critics, Bloomberg created a program of third grade retention, a policy which later came to include fifth grade, extolling it as "the end of social promotion."[6] In theory, those students left back were then supposed to receive additional help, though during the recession this, in fact, scant support would drop to virtually nonexistent. Bloomberg's megalomania had been highlighted when he fired two members of his Panel for Educational Policy, on the spot, when they questioned using state tests as the sole criteria for not promoting a child.

Yet this new policy couldn't alter the manifest absurdity of the status quo: kids who scored a 2, "below grade level," on the state tests—even a low 2 which corresponded to an D-/F+ in grade terms—passed to the next grade as a matter of course. Meanwhile, those students whose reading level, assessed by their teachers, measured a full grade behind were also routinely promoted. No, really. Despite his abhorrence of "social promotion," in fact the Education Mayor's legacy would turn out to be the highest promotion rate in the city's history.[7]

Bloomberg's "my way or the highway" top-down management style meant that all accountability was with him, particularly salient in next year's election in which credit or blame would result in his fate. But his arrogant approach left teachers and parents out of decision-making, notwithstanding the fact that he had already won many parents' votes in his mayoral campaign in 2001, when he promised to reduce class sizes. Though he had even referred to research singling out overcrowding as highly negative to student learning, Bloomberg had not honored that expensive assurance, so now a parent group, Class Size Matters, was avidly lobbying the DOE for smaller class sizes. We joined the parents in their demands, since to any teacher the issue was a no-brainer: the fewer the students, the more individual attention we could give, the better the quality of education we could provide. Duh.

All of a sudden, we no longer had the reading program "Success For All." Despite my dislike of its impossible pace and rigid scripted format, it turned out SFA had yielded reading gains four years in a row for my school as well as others. Nevertheless, the program was unceremoniously given the heave-ho by Diane Lam, with the blessing of Joel Klein, of course, without so much as a phone call to its developer. Success For All's excellent results, obtained at an investment by the city of twenty-seven million dollars, were ignored, probably because Lam did not approve of the explicit phonics involved in the program.

By March, Lam herself was thrown overboard, the first of several Bloomberg officials to meet an ignominious end when she proved involved in a nepotism scandal and was given the axe. Yet her fanatical constructivist legacy lived on to rob lower-performing students of the logical, systematic pedagogy that might diminish the achievement gap.

The city's scandals were nothing next to the revelation of the grand daddy of educational cons, one so big it would bring about the demise of learning for a generation, as well as threaten the future of the nation itself. The No Child Left Behind law had ridden the coattails of the oft-invoked "Texas Miracle," a phenomenon of soaring test scores and plunging dropout rates, made possible ostensibly by the accountability Texas required of its principals.[8] In return for cash bonuses of up to five thousand dollars, principals who had signed one year contracts would deliver district-mandated numbers for low dropout rates and high test scores. Those who failed to make the numbers were demoted, transferred or fired. The result of this program was thousands of disadvantaged children in Houston, for example, had the astonishing dropout rate of just one and a half percent. That is because the dropouts were not counted, instead being hidden by classifying the missing students as transferring, getting a GED, or returning to their native country.

Though top people in the education system were aware of the faked statistics by the year 2000, that did not stop Bush repeating the false claim of Texas's success as a mantra during the election. Nor did the sham story inhibit Rod Paige from accepting Bush's gift of the highest education position in the country, secretary of education, in itself a corrupt gesture, a blatant payoff for Paige's phony education record which helped get Bush elected.

In the next couple years the deception had been publicly unmasked when an assistant principal—who had seen literally hundreds of his students drop out every year, yet his school reported a zero dropout rate—questioned the figure; the Texas Miracle,which extended to other Texan cities, was busted as a massive scam. When the investigation was finished, the city's dropout rate reached national urban numbers, forty to fifty percent.

Another cause for Bush to gush had been the sensational Texas test scores of tenth graders. The results of these, too, were found to have been cooked to enable principals to keep their jobs. Higher scores were effected by preventing low-achieving kids from taking the important tenth grade test at all, principals simply keeping them out of tenth grade. Some kids were kept in ninth grade three years in a row, even though they had passed all the classes, then skipped into eleventh grade. This meant that they didn't have enough credits to graduate and many ended up dropping out. Some had not been given, expressly, all the correct classes to take in ninth grade, and were told they would have to repeat the grade.

They had all served their purpose, unwitting pawns to the principals' accountability agendas, their absence from the tenth grade test destroying their futures—but boy, how impressive their schools were. Ultimately, the sham Texas Miracle was exposed nationwide when the show *Sixty Minutes II* televised the despicable, indeed evil, saga; naturally Secretary of Education Rod Paige declined to be interviewed.[9] Since NCLB had been based on a criminally-created mirage, then, the handwriting was on the wall indicating the inevitable destruction of that myth, as well.

Meanwhile, for New York state it was business as usual, the fourth grade state math tests administered, as ever, in the spring. After the test a Teaching Fellow with a fourth grade class told me of a highly illegal event: during the test, Guido's flunky, whom he had brought from his previous school, the corkscrewed math coach staff referred to as Miss Piggy, told the teacher to leave the classroom when she entered. When the test was finished and the teacher came back, the students said Miss Piggy had told them the principal had sent her to help them, providing them with six answers per child and correcting their mistakes. The shocked teacher had the students write statements regarding what had happened, and delivered them to Guido. There were emails back and forth between her, the AP Dubrow and Guido, but the end of the school year was approaching and nothing was resolved. The matter was a big secret; I was one of the few people who knew about it.

Finally receiving my master's degree in education, embellished grandly with a commencement speech from President Clinton, as the year ended I applied for the art position again for the upcoming year. Guido was adding another art teacher, and there was even possibly going to be an art room.

I continued looking online in the teacher's transfer system, however, only schools similar to my current one were looking to fill that position. I figured I may as well stay. I had passed my first goal, fulfilling my contract to the Teaching Fellows. The next year I would be focused on getting tenured.

4

After a stretch of summer rest, the only real score to being a teacher, though truly not an indulgence, but a necessity, September came and with it the luxury of an art room I would be sharing with the other art teacher. She was the Teaching Fellow who had taken my place as a fifth grade teacher the year before. Since then she had become chummy with Guido, accompanying him and his janissaries on his Friday night tears. From the get-go he gave her precedence over me, in scheduling, supplies, extra perks—whatever came along. His solicitude was conveyed in earnestly whispered *tête-à-têtes* outside the room. For her part, as an art history major she was qualified and her drawing was fine for elementary art.

On the first day of school Guido had addressed us at a faculty meeting, flooring us all when he declared we would be observed five times in the coming year. Our observations by an administrator, always the biggest component of our rating for the year, tended to be, thankfully, just once a year. His edict of five observations was ugly, unnecessary posturing: the preening effect was of him thrusting out his unimpressive chest to dominate after a summer bereft of power. Though his threat was intimidating—we all had sufficient work and stress without the triple dose an observation involved—we took it with a grain of salt: given their busy schedules administrators would never have the time to do that.

In fact, Guido's threat turned out to be an empty one. In that sense it was not much different from the bomb threat we got one morning. The telephoned bluff, probably from an irate parent, incurred a botched report to police and equally bungled evacuation into the rain. The crisis was so mishandled a bonafide threat would have done us in, though it was hard to imagine *any* explosion, given the paucity of even neural combustion in the place.

As the year proceeded, we alternated months in the art room. For Extended Day tutoring I had been placed in a fifth grade class taught by the boorish blowhard Sanchez, a teacher who did not speak so much as trumpet. In the fall, Sanchez's students were cramming for the state test in social studies, an annual frenzy which only lasted a couple months prior to the exam. After that, social studies was throttled back. Subsequently, even that cursory nod to social studies was jettisoned when the fifth grade state social studies exam was eliminated, subjects other than math or reading deemed extraneous in a culture of "I test, therefore I am."

Meanwhile, the hair-raising ignorance the students displayed of things historical, cultural, and especially geographical, was downright chilling. New York City, according to one, is a continent. Cleveland, a boy insisted, is a nation. During a discussion of common holidays another, the bravest of dozens of eleven and twelve-year-olds who did not have a clue about the origins of Christmas, hazarded timidly, "Is it the birthday of the Baby Santa?"

From my first day teaching I had noticed this remarkable lack of basic knowledge, not just in social studies, but in every field, information the general population takes for granted. Apparently the kids were not getting this understanding at home. However, that did not explain why, when we taught something to them, the majority still did not know it.

At the end of an art class, my teaching materials in hand so they could not peek at what I had posted before, I asked them to name the artist, style or concept we had been working on for nearly the last hour. Except for a couple kids with the lights on, invariably nobody could answer. After a few unnerving displays of these blank expressions, I resolved to drill the class periodically through the lesson, covering the board and making it a competition to remember what I had posted. That repetition only increased the number of students who responded correctly to about half; invariably there were some that did not know it even by the end of the class. Following instructions was an equally challenging endeavor: I could repeat them three times and there were still several who had not listened to those. I had to resort to virtually chanting whatever they needed to know, mantra-like, at intervals throughout the class period. Matisse, Matisse, Matisse. Collage, collage, collage.

Of course, they were not all this unresponsive. But when faced with several, the energy required to teach these kids was nothing short of herculean. Nevertheless, my inward impatience with them never blinded me to the circumstances which had brought them to that place. In time I would discover that the "toxic stress" of poverty—equally the source of disturbance to their irate parents— had also impacted the kids' cognitive abilities, literally altering their brain's structure: working memory, crucial to learning, had been damaged.

Naturally, one of the biggest frustrations of trying to educate our population was the widespread nonchalance accorded homework, as well. A duty supposed to be the bane of the kids' existence was instead, ours: huge proportions of our students did little or not even bother at all. Regular fallout from this non-engagement, on the part of kids *and* parents, after all, was typified by a fifth grade teacher who spent an entire Sunday planning a week's lessons based on homework assigned the Friday before: only eleven out of twenty-eight kids did the homework, so the planning was for naught.

The pervasively low caliber of such a large proportion of students throughout the school elicited the question, why were these kids not in special ed? I discovered teachers were not even allowed to suggest the special ed option to families. In fact, years later instructions for parent-teacher conference day would still specifically dictate, "Do not state or infer that a child should be evaluated by special education. Do not state or infer any disability or handicapping condition." Parents had to come up with the idea themselves, then go through a morass of red tape to make it happen.

Obviously, the special ed smaller class setting, limited to twelve children, with a teacher and a minimum of one paraprofessional (plus as many one-on-one paras as required), was discouraged because it was expensive, considering how many could be warehoused in the larger "regular ed" classes. But I knew of teachers who, at least unofficially, put forward the advice that a child would do better in a "more intimate setting"—the euphemism for special ed. The process could take months of interviews, observations and meetings of expert committees. All this time the candidate, often desperately in need of a dedicated para, might be bouncing off the walls in their mainstream class, completely wrecking their education and that of their classmates.

Perhaps the most idiotic aspect of the special ed process was the bizarre power accorded the parents: though manifestly unqualified to make a judgment, they could, and often did, refuse the placement, dooming their child and those in his class. Equally, they had the right to decline the best placement for their child's needs (one reached through meticulous consideration by the evaluators involved) simply because the child would be picked up and dropped off by a school bus every day. Again, this conclusion resulted in the child being placed in an inappropriate slot in our school's general special ed class, regardless of being ill-equipped to address his issues. Naturally, the child, his classmates and the teacher all suffered because of the parent's imprudence.

Considering the vast majority of kids struggling or not even bothering to, the handful of diligent kids, many from Bangladesh, was a miracle of clemency. Indeed, every June a girl from this group was the fifth grade graduation valedictorian. They all had in common structured, caring families with iron-clad discipline and industrial-strength educational values. Without these students, the only ones to usually score four (above grade level) on state tests as well as report card grades, the school's stats, already impossibly low, would have been downright irredeemable. In the imminent disparagement to come of teachers and their unions as scapegoats for the failures of NCLB, these high-achievers would be a testament to the competency of our staff, consistent proof that our teachers were highly effective when the kids and parents pulled their weight, too.

In fact, in every grade there were just one or two, at most less than two percent of the students, who could realistically be headed into medicine, law or some other top profession. We could visualize more manifesting as cops, firefighters, and others at the backbone of the middle class, and still more as lower-skilled technicians in service industries like health care. Unfortunately, in the absence of expensive psychological and academic interventions, a number of our kids were inconceivable in any but the least demanding pursuits, looking forward (or not, rather, anticipating any eventuality, that was the problem) to continued hardship with menial work at minimum wage. Just like others in my Teaching Fellow cohort, my initial idealism had undergone a sobering evolution in perspective, and swiftly: even though we naturally wished them the life of their dreams, disappointingly, the most compelling contribution we could probably make to many would be keeping them off of welfare and out of prison. Still, by nature I could not help leaving the door open: I had always felt anything is possible. I was not going to alter my philosophy now for the kids—especially not for the kids.

While Klein insisted on pedagogical conformity with his authoritarian vision, he began a *fatwa* against the teachers union, his criticism concentrating on three aspects of the teachers contract: tenure; regular, incremental pay raises; and seniority privileges granting teachers with the greatest longevity the best assignments. Of these issues tenure was the hot button, sexy one, foundational to the reform movement's platform that teachers are not only incompetent but untouchably so. In fact, despite the dexterous hackle-raising the reformers coaxed from an easily manipulated public, tenure isn't a free ticket to never-ending employment, merely a guarantee there be a just cause to be fired, one established in a fair hearing. Once afforded this due process, if a legitimate reason is determined, teachers are terminated like those in other professions.

In attacking tenure, solicitor Klein wasn't beyond denying us a simple right to justice. Besides his resentment of our basic union rights, Klein championed incentives (merit pay) as well as more money for teachers who work in the most challenging schools; the pervasive unpopularity of Klein's micromanagement of instruction, however, hardened teachers' resistance to these innovations.

Klein's position was just the local version of a primarily right wing education policy trickling down from Washington and special interests, a campaign to destroy collective bargaining rights and privatize education masquerading as an initiative to fix the low achievement of disadvantaged kids.[1] Concerns such as the anti-government Koch brothers, armed with over seventy-two billion dollars and an extreme free-market ideology, sought to launch a putsch for privatization, their aim dismantling the public education system and exploiting its billions in funding.[2] Both privately educated, one of the Koch's initiatives, Americans For Prosperity, would be unleashed at the local level to place like-minded officials on school boards not simply to force schools into a business model, but even to rid society of written-in-stone mandates like desegregation. In the fall of 2013, for example, three hundred fifty thousand Koch dollars would be deployed successfully in the school board race in the suburbs of Denver, completely overwhelming the resources of local grassroots groups. Taking a page from the Karl Rove playbook, the propagandistic attack included mass e-mailings to parents of blatantly false information, scoring a direct hit and electing several reform candidates.

At the state level the American Legislative Exchange Council (ALEC), two thousand conservative legislators who espouse privatization in every corner of the public realm, has been the backbone of the reform agenda, providing pols and other heavies with talking points and scripted speeches to further its cause, one custom-worded bill at a time, backed by a custom campaign donation (we can thank ALEC for the various state Stand Your Ground, Voter ID and Parent Trigger laws).[3] Besides exerting political pressure, in time private money would reveal itself to be the catalyst behind all aspects of education reform, despite the threat these private concerns pose to the democratic promise of an equal, quality education for all. The American vision of education as a social responsibility was giving way to a less noble distortion: an institution dedicated to the public good was now seen simply as another opportunity for private plunder.

But remaking education was not only a neocon agenda. "Neoliberal" Democrats were on board as well, focusing on the right of high-needs children to the same quality education as their advantaged, usually white, peers—the phrase "civil rights" being their operative cover. Yet all reform proponents equally grasped the most expedient, facile solution, one which would leave untouched the powers that be, was to punish someone in the triumvirate of parent/teacher/child who impacted a student's academic achievement. Rather than methodically sort out the tangle of variables responsible for the poor national performance, better to simplistically seize on the low hanging fruit of teachers as the culprit, with the added conservative bonus of busting unions. The phony elixir of NCLB, forced down the gullets of increasingly desperate local affiliates unable to raise test scores, would toast a decade to come of a new national sport: teacher-bashing.

The months I did not have access to the art room I resumed my gypsy traipse from floor to floor and class to class. Laden with shopping bags full of supplies, I backed into the door of a class as a cheer went up: partly for me, partly for art, but mostly because it was a reprieve from fractions, decimals and all manner of left brain afflictions. The classroom teacher, a few gray hairs the worse from a morning of wrestling learning into grudging cerebellums, beat a hasty retreat to the hallway, fleeing the classroom for a well-earned preparation period. Now and then a teacher stayed back to lesson-plan at the back of the room; however, for the most part when they saw me they were more than ready to get out of Dodge.

Visiting so many classrooms, I came to connect the dots: if the teacher were messy, disorganized, out of control and nonchalant, then so, in general, were the students. Conversely, if a teacher were organized, alert and in charge, that civil tone bled, at least somewhat, into my art period. Better still the rare teacher organized to the point of anal, controlling to a dictatorial degree: though I could not speak for the mental health fall-out from a year spent in this environment, entering a room of silent, possibly traumatized kids with folded hands on cleared desks, ready to work, was a windfall for me. As clusters, given our tentative hold on the class's behavior, we did not appreciate the teacher leaving the class in a state of chaos.

Most teachers addressed the class using the casual, in fact, fitting, "boys and girls." I said, "Good morning, ladies and gentlemen." I was bent on brainwashing them into being such, admittedly a lame, almost superstitious ritual to ward off behavior I was ultimately powerless to prevent. At least it was a shot at a structured formality, a safe place for me to teach and them to learn. Then I would enlist the aid of monitors (kids always clamor to help) to hand out materials, table by table. Meanwhile, I set up posters of art and my own exemplar springing from those influences, using magnetic clips on the chalk board. The kids were never good at transitions, and depending on the class, this moment could be dicey.

The conversations having already started, I sang to the class "Stop, look and listen!" and they responded, singing, "Okay!" It was really useful to get their attention and signal them to yes, shut the fuck up, we are starting. As the years passed and I kept using the jingle with older classes just to maintain the routine (keeping things predictable fosters structure and desirable behavior), I would say "Stop, look and listen!" and the nascent smartasses would yell, "No way!" What happened next hinged upon where we were in the project: a lecture/discussion, modeling different skills, students guided at accomplishing skills, independent work, and at the end of projects, a reflection where we evaluated and shared the work. When the students worked on their own I made the rounds of the room, conferencing.

It sounds normal enough, though a fly on the wall could attest otherwise. First of all, from the second I entered the room my adrenals jumped to attention, my shoulders tensed for combat. Based on the number of resident hellions in that class, my pulse began to pick up proportionate speed. I was still pretty green, just trying to negotiate the tension between my natural civility and the brutality they seemed to require—yet I could not accept the idea that I had to be monstrous to get them to behave. Anyway, they would never have bought me as that.

Though the kids were so versed in classroom rules they were practically branded with them, the inexorable juggernaut of defiance made its initial lurch forward, sending out appraising feelers to gauge how far they could go. Since I was "nice," this meant, for all intents and purposes, it was party time, at least for the insurgents. For me, however, it was on.

The entire period, while I attempted to teach art, was in fact a tug of war: a kid got up, I lost a few inches. I made him sit down, I got them back. Succeeding in getting a table quiet put me in the lead. But then, when two tables erupted, I was in the red again. Sometimes, losing it, my vicious, booming voice would catch them off guard, gaining me quite a bit of ground—but only momentarily. Arguments gave them the upper hand once again. Resolving them gained it anew. And so it went, on and on for fifty minutes. A fistfight set me back completely to vanquished mode: violence was the height of stress, plus I would lose my lunch and prep period to calling parents, writing testimony and injury reports. GAME OVER. On to the next contest—the next class.

I did not have one job, but three: teaching art, controlling behavior and ministering to the relentless, overwhelming neediness. The added responsibility was addressing logistics: constantly monitoring the clock, getting in and out, with all of my supplies (stealing was rampant, while methodically snapping crayons in half, a hobby for many), and the room cleaned up, on-time to get to the next class. I revisited this quadruple obligation, plus the Extended Day tutoring, twenty-five times a week. In between, I was racing to prepare materials or lessons to come, the timbre of the day ranging from very busy to downright frantic.

Given the giving essence of instruction—a prodigious push of mental energy, charged with equal emotional fervor—an undertaking so fueled by the brain and the heart would be dissipating even with classes of adjusted children. But my added cameos as the Marquis de Sade and Mother Theresa meant I could barely move when I got home, there was simply nothing left of me. Immediately flinging myself on the sofa, which grafted itself to my butt for the rest of the evening, my most demanding exertion was pressing a remote button to conjure John Stewart's or other comic consolation from the night before. I was turning into a horrible mother: making dinner required a rise Lazarus style from the sofa I was barely able to effect. Fortunately, my son did his homework without any kvetching from me—I was in no condition to Tiger Mom. But if he behaved in a way even slightly reminiscent of what I had endured at school, I would fly into a rage, the one I could not have in front of my students. At the end of an endless week, Friday nights I hit the sack as early as a nursery-worthy seven o'clock.

Despite the notion of accountability Bloomberg was taking every opportunity to drum into us, no-bid contracts with city suppliers were burgeoning under his administration. Indeed, in the DOE he had created a whole new Office of Accountability, notwithstanding the forced demise of the apparently useless Office of Teaching and Learning. Going forward, the sweetheart deals and exorbitantly paid consultants would multiply, several not surprisingly ending in fraud and charges of criminality.

Klein continued his push to create charter schools using public funds, encouraging the privatization of the public school system. As he voraciously courted the NCLB tenet of "choice," Klein aggressively raised philanthropic donations for nonprofit charters (it was all the rage for hedgefunders to sponsor schools, now called "edupreneurs"). Most of Klein's enthusiasm for charters stemmed from their lack of unionized staff—he had complete power over them—even as, ironically, charter schools owed their existence to the national teachers union. In 1988, the head of the American Federation of Teachers, Albert Shanker, had the idea to create a small school focusing on at-risk and dropout students, but funded by the public system. Yet by 1993 Shanker reversed his support for charter schools when for-profit business entities advanced their agenda of privatization.

Anyway, given the union's protection of teachers' rights, along with its fight to maintain a state cap on charter schools, Klein was certainly no friend of Joe Hill. Charter schools sprouted in brand new buildings as well as empty rooms in existing public schools, battles then ensuing for the use of common spaces, like cafeterias and gymnasiums. Most controversially, Klein's failed initiative with the help of the Gates Foundation—new, multiple small high schools replacing large ones, established within a former high school building—then forced overcrowding in the remaining traditional large high schools. Through it all, Klein's *raison d'etre* was ostensibly to raise the dismal city graduation rate, about fifty-four percent of students.

The usual grind was enlivened one day when Guido called an emergency faculty meeting in the library after school. He announced that the custodian, when cleaning the fourth floor staff bathroom, had discovered a plastic baggie with cocaine residue in it. Guido went on to make a cloying pitch worthy of a Twelve-Step program, extolling the virtues of our school "family" as a support system for the unfortunate lapsed one (squirming) among us. He went so far as to paternalistically encourage the sinner to unburden themselves to him personally, so he could shepherd them to resources and redemption. Yet the frenetic behavior of a cokehead did not square with the zombie mien of the bone-weary teachers—after all, the school was a set for a George Romero movie.

In January it was a year since the debacle in the special ed class that had gifted me with a letter in my file. I guess I was due for another raking over the coals when Sanchez's fifth grade class was in my room for their regular art period. I had taught the kids how to etch a design on styrofoam plates, then roll a brayer with ink onto it and print the image on paper. The queued students were impatient to get a turn with the ink and one girl, Marielly, cut the line and hovered by me, a determined pest. As the atmosphere became chaotic, I kept telling her to get in line and fending her off, getting more and more flustered as I tried to manage the tough logistics of the lesson, while maintaining the all-important management of the class.

Finally fed up with her hectoring, I told Marielly she would not be printing at all because of her behavior. She was furious and started grumbling to her friends. Meanwhile, the class finished and so did any further attempts at teaching printmaking: regretfully, it was too complicated procedurally for one teacher and twenty-seven unruly kids. The next day I got a letter that I must meet the principal in his office accompanied by my union representative. Once again, I had no idea what it was about.

As it turned out, I was accused of "corporal punishment" in the form of "verbally abusing" the accuser, Marielly. She had gone to her teacher, Sanchez, claiming that I had called her an "idiot." This statement was backed up by "witnesses," her friends, who also asserted they had heard me say that. For her part, Sanchez could have stopped the whole thing in its tracks by saying I would never say that, the girl must have heard me incorrectly, anything to stop her from incriminating another teacher. We had all encountered situations where you could tell the angry child just wanted to get the teacher in trouble, and we would diplomatically dissuade the child from pursuing it. This was not just out of loyalty but because the students' motivation was transparently false and self-serving.

The fact was, some kids, though thankfully only a small percentage, were extensions of defensive parents who were always ready to blame/work the system for some benefit, if only a brief sensation of power. So Joelis, the child who had pretended I had shoved him, had been raised on parental plaints of discrimination or whatever injustice would advantage to play *the man*. As the bad seed of these conniving "victims" the kids had big chips on their shoulders and a sense of entitlement just as gargantuan.

Inexplicably, since she and I were cordial, Sanchez had egged the student on with her complaint. Moreover, girls with whom I had enjoyed a warm relationship for years were suddenly capable of the most astoundingly evil, dishonest declarations against me on behalf of their friend (with whom I had previously been amicable as well).

For no apparent reason, since it was my word against theirs, Guido chose to believe them; had I been one of his cronies I would have undoubtedly fared better. Despite an eloquent written rebuttal and doggedly grieving the finding in three separate stages over the next few months, I received a second letter in my file. Once again I would have to wait three years to get it removed. Now my file was beginning to show a pattern of "corporal punishment," a theme which if left unchecked could get me tossed out. The injustice

94

dispirited me and only worsened the despondency I felt about my thankless teaching gig. Especially unsettling was the lack of fealty between teachers in the face of student assaults.

My immune system reacted typically, acquiring an especially nasty respiratory infection. My constitution was no match for the savageries of students or staff: flayed further with every violation, I had become a Proustian delicate incapable of withstanding the childish malice of the place, particularly in the viral swamp of endlessly congested, hacking kids. Indeed, at times the building struck me as less a school than a walk-in Petri dish.

Meanwhile, the state math test cheating event from the previous year was quietly simmering. The statements the students had written the year before had "vanished" and Guido was doing nothing about Miss Piggy's infraction except to promote her to assistant principal. He might have succeeded in burying the whole affair had there not been damning emails implicating him, Miss Piggy and the assistant principal in a cover up. The teacher had her former students, now in fifth grade, rewrite their statements from the year before.

A letter tipping off the media turned up at the *New York Post*, which published an expose of the cheating and cover-up, ever panting to launch an attack on schools. We all ran out at lunch time to buy the newspaper. There was a picture of Miss Piggy and an account of the dirty deeds, with a quote from union rep Graham accusing the principal of trying to protect the assistant principal. (Both Graham and the teacher involved denied contacting the *Post*.)

The school was ablaze with excitement. The next day Randi Weingarten, the president of the UFT, came to speak to us in the library. People were so whipped up, I half expected torches and pitch forks to be handed out to complete the Bruegelesque scene; that is the least we could have gotten for our union dues. However, we were simply advised to stick together and not speak to the press, the DOE would be conducting an inquiry. People secretly in the know were whisked out of school by the OSI (Office of Special Investigations) to be interviewed offsite, kid-gloved rendition.

From there, the plot just thickened. Graham had been getting harassed by Guido for the media coverage, and during a parent-teacher conference night shortly after, the grapevine reported, her adult son came to school and threatened him, prompting the besieged principal to take out an order of protection. In a twinkling Guido used his principal prerogative to punish by checking Graham into the home for wayward educators, the Hotel Rubber Room. She languished there for months in typical DOE holding pen fashion, assigned nothing to do while collecting full pay.

In the meantime, Miss Piggy disappeared. Far from being fired or punished in any way, thanks to the crawling pace of the process, she kicked back in another Rubber Room to enjoy a prolonged latexed vacation. As a matter of fact, in the spring of 2010 the *Post* would publish her picture as an extreme example in a story condemning Rubber Rooms: she had spent five years there before being terminated, on full salary of one hundred twenty thousand dollars a year, while the case was investigated. Apparently Guido's appointment of her as assistant principal just prior to her fall from grace had been calculated to gain Miss Piggy the greatest subsequent taxpayer remuneration.

About a month before the end of the year, Guido called the staff together for a brazenly specious announcement: because he did not want to drag his family through the investigation of the cheating scandal (he was actually going to be brought up on charges), he was resigning. Given Guido's transparent culpability, the presumption was dazzling. Notwithstanding the opprobrium of his weekly binges, he could not brook the public indignity of being fired. Another player in the case, the AP Dubrow whose complicity in the cover-up was documented through emails, left on her own to become a principal in another school. The lengthy process finally caught up to her and after years, she too was fired. However, both she and Miss Piggy made out like bandits before getting the ax.

In previous years, I had been leaping through the hoops: exams, training and degree work, required to get the state teaching license. Now I completed the last task, a video of me teaching an art lesson to a third grade. Three months later, with a wheezy sigh (still sick) I opened the letter declaring my official certification as a licensed teacher.

Despite our Teflon-coated super-veterans with their decades of masochistic longevity, it is an educator commonplace that each year at an inner-city school is equivalent to five years teaching at a school in a good area. According to this calculation, a brilliantly apt one with which my very bones concurred, I had already done fifteen years. No wonder I was so spent: at the cellular level I was almost ready to retire, considering all the years I had worked prior to teaching.

Given the chronic shortage of classrooms, it was unlikely the next principal would approve an art room for the next year. I seized the opportunity my current space provided by embarking on projects that would otherwise be unfeasible. For one of these, I showed the kids examples of modern American art, detailing the colorful personalities who had created it. Then I unfurled a huge roll of white paper down the length of the room and manned the kids with jars of various colors of paint. "On your mark, get set, go!" and we were off, splashing, spraying and splattering splotches of color in a convulsion of Abstract Expressionism. Even though I only dared do this with my smallest, best-behaved group, the aesthetic maelstrom extended into the hallway as the budding Jackson Pollacks headed to wash up in the bathrooms, slapping their handprints onto the corridor walls. As I finished washing away the psychedelia, I saw Guido giving the new principal, a woman, a tour of the building.

The last week of the school year the June heat exhaled its dragon breath, clutching the building cruelly in a now-familiar rite of summer passage. To the whirring accompaniment of the ineffectual giant fans, the polyestered bottoms of proud parents stuck to their seats in the auditorium, cameras ready as "Pomp and Circumstance" blasted from a boom box in front of the stage. Kindergartners in bouffant hair, chiffon dresses and high heels, the boys with gelled hair in miniature suits, proceeded to the stage where they were lauded for their achievement. In the ceremony that took place a couple days later, equally dolled up fifth graders sported lurid robes and mortarboards of questionable shiny fibers, an unwelcome revisit of seventies prom attire.

The implication was that the completion of one year and six years of school, respectively, was some kind of accomplishment, though they were legally bound to be here. The hype with which these faux feats was celebrated only stoked the anticipation of an equally facile New York City high school diploma (given the ease of the Regents Exams, in fact, hardly a misperception). At least that, however, required another seven years of school.

The parents, dressed in their finest for the occasion, had brought helium balloons, flowers and at least one, a penchant for pickpocketing: a teacher missed her Blackberry during the ceremony. Another time, during a performance a supervising teacher left her good shoes nearby—those vanished as well. Though the majority of parents were decent, it came with the territory.

A few weeks later, on the last day of school I got my rating sheet, and with my third year of "S" for "Satisfactory," tenure; I had passed my second goal. There was the usual staff party that night for the end of the year but I did not go. Teachers who attended spoke later of how plastered, then maudlin, Guido became. Soon after his disgraceful departure from the New York City system, Guido moved to a better job as a principal in an upscale town. Despite the havoc and expense he had unleashed on the city (we found out later he'd blazed a spectacularly outrageous trail in the school before ours, too), he had emerged unscathed, his scot-free disentanglement resulting in no consequence save a better job in an easier district, not surprisingly, one in which he was said to have outstanding connections.

5

Principal Dearest, as I would come to nickname the new principal, had presented herself to us prior to the end of school. A middle-aged woman with graying hair, her chiseled bone structure rendered her Mt. Rushmore-handsome, giving the impression of, well, testosterone. She addressed us in the school library while we sat breathlessly on the edge of our seats, straining for a hint of what was to come; the timbre of the school and our individual existences depended on the tone she would be setting. Introducing herself, she referred to her approach to education as that of a "lifelong learner," trendy argot we heard in graduate school and professional development consistent with the educational flavor of the moment. Because Principal Dearest had decades of teaching experience (which we naturally equated with empathy for teachers), we were convinced we had a winner at last.

Later in September, though she nixed the art room in favor of opening another grade classroom, a chance meeting with her in the auditorium persuaded me we had nothing to fear. I unburdened myself to her, telling her of the last two principals we had had and noting her experience encouraged us to believe we had found someone normal at last. Good-naturedly, she told me she did not know how "normal" a person could be that had done this job for so long, and that she had her faults: she could have a bad temper, for example, though she usually apologized for it afterward. I dismissed her insouciant allusion in what was a delightful, promising encounter. At one point she mentioned that this would be her last job, that she had five years left to retire. This last piece of information, though thrown out informally, would prove to be a source of sustenance in years to come.

Anyway, the days of preparation we had before the opening of school were dominated less by our anxiety over the new principal than by a more immediately malevolent female named Katrina, in hindsight, an inauspicious beginning, to say the least. I could not sleep thinking of the people in their dark attics, the water up to their chins; the Superdome outrage just added to a horror I monitored obsessively with equal measures of indignance and compassion. The black child in the Sponge Bob tee shirt who famously appealed during his fifteen minutes, "We jus' need some help out here—it is so pitiful..." was one of the kids I was teaching.[1] I was appalled by the staggering callousness, incompetence and corruption the disaster highlighted, as if Bush could have wreaked any more destruction on the country. The symbolism trumpeted the *coup de grace* for a nation in obvious, precipitous decline.

Record results from spring reading and math tests were announced, just in time to enhance Bloomberg's chances for re-election, his success almost certain given his unlimited resources to buy ads, conduct spin and deliver misleading soundbites.[2] What the public did not know was the lame state tests, scored 4, 3, 2 or 1, equivalent to A, B, C or D, were pathetic indicators of a child's actual knowledge. Students could move up from the lowest level 1 to level 3, grade level, simply by guessing. Moreover, what the state viewed as "proficient," level 3, was so diluted, only the deluded would imagine such aptitude could result later in even high school graduation, much less getting into, or through, college.

Our anger continued with Klein's authoritarian approach and his strict pedagogical mandates. Now more than ever at teacher as well as parent protests, the educational fascism provoked the chant, "Let teachers teach!," a mantra expressing the frustration and demoralization shared by everyone. With the good salary raises negotiated in the new union contract Bloomberg sought to soften the DOE's tyranny, while not only buying continued union support for himself as mayor, but thinking ahead to a campaign for president.

As usual I was waking early, taking the 4 train up to the Bronx. Though I had valued walking to work for years in Manhattan, I never knew how much until I no longer had the opportunity. Six flights of decrepit steps down into the bowels of the Fifty-Ninth Street station I waited, dodging the metronome of drips coalescing rhythmically in the ceiling's textural chaos of peeling plaster. I marveled at the decay, literally awesome given its situation not only in the "Greatest City in the World," but at this tony neighborhood stop, the one for Tiffany's.

The humidity was always more oppressive, the temperature twenty degrees higher, than at street level, so this meant in the late spring, sweating torrents when merely standing still. The experience lurched into miasmatic mode when a train arrived or departed on the other side of the tracks, the stagnant air stirring and sending up wafts of urine. I learned to hold my breath at those times, though there was invariably some other horror to contemplate, like a super-sized rat strolling desultorily along the tracks, or a glistening mound of fresh sputum.

When the train arrived, the sensory assault continued as I pushed through the clumps of babbling Bronx Science High School kids to stand against the back door, riding the train freestyle like a careening surfboard until One Hundred Twenty-Fifth Street, where I usually lucked into a seat. Thence I was treated to the treble throb of my seatmate's low-rent headphones, emitting techno beats so disturbingly discernible, they were surely counting out the remaining moments of the listener's hearing. At the first stops in the Bronx, neighborhood high school kids would get on, adding to the cacophony, the gum-snapping adolescent girls holding conversations so loud they had clearly already gone deaf, their vapid dissertations so obtrusive I longed for my own deafening techno.

Their jejune discourse, especially when accompanied by boys, was peppered with curses, vivid sexual references and lots of "nigger" or the affectionate "my nigger." Whether it was a good thing to de-charge the word of its fraught history and intensity, in fact, reappropriating it through casual use—or a bad idea, disrespecting that same history and all it stood for—the social

101

phenomenon of flinging this grating word around was one I found hard to appreciate. Though I could not totally divest myself of the offense it caused me, it was interesting to note how over time the word lessened in power as I heard it used, as a stand-in for "man," really, more and more.

Anyway, it was hard to focus on that effrontery when a male creature next to me stretched out in loutish oblivion as if in his own trailer, an attitude of such primitive entitlement it rang territorial. Often I found myself sitting next to this genus of jerk, a hard-boiled macho man with beefy thighs akimbo. The spread of his legs, as much as ninety degrees, reliably indicated the relative measure, geometrically, of his rank as an asshole. His obnoxious requisition of my leg room forced me to solder my legs together. Even more imposing than Mr. Testosterone was the squad of jumbo people living the (maximum) maxim that three hundred is the new two hundred. Often an amorphous mass of avoirdupois was wedged next to me, forcing me into painful contraction, my only salvation my bid to imitate the invertebracy of Gumby.

Then there were the beggars and hustlers. I remembered how they had mercifully disappeared during Law 'N' Order Giuliani's tenure, but now they were back with an infuriating vengeance under Bloomberg, tormenting a captive audience of hapless passengers, guilty of nothing save the desire for some peace on the way to or from a hard day's work. A variety pack of them stalked the 4 train often in the afternoon (apparently they slept in), a profound annoyance at any time, but particularly galling for the zombies like me who populated the trains then. As drained, barely sentient members of the Living Dead, if we had gotten a seat we only wanted to sleep. But they all had their *schtick* to jolt us out of our low blood sugar catatonia.

Several were youthful types who announced with disarming honesty, calculated to cajole, that they was not sellin' candy for no organization; no, they was sellin' candy to stay off the streets and put some money in they pocket. They were actually delightfully expedient compared to the hardcore mendicants who got on, blasting us awake or interrupting our cherished interlude of reading with a bellowed apology for disturbing us. This did not stop them from launching into the same sob story year after year. One recited his tale of woe, a litany about his wife dying in the fire that burned down his house at Easter, so many times, I resisted the urge to get up and tell it myself.

His intrusion was always the worst of them all, getting on at One Hundred Twenty-Fifth Street, imitating the sound of the doors closing, a tedious impression which he alone found hilarious.Then he proceeded to speechify in his Jamaican lilt, right off the bat excusing his invasive behavior, inveighing against the "haters," apparently those of us who, deservedly, well, hated him. A round of cliches about love and peace was followed by an evangelical ditty, later replaced by a litany of all the types of exotically-named weed he would be happy to accept as a donation, a recitation he judged dazzlingly Noel Coward-like. You just wanted to "extinguish," B. F. Skinner-style, his behavior by ignoring him, in which case at some point he might have given up. However, there was always a handful of dumb asses who *did* find him amusing, a couple of whom would give him money. The haters just had to grin and hate him, because that sparse encouragement meant he always came back.

But that idiot, and a cast of others who used the 4 train as their rolling podium, were small fry irritants compared to the world-class provocation spewed regularly by a Jehovah's Witness. Striking at the crack of dawn, the stupefied passengers were punched awake by the (in no way at that time) good news that Jesus is coming. Discharged robotically by a Hispanic simpleton channeling Jose Jimenez, the rote scripture disruption and the fact that we were literally hostage to it, incensed me. After a few instances of this guy's oral predations I hurled a sermon right back at him. I shouted at him that the train is not a church. He had no right to bother us, it was not Christian. Jesus would never do what he was doing. He should pay for our train tickets if he wanted to do this. How dare he talk about sinners when he is committing the biggest sin of all: bad manners! He droned on imperviously, occasionally parrying with an apparent default response: "Eet's a free country."

This impelled me to deliver an impromptu lecture on the separation of church and state, and the inviolability of the train, being public property. Rejecting this edification, he continued his nasal dirge about the dayveel and pairrrdeeshun and the unbelievers burning in fire and brrreemstone: in fact, everything I wanted to happen to him.

Usually people, startled awake by him, then by my surprising invective, looked at me curiously with no sign of solidarity; their bovine stares of glazed apathy only riled me further. One time, though, I happened to have on each side of me men who were also fed up, and the three of us ganged up on him. Our sustained attack, though hardly the biblical proportions he deserved, may have been the *coup de grace*, because I never saw him again.

That was a gift, because just about any discomfiture was preferable to his Rapturous drivel—even the perv exposing his cyclopean junk under a newspaper as I got on one day. Though I knew I should join the women who fight back by taking a picture of IT (*Ben Hur* letters) with my cell phone and posting online, I was scared that IT, attached to him, might pursue me out of the train, opening a whole new can of worms (big ones).

Aside from those punctuations of random skeeve, the banal ick factor of the daily commute was sheerly being packed together in compulsory intimacy; when the doors opened it seemed a cascade might tumble out with the Marx Brothers in tow. Amazingly, since I had been doing it for years now, there was still that surreal quality when arriving home downtown after a day in the Bronx. Though a quotidian ritual, the cultural chasm never failed to amaze.

At school, in the meantime, the alarming lack of basic math skills persisted. Fifth graders, even older, held-over teenage ones I was assigned to tutor in math in Extended Time, still could not quickly state what two times seven was, responding with a helpless silence or the few who were motivated, using their fingers. Had the elite educational developers of Everyday Math not, in fact, done the math that basic skills were a nonnegotiable, requisite foundation? How could school district administrators fail to connect the neglect of core knowledge with low test scores? Because the fact was, multiplication times tables were not part of a math program that had been driving teachers and students alike, crazy.

No wonder constructivist math programs lacked supportive research evidence. As the years went by teachers' exasperation with the method would just increase, their complaints falling on the deaf ears of school bureaucrats boondoggled by the theoretical jargon of educational "experts" invested, perhaps even literally, in personal financial terms, in the progressive math curriculum. The harsh fact was, students were not mastering basic operations, which were taught in a needlessly labyrinthine way. Simple multiplication facts were not known because of the program's view of old-fashioned drilling as anathema. Instead, "critical thinking" used to understand a concept was emphasized, not the ability to perform an operation and get the correct answer. In fact, weren't they both important? And given the plethora of time-constrained tests, the lack of snap facts at their fingertips clearly doomed them to failure.

The upshot of this approach was, kids were going into middle school not having the knowledge or skills needed to proceed to the next level. Moreover, even if they *were* able to understand a concept, Everyday Math would confound that comprehension by leaping from topic to topic to demonstrate alternative methods. Incredibly, that illogical system, called "spiraling," provided no time for the kids to even practice. Anyway, providing different approaches seemed pointlessly confusing to kids hard-pressed to even integrate a traditional algorithm; the gratuitous luxury of exotic operations seemed more appropriate to advanced kids who had already mastered the basic operation.

Further baffling was the abrupt insertion, at intervals, of sophisticated math the students were developmentally helpless at that age to understand, like algebra and geometry. Perhaps the most incalculable idiocy was the program's emphasis on calculators over the development of personal computation skills, a clearly disempowering idea which had been researched as negative to children's math learning (duh).[3] As ever, the cooperative aspect of the math program was troubling, too: the kids were only able to perform in an authority-enforced structure, so given the freedom to construct their own learning, instead they were constructing their own entertainment or fighting.

Ultimately and inevitably, the National Council of Teachers of Mathematics would issue a new directive underscoring the importance of core math skills.[4] Though our teachers tweaked Everyday Math to address our student population, the results of the program were, naturally, a majority of kids with glazed expressions. They did not have to focus anyway: the capricious nature of the program meant the subject would be switched so quickly, why bother to engage now? In fact, Everyday Math seemed an apt metaphor for the ADD that characterized the cognitive style of so many of our kids, with much the same damaging effect.

Since we did not have an art room this year, the other art teacher and I put our stuff in a closet on the fourth floor. Meanwhile, day-to-day I kept my supplies in the science room where I hung out with other cluster teachers. We were pals, particularly since we shared the same secondary status among the kids and we could compare/moan about our scraps with the celebrated behaviors in each grade. I became friends with a new Teaching Fellow, Paul, who was supposed to teach ESL but had been placed in science. He was as cheeky as I was irreverent, and we loved the same kids, like Reginald, a West Indian goofball in kindergarten whose wicked Mashed Potato was so disarming it almost cancelled out the fact that he interrupted every teaching attempt with a loud nonsequitur. Anyway, Paul and I leavened the levity level with our jokes and Rabelaisian hijinks: we dressed the science room's resident skeleton in my motorcycle jacket and, not missing a "teachable moment" as it is called in the industry, placed a cigarette between his teeth.

My first couple years, there had been a paraprofessional in each kindergarten classroom, a necessity the DOE suddenly deemed a luxury and so relegated to the past. The veteran teachers spoke wistfully of the days when there had been a para not just in the kindergarten but in *every* classroom, a prospect of eased behavior management that made me salivate. Indeed, just ten years before a kindergarten class of twenty-eight had the luxury of two teachers and two assistants! Now the city had taken a buzz saw to the remaining "superfluous" paras, so ours were placed forthwith expressly in special ed classrooms where they were legally mandated.

Now more than ever, without the extra help, the large kindergarten classes of unsocialized kids embodied a public service announcement, nay command, for universal pre-kindergarten. The halcyon days of sand boxes, water tables and socialization were a distant memory: in recent times kindergarten had transformed into first grade, with letters, sounds and early reading, actual work, the order of the day. But many of these kids were just four years old for the first half of the year, barely out of toddlerhood. Moreover, shockingly, over half of even the five-year-olds had never been exposed to the alphabet, colors or numbers to ten, information considered rudimentary in better-off families (and an inexcusable predicament considering the ubiquitousness of *Sesame Street*). Since these same children, expected to switch their intellects into overdrive, overnight, had never been taught to take turns, share, wait in line, or any of the social functions comprising the foundation for academic exploration, a pre-k emphasis on social skills would make all the difference, especially in the absence of the treasured kindergarten paras.

"Lunch Duty," now a voluntary assignment, had at one time been part of a teacher's day, until the union rightly negotiated the obligation away. School aides, part-time workers from the neighborhood, were a more appropriate choice for a position calling less on master's degrees than good, old reliable bossing and mammying. With budget cuts also reducing the school aide allotment, Guido had enlisted a few of us to beef up their ranks; in return we missed teaching a class for that period. This entailed supervising one grade at tables in the cafeteria, while another played outside in the yard. If the weather were inclement that group would move to the auditorium to "watch" (blab over) a blaring movie. Like punished classes prevented from going outside, there the kids squirmed in the dark, wasting precious moments of youth in the thrall of product placements with a side of animation.

This year, as I continued my turn in the cafeteria, I knew I had had enough: at this point it was hard to see lunch duty as divine dispensation from teaching a class. The main cross to bear was the cochlea-shattering noise, but there were other asinine contingencies as well. With characteristic misguidedness, the administration sought to ban talking from the lunchroom as well as the auditorium, imposing this senseless regulation through the barked prohibitions of school aides as well as Ms. Moore, an assistant principal.

This presented a quandary for me, as I could not in good conscience tow the company line: I believed the kids were entitled to talk at lunch, considering they were not (at least officially) allowed to talk the whole rest of the school day. Anyway, it seemed to me the twenty-first century cafeteria gruel was enough of an homage to *Oliver Twist* without promoting further child abuse; to deny their need to socialize was not only an inhumane idea, but an utterly unenforceable one. Thirty seconds of silence was all the kids would give—after that grudging token, of course they resumed their talking, regardless of the shouts, the whistles, the threats, the counting to threes or else. After awhile a particularly harsh ultimatum would spur another thirty second reprieve, then right on cue the tumult would start up again. The volume of the forbidden chatter ricocheting off the tiled walls was ear-splitting, yet that did not seem to phase the kids in the least.

Assistant Principal Moore, who though mild-mannered, even passive, was the administrator in charge of the manicotti-munching mob of older kids, in one of Denial's Greatest Hits, ordered me to quiet the students (something she herself had never been able to do). Put on the spot, my dilemma was thrown into stark relief: not only did I support their right to talk, but I was not about to gain cholesterol digits in my battle to silence them, especially to win only a thirty second nose-thumbing. I had to marvel, in fact, at the silliness of the campaign as well as that of the stickler Moore. Clearly she did not acknowledge the nature of the beast, that the doomed quest was like bringing a hurricane to heel.

Moreover, any effort on my part to subdue their exuberance, in meeting with certain failure, would cause me to lose face. I needed that face—oh, how I needed that face—to garner respect in my own art classes. Why should I sacrifice any hard-fought street cred I had won over conversations of which I not only approved, but could never hope to stop? From then on I avoided Moore until I could get out of lunch duty; I was not suited for the job anyway. Being a child trapped in an adult body, I naturally sided more with the kids than the administration: if a food fight had ever erupted, I might well have been the instigator.

The year's starring challenge, Jah-ira, was an extremely large, violent kid in third grade so difficult he necessitated his own private male staff member to squire him around. The teacher was thus prevented from the small group tutoring that was his actual job. Instead of learning, to keep the rest of the school safe Jah-ira was rewarded and propitiated with entire days playing games on the library computer. Fortunately, he was ultimately shipped off to a special, special ed setting, District Seventy-Five, more appropriate to his propensities; by the age of sixteen he would be a dropout and father of two illegitimate children, the deadly diaspora of his DNA a ticking time bomb for the neighborhood.

But despite Jah-ira, somehow this year there were fewer extreme "behaviors" in the school, maybe because the population had dropped since my first year by a couple hundred, and so the proportion of any type was smaller. In fact there was no definitive reason for this change, though some said it was probably due to other schools opening in zones next door, siphoning them off. The improvement in the kids, even if it was slight, raised my spirits. But just as important was the fact that the new principal left us alone, either because she was involved in her own learning curve, or (pinch me) because she was decent.

Then came the December transit strike. As we were still required to be at school, regardless, the six stranded Manhattanites had to pack into the music teacher's Volvo, meeting at different rendezvous points throughout the backed-up city. This went on for a week till finally the strike was finished. Although it was a logistical headache, the camaraderie in the car was fun, as well as the typical gossip/whinefest that characterized wherever two or more are gathered.

One of the Manhattan-dwellers, Allie,was a colorful debutante Teaching Fellow with an Ivy League pedigree and a posh lifestyle hilariously at odds with her day job. Her perky preppiness, from her Topsiders to her Lacoste-topped Talbot's skirts, never failed to provide an entertaining counterpoint to the drab atmosphere of the school. On Mondays, sometimes reeking of vodka from a bender in the Hamptons the weekend before, she was more often than not on her cell phone, making plans for an upcoming ball. Indeed, her teaching job was little more than an interval between social engagements. As a professional prepster, she loved theme parties and was always enlisting helpful ideas for her next costumed incarnation. Indeed, the trust funder declared that her DOE paycheck was sufficient only for the cab fare required to conduct her prodigious social life. She taught three years, just enough to get tenured.

Every school has a UFT representative as well as a delegate. Graham had been our rep for years, and now I was voted delegate. This meant I did not deal with day-to-day union affairs in the building but was a back-up, going to the monthly meetings downtown and there in case the rep was unable to perform their duties. Immediately, I became aware of the fact Graham did not go to the required meetings. Unlike Graham, who seemed to use the position mainly as a way to stay in solid with the principal, as a true activist I loved going to them. In the meantime, the standing apathy in the school was appalling. Disgusted, I focused my political energy in New York and Washington, plying my militancy at union and other protests.

The intense emphasis on state tests persisted, now expanding to include third and fifth grades, the drive for higher scores shackling teachers' instructional creativity as much as the totalitarian directives from the city. Teachers felt they were not in control of their classrooms, just soulless robots, shoulder to an inexorably accelerating wheel of madness. The unlucky kids, equally rats in a maze of experimental educational reforms, were not any better off, the deadly test prep continuing to alienate further, already disengaged students. Yet the blank trust placed in the scores continued, unchallenged: complex factors including the subject tested, specific material, connection with the curriculum, quality of the tests and more, were simply disregarded. Frequently we still noticed mediocrity, ambiguity and even mistakes, not only on test prep materials but on the tests themselves. Moreover, results of the tests, meant to prove the proficiency of students and teachers alike, represented only a tiny part of a student, ignoring multiple variables in the child's psychological and educational development.

Notwithstanding their unreliability, the tests loomed over us like an omniscient Big Brother: even the second graders, as yet in an untested year (their turn at the standardized guillotine would be imminent), were filling in bubbles for their worksheet answers, pawns already training for the stultifying years ahead. NCLB had mandated the tests so school districts would narrow achievement gaps or incur penalties, yet the ever-present tyranny of the tests was a never-ending punishment in itself. Moreover, the testing hysteria was in fact widening the achievement gap, deepening the gulf between higher SES students getting an authentic education in schools exempted from mandated curriculum and test prep, and the disadvantaged students forced to endure a faked but "accountable" "education."

By January, the kids had passed the modified honeymoon period long ago and were well into Wild West mode. Once again I found myself exhausted; as ever, I could not imagine *any* activity, much less a social life, on the weeknights, barely even, on the weekends. I had to see people during vacations, which was the only time I felt part of the Land of the Living, otherwise, the energy deficit was just too extreme. I had added that to my beefs with the teaching business: the job wrecked all chances of a life outside of it. Even the young classroom teachers just out of college went home and slept every day, waking up to plan and do paper work until late at night. I did not have that work to do but I had a kid to raise plus now that I was fifty, a dearth of mojo as pronounced as their lack of time. In that sense the job required self-sacrifice far beyond the direct commitment of the school day.

The result was that everyone was constantly living for the weekend, the holidays, the vacations, and especially, summer vacation. The number of days until summer was always of fascination to all, measured in tally marks like a jail cell countdown. In the meantime, every free day that came along was a godsend. In the fall I gave thanks to the Jews for their holidays, so welcome even as we did not have a single Jewish student and only two Jewish teachers among almost a thousand people in the school. Indeed, every holiday was a piece of heaven. In my first year a veteran told me, "March is the hardest month because there is no holiday at all."

I remember thinking that was a terrible way to live, always wanting to be somewhere else. What an obscene waste to be able to grind slave-like through the unbearable only because the beacon of the bearable shines weakly from a future day of respite. Yet I found myself doing the same, fortifying myself every day with the thought that I could make it through that day, or week or month, to the blessed time when I could relax.

It was crushing to note, the new principal for whom I had entertained such optimism, had begun to persecute a couple new teachers, dipping her toes in to test our tolerance for tyranny. Satisfied she would get no resistance, Principal Dearest became further emboldened, most likely encouraged by the apple-polishing of Guido's fulsome friends who were busy as beavers making themselves indispensable to her (just as they had made their busy beavers indispensable to him). According to a rumor making the rounds, Principal Dearest was literally crazy, appointed by the superintendent as our principal as revenge for the cheating scandal involving Guido, who had been a district favorite. Though the specifics of her placement remained vague, over the year Principal Dearest had been developing a reputation for erratic behavior which, if not indicative of mental illness, was at least a touch bi-polar. One did not know from one minute to the next where her mood would be, and many was the time we would hear her yelling at a teacher or a class in the hallway, only in the next minute to soften and coo maternally.

The school uniform was increasing in popularity, probably because parents wisely saw it as, if nothing else, a chance to save money on clothes. The zealous new principal applied a Mafia strong arm to the appeal of the white and navy togs: only the kids wearing a uniform were allowed outside in the yard at lunch time. This harsh decree lasted only a couple weeks, proving ludicrous and insupportable since the auditorium couldn't seat the multitudes of fashion victims still in the majority. More to the point, Principal Dearest had no legal right to order the uniform under any circumstance, and once the perturbed parents got up in her face, she was forced to desist.

Undaunted, Principal Dearest's oppressive style surged onward and upward to greater opportunities for severity, her pronouncements swift and draconian. Doffing her hat to the Nazis, for example, countless times when even a couple of kids misbehaved, their entire class would be punished, and severely so. When two classes came back late from a field trip, no fault of their own, but the trains, they were banned from taking subsequent pre-arranged ones, trips the kids had paid for and anticipated with excitement. Their feelings, as well as the time and academic preparation by the teachers, did not mollify Principal Dearest: she had issued her edict, and just like her determined, scowling jaw, it was etched in stone.

Principal Dearest fired a new teacher whose personality she did not like after just a few weeks, using her prerogative to terminate the untenured with scant cause and zero opportunity for a second chance. Though Principal Dearest left me alone, like everyone else I started to read her expression when she approached from the end of a hall, and if it was portentous I avoided the encounter. Once again, it seemed we had another Cruella, but a crazier, more unpredictable one, according to many.

Near the end of the year she burst into the science room and as opposed to asking, screamed at us to clean stuff piled on the unused students' computers, which we had nowhere else to store. It turned out some higher-ups were to visit the school and Principal Dearest planned to show them the room. Obviously she wanted the computers to appear in use by the students, though in fact in most rooms they were nonfunctioning props. Considering our paltry, unintended misdemeanor, her superfluous hysteria did not augur well. We were not alone in finding Principal Dearest unprofessional:

by the end of the school year she had achieved a hazardous reputation schoolwide. Once again demoralization set in.

Adding to the feelings of insecurity Principal Dearest engendered was the haphazard fashion with which much of school business was conducted. She seemed incapable of juggling or prioritizing, abilities obviously necessary to her managerial position. Despite a huge wall-length dated planner in her office, by-the-seat-of-her-pants was her preferred mode of dealing with daily duties. Given the day-to-day disorganization, when something unpredicted arose, that really threw her, and therefore the rest of us, for a loop. Principal Dearest sometimes copied hundreds of already-late letters to go home without proofreading them, then when mistakes were discovered, recalled them ten minutes before school ended, creating gratuitous chaos during dismissal.

On other occasions she would make decisions only to reverse them, without explanation or advertisement, shortly after. Sometimes it felt like we had been left in the dark, groping about for a Braille leadership we could not decipher. Principal Dearest was purportedly a graduate of Bloomberg's Leadership Academy crash course for principals; perhaps it was there she had been schooled in "Slapdash Management 101," "Rush to Judgment 218" and one she would employ vigorously in coming years, "Bullying For Dummies 309."

When the time came to give us our yearly ratings, Principal Dearest called Paul on the carpet. Even though he was good at teaching science and observations of his lessons had proven satisfactory, he had been absent or late too many times and she intended to fire him. When he asked for a second chance, she relented; he came out of her office, relieved and grateful. Inexplicably, she then called the district office and told them he was fired.

Bewildered by her reversal, he went back to her and pleaded his case again. This time she had the added effect of tears of compassion streaming down her face, assuring him that he would indeed be back the next year; the school secretary told all of us later how she had heard Principal Dearest say those very words. But shortly after Paul left her office, relieved again, his cell phone rang: it was the teachers union rep. The principal had called: Paul would be getting an unsatisfactory rating and terminated as of the last day of school. This back and forth had all happened in a single morning.

Whether these head-games were cruelly intentional or simply a bipolar biproduct, either way Principal Dearest's fickleness and casual treatment of a vulnerable human being resulted in the ruination of a life and the loss to the system of a growing but effective teacher, and one whom the kids loved. For a long time after, students and teachers alike asked after Paul and expressed their interest in his welfare. Because of his bad rating, Paul could never again teach in the city system, and he had to drop out of the Teaching Fellows master's program and pay the city back for the classes he had taken. He ended up going abroad to teach ESL, where he received stellar ratings.

But back in the States, even years later, Paul had difficulty getting employed as a teacher with that termination on his record. After all, when arguing your defense to a civilian, it is impossible to adequately convey the banal sociopathy of an NYC principal; the legacy of Principal Dearest, and so many others, lives on in shattered lives.

Paul was just another martyr to a principal's insatiable blood-of-a-teacher-lust. *Plus ca change, plus c'est la meme chose.* What was with that, anyway? There was most definitely a personality pattern here, and not just evident from what I had seen in my school, but substantiated by the experience of other Teaching Fellows in theirs as well. Was a malformed, fragile ego in need of constant affirmation an official prerequisite for a "leadership" position? Exactly where do "callous disregard for humanity," "vampirical cannibalization" and "soul murder" rank in the DOE's job description? That such flotsam left behind in the trajectory of human evolution, is magnetized to the petty fiefdoms of the schools, is an extraordinary and telling phenomenon. The hierarchical system inherently fosters a nurturing environment for those who crave power, regardless of competence, an institutional enabler of despotism. In such an atmosphere neither talent nor skills are necessary, only relentless ambition, grandiosity and enough emotional intelligence to manipulate the connections that make ascension possible.

The majority of teachers lack this venal perspective. Motivated by their love and desire to help children, teachers represent the emotional heart of the school. Even money cannot tempt them to leave the classroom; that would negate their reason for being there. Those who leave teaching and the hands-on experience with children for administrative positions, such as assistant principals, demonstrate no such commitment: with their interest in remuneration, their motives are as self-serving as those of teachers are noble. At the greatest remove from the kids, and in the most egocentric niche of all are the brashly mercenary principals, whose lucrative, but more fundamentally, alluringly authoritarian positions, deftly bespeak their love of power over the power of love.

A system in which everyone begins as a teacher, then, over time separates out the givers from the takers, the latter exploiting their advantage to control those pure-motived souls below. The systemic imbalance rewarding most those who deserve least so skews the educational landscape it cannot but add to the dysfunction. After all, research shows the most critical school component in a child's academic success is a qualified, quality teacher.[5] Like others in the reform movement, Bloomberg had not done the math (or arithmetic, rather, given our superannuated mindset) leading to the logical conclusion that empowered, respected teachers graduate empowered, respected students. The best public education systems in the world value teachers—in Finland they have done the math, a calculus made years ago.[6]

Since late spring when the annual teacher transfer website resumed, I had been looking at options to leave; nothing interesting was available. Though the new principal had made a wacky (charitably) debut, I was willing to chalk that up to her first year jitters (too charitably, as it would turn out). So, considering how fond I was of so many of the kids, I made my peace with staying another year. (In hindsight, I should have booked my ass to the nearest exit.)

Principal Dearest brought her husband to the June end term party. He told one of the teachers his wife had said if she were not a principal she would like to rule the world. Uh oh. A harbinger of things to come? Film at eleven.

6

Our second year with Principal Dearest, since Paul had been fired, I returned to a school bereft of goofy companionship. Whenever Reginald, now in first grade, did the dance that Paul loved, I missed him that much more. The science teachers moved to a new, smaller room and had to give the skeleton away, so stripped of my Goth coat rack, once again I hauled my jacket from class to class.

I was still longing for a schoolwide rewards system to succor the sucky behavior. Since that was not happening, this year I started my own raffled prize at the end of every class, for grades two through five. The two younger grades I could sticker, a way cheaper enterprise. I brought a little shopping bag with all manner of prizes to every class, then at the end of the period I would reach into an envelope with that class's names in it and pull one out. If that child had been behaving they could pick a prize, if not, I would go back in until I found a deserving one. Kids could win over and over, but if some who behaved were nonetheless unlucky, I let them pick a prize at the end of the year. Those who did not behave like ladies and gentlemen, well, they would never win.

The lower-level, impulsive kids generally picked an instantly gratifying prize like candy, whereas the higher-level kids picked prizes that would outlast the moment, like a pack of markers. This bore out a famous study in which a child showing impulse control receives two marshmallows in return for waiting, while the one with less self-control only receives one, but immediately. The study accurately predicted the children who would go on to become academically successful, accomplishment being contingent upon delaying gratification when necessary. In my school, unfortunately, the candy tended to be the prize of choice.[1]

The raffle, though it became a mainstay of my classes, never brought the desired order I had had in mind. Second graders new to it and still in the thrall of adults were most prone to respect it. In other grades by the middle of the year many, except the kids who behaved well anyway, had scorned the prospect of a prize in favor of talking or playing around. Clearly, if I were to buy more expensive prizes, the behavior would have improved concomitantly, but with so many students, that was not an option.

Yet without fail at the end of every class when I announced the raffle, ironically the room would go quiet and even jerks who had marauded through the entire period would sit with their hands folded, even, waiting (as if) to be picked. So ultimately, the real benefit of the raffle proved to be its value not just as part of a structured routine, but as a means of gathering the class together at the end into a calm, collected mass to be handed back to the returning classroom teacher.

Just before the Columbus Day holiday, Principal Dearest told me a grant which Guido had applied for had come through: a volunteer group which beautifies the schools would be coming in late October to paint the auditorium. Since I was a designer, she asked me to recommend a color for the trim (I chose calming and dirt-hiding slate blue) and to sketch some appropriate motifs for the panels between the auditorium windows. I spent the three-day weekend doing just that, drawing musical instruments, musical notes, dance motifs, ballet shoes, etc. to scale on graph paper. Pleased with the results, I handed the pages of designs to the principal's secretary the Tuesday after we returned.

In the days following, though I passed Principal Dearest in the hallway several times, she looked right through me as if I did not exist. Considering we were doing a project together, her aloofness was puzzling. Finally, absolutely stumped by her sphinx-like mien, I went back to the secretary and asked if she had given the principal the designs. Of course she had, and she had loved them—had the principal not told me?

Crazy Principal Dearest never did mention the designs. One day I passed her in the auditorium on a ladder with an overhead projector, sketching some elements of the designs onto the wall with a pencil. Still, she said nothing to me. I knew she liked them, since she had told the secretary as much and was indeed drawing them on the wall; I could not help thinking a principal should have more pressing business. Now, the fact she had said nothing, nor asked me, the trained artist, to execute the wall sketches, was frankly weird. I did not know whether to feel angry or just bewildered by her gauche conduct: Principal Dearest was simply inscrutable. She left off copying the designs after one panel, anyway.

A couple weeks later we came to school one Monday to find the auditorium and outside foyer transformed: the volunteers had spent the weekend there, though painting only a few scattered elements of my designs throughout their own hodgepodge of murals, several unfinished. Those completed had less sophistication than a highway exit McDonald's tribute to the Hamburglar, with even less success in their drippy execution. One lurid entry had some cartoonish ducks with the platitude, "Literacy Through the Arts" below it for no apparent reason other than as a voguish genuflection to the dictums of NCLB.

The whole effect was tacky and puerile, as if our own students, and untalented ones at that, had painted the scenes. On top of that, instead of painting the trim the slate blue I had suggested, Principal Dearest had chosen a shade of brown so Spot-on dog shit that it registered as a Martha Stewart impulse to coordinate the interior of the school with the exterior sidewalk. The effect was repulsive and between the trim and the new "art" on the walls, it felt like we had been totally punked by the meddling volunteers. I had certainly been dissed by Principal Dearest, spending a long weekend on designs which were neither acknowledged nor used.

The hit-or-miss administrative disorganization begun the year before now coagulated into a chronic gelatinous slick of uncertainty; the tenuous management could slip at any moment. The frantic announcements, recalled papers going home and lightning reversals of decisions—all more often than not, last minute—just contributed to the free-flowing angst. All of this was avoidable, of course, with foresight, planning and decisiveness, but Principal Dearest had a propensity for fixating maniacally on isolated issues at the expense of others with arguably higher priority.

At times the only consistency was inconsistency in the bananas republic the school was becoming. Principal Dearest screamed at a first grade teacher for letting a couple straggling students finish breakfast before the class went upstairs, yet the very next day excoriated the teacher for *not* allowing students to finish their breakfast.

On top of all the other craziness, Principal Dearest's dearth of emotional intelligence meant she also lacked boundaries delineating appropriate speech, with no qualms about cursing like a sailor at the assistant principals and in staff meetings. Indeed, her salty vernacular extended to raunchy comments about boobs and other lady business, as well as the occasional dirty joke. Once I walked into the office to hear her finishing a tirade about a boy who had gotten in trouble for drawing a dick on the stairwell wall. "...What is it with men and their penises?" she bellowed down the hall to the staff's amazement, startled classrooms of first graders craning to hear better.

I too had noted that omnipresent priapic preoccupation: when I went from the fifth grade to the first grade with individual cans of clay for sculpture, invariably a six-year-old would open one and be presented with the classic delight of pre-adolescent boys: who could forget, yes, the old reliable, dick and balls. The younger child would usually say something like, "Oh look, they did not make the bun big enough for the hot dog!" and I would nod in agreement.

Halloween came. Since I had reached critical mass with the religious fanatics brainwashing their kids about the Devil's Birthday, I decided to go into more detail than usual with the Celtic cultural history, elucidating the harmless tradition of scary costumes (I might have mentioned the especially frightening Barbie princess ensemble, a pedophile's delight) and trick-or-treating. My aim to enlighten completely backfired as, despite my repeated disclaimers, a couple kids went home and casually mentioned that evening, over the arroz con pollo, that on Halloween the dead crawl out of their graves to haunt living people.

I was dispatched to Principal Dearest's office for a dressing down, complete with the asinine pronouncement,"We don't teach religion in school!" My remonstrance that I had been teaching social studies fell on deaf ears; when parents got inflamed, Principal Dearest, like any egomaniac incapable of receiving criticism, always did the same, conveying their wrath as a new, more vicious Wrath 2.0, to us. She banned the teaching of Halloween at all henceforward. Other teachers continued in the way they always had: not teaching it, exactly, just focusing on the cute aspects of its morbid decor, without explanation. Cuddly vampires, adorable ghouls, Hello Kitty as a voodoo doll.

Since Halloween costumes had never been allowed for students, Principal Dearest came up with the idea of a "Parade of Characters." With a nod to that darling of NCLB nomenclature, "literacy," the lower grade classroom teachers had to devote hours to making costumes to represent a work of literature the kids were studying. For example, *The Cat in the Hat* required the whole class to be dressed as such. Then on Halloween, the classes would go out into the hall and march around the school to be admired for a few minutes, then return to their classrooms. The joyless exercise was designed to pay lip service to both Halloween and the reform movement, kiddie frivolity trumped by the fashionable notion of "accountability." Never mind that it had required teacher hours, student time and materials that would never be used again—it could be touted as "best practice," another modish catch phrase of the current educational *Zeitgeist*. Principal Dearest loved this empty ritual so much she revisited it every Halloween, so legions of very hungry caterpillars, gingerbread men, seven dwarves et al glumly sauntered through the corridors in feigned festivity, when all they really wanted was to eat a Kit Kat bar—dressed as Chuckie.

But out on the streets after school there would be just as many tiny Freddy Kruegers or diminutive Ghost Faces from *Scream*: in the neighborhood, wholesome interludes of quality time involved families gathered around the television for a heartwarming slasher movie. That the kids had even glimpsed these was disquieting, but in fact they were downright aficionados of the horror genre, with multiple viewings under their elastic belts. Their frustrating habit of talking during classwork time was never harder to stop than when the conversation turned to the latest theatrical release of blood and gore. Indeed, the kids competed for bragging rights, often viewing this graphic swill at an early discount, thanks to the profligacy of pirated DVDs sold by African guys on the Bronx sidewalks.

The only entertainment as compelling as *Saw* was video games, a ubiquitous addiction so devastating to kids' futures they should be classified as an illegal substance. As if purposely invented to perpetuate the blight of this generation's ADD, the numbing, electronic barrage accustoms the victims to a lightning-paced world of instant gratification passively conjured with no effort at all. Ironically, their physical bodies languish while their buff avatars maraud wildly through the most popular games, the ersatz action pathetically standing in for an actual life while the repeated, ascending thrill of fake violence desensitizes them to its evil in the real world.

What is more, the mindless influence, no favor to already tranced-out kids—in usurping the pleasure of reading books and creative, mental activities—has stolen imaginations as well as brain cells. School will never be able to compete with these enhanced, facile fantasies because these kids are most animated by, well, animation.

But horror movies, video games and third in the axis of evil, unlimited television, are mere fittings of a childhood deprived for some of an adult in charge. Of course, there are many good parents in the Bronx. But for the unlucky kids, these electronic distractions are joined by late-night unsupervised romps through the streets, post-midnight bedtimes (so they sleep at school), smoke-filled rooms (some kids' clothes and hair reek of cigarettes, the second-hand attack at least part of the reason for the mysterious skyrocketing asthma rates in the Bronx) and no enforcement of homework. Plus, of course, drama, violence and whatever is inappropriate: probably some are seeing porn, too, if not actively creating it.

Over and over, it is the parent you long to slap silly, like the slutty mother who, a little boy told me, kept him awake every night while she had sex with different guys in the next room: at school he kept falling asleep on his desk; or the baked parents who rolled into the school office in a cloud, as if Pigpen had spliffed on some very pungent skunk weed; and the father of a second grader who, she said, told her to stay away from his "weeds." Plus as much as most parents would never wish harm on their children, every day I passed an unconscious parent either cursing in front of their kids or subjecting infants in strollers to heavy duty rap music blasting from boomboxes right next to the baby's ears. Not only was the parent forcing a precocious resonance with the beats of percussive anger, the hapless child would go deaf or perhaps worse, go through life subconsciously obeying the dumb ass edicts of Lil Wayne. Moreover, though they were often in the news for fatally attacking children, next to the baby walked the de rigeur ghetto pet, canine extension of the macho *poseur*, the family pitbull. Given the overwhelming load of toxic stress assaulting these kids, free parenting classes would be simply beyond valuable.

Now five years old, in January the No Child Left Behind law was up for reauthorization. As it turned out, the Bush Administration had never provided the money to fully implement NCLB, yet states were to comply with all provisions of the program or lose federal funding, incomplete as it was. Thus, states had to make cuts to to everything that would not result in higher test scores: arts, social studies, science and foreign languages were stripped away, as well as materials like books and school supplies, with extras like afterschool programs and field trips relegated to history. In NYC we continued to have limited access to all of these through the city education budget, as long as Wall Street and the rest of the city's economy provided the tax base to do so.

I could not imagine NCLB would be renewed, given its focus on test scores to measure accountability had resulted in educators "teaching to the test" at the expense of actual instruction. Indeed, time, money and energy had been diverted into test prep and testing to the point where an authentic education, with its intrinsic stimulation, impetus to a love of learning, and character-building, had become a distant memory of a time less irrational. Test subjects: reading, writing and math, along with test-taking strategies, had been deemed the only knowledge worth knowing since the school and its teachers were judged solely by students' ability to deliver the scores. Moreover, just like other states overwhelmed by impoverished kids, ELLs or disabled students unable to pass the tests, New York state had responded to strict NCLB requirements by watering them down so they were conducive to student performance, and to officials maintaining their jobs.

States could also lower standards to heighten achievement, meaning the bar for achieving "proficiency" was lowered, allowing students to pass more easily. But even the easier tests were too difficult for the special ed students and ELLs, and cultural biases reflected on the tests, such as vocabulary words, or prior knowledge, assumed to be known by everyone, still put many disadvantaged students at an even further remove of success.

Unlike its swift inauguration, at least now NCLB was being subjected to scrutiny and discussion. Temporarily extended, the law would be stuck for years in congressional committees while politicians debated its controversies. Hopefully, the powers that be were finally learning what a majority of concerned parents and educators already understood: NCLB had turned out to be a simplistic approach to a complex problem, blaming schools for student failure to achieve, while so many other variables were, in fact, at play—poverty and all of its accompanying negatives; students with disabilities; students who do not speak English; obsolete school buildings and equipment; large class sizes and decimated budgets, among other factors. What living organism thrives when starved?

The snows came and with them many absent teachers, though now regular substitutes were called and actually showed up, so the clusters were spared. I was constantly coming up with new lesson plans to engage the kids, keeping the good ones to recycle a few years later. The best were based on art history. For example, we studied Andy Warhol along with rendering facial expressions; the result was a multiple self-portrait with different feelings, in Pop Art style. After learning about the oldest art from the caves in Lascaux, we drew our own versions in oil pastel on crumpled brown paper to imitate the rock surface. Studying ancient Egypt we wrote our names and titles of our art in hieroglyphics, making tomb murals in the Egyptian style.

A Pixar exhibit at the Museum of Modern Art, with stunning animation renderings for characters from the popular movies, proved really inspirational, since the kids knew the movies by heart. Using the catalogue and posters from the show, the kids designed their own characters, and many an animator was born from the project. In a lesson which had me wearing a *Cat in the Hat* hat from class to class, the younger kids designed their own Seuss-influenced character with a silly name and a rhyming sentence to go with it.

As ever, I sought to imbue a love of creating and the best way to achieve that was to present them with imaginative opportunities. Though often kids would announce their goal to be an artist when they grow up, in truth, not more than a couple per grade (out of one hundred twenty-five) had sufficient talent to make that a reality. But at least another handful were skillful enough to go into artistic fields, like visual display, fashion or interior design.

When illustrating figures, the kids tended to leave them white like the paper background. I pointed out that unless they are a ghost—ha, ha—nobody is that color, not even people who are called "white" (okay, I lied, but none of them knew Conan). For that matter, nobody is "black," either. We are all brown, actually, we just go from palest to darkest brown. Given the mix of heritages in the school population, every shade was represented, from veiny translucence through cafe au lait to near-ebony. The class pack of crayons I used to teach included one brown; I taught the kids to use it with differing pressures to give people a natural skin tone. My brown theory was practical, but I especially liked the sense of cohesiveness the inclusionary concept emphasized of a brown *us*.

My premise also challenged a riff I had heard too many times around school: African American and Hispanic kids would refer to each other as "black" or "white," sometimes just stating a visual fact, others with a tinge of racism behind it. If the color bias I had seen talked about on *Oprah* years before was still around, it would be my pleasure to proselytize it out of existence. However, a few times I would be accused of being "racist," in fact, by unhappy kids I had disciplined. "You jus' sayin' that to me cuz I'm black," or "She got a problem with black people." Whenever the race card was played you could hear the parents' knee-jerk defensiveness expressed in the child's declaration. But even the rest of the kids did not buy the Johnny Cochran treatment: I had not punished the kid for nothing, and kids of the same color were left alone, so where was the logic?

Starting with a couple classrooms, we began getting huge computer screens in the front of the room called Smartboards, the result of a grant. Taking the place of the traditional chalkboard, and using their connection to a laptop computer, they were able to deliver state-of-the-art technology to the class. Whatever was on disks, the teacher's hard drive or on the Internet could be presented to the class. We could write and draw on them, too. I was excited to use them to teach art, however they needed frequent tech support. Also, since sufficient training on them was lacking, some teachers ignored them in favor of dry-erase boards they still had. The Smartboards certainly gave the school a more modern look, even though we still did not have air conditioning.

One morning Principal Dearest was in a bad mood and required an ego pick-me-up, so a drive-by attack was in order. I was in a fifth grade in which we were making large sculptured paper snowflakes, stapling pieces of them together as the kids finished the parts. The class was loud, and that was always an incentive for the principal to smell bad "management," still the operative industry lingo for "discipline." I had given up trying to hush fifth grades as an exercise in futility—though the noise was irritating it was healthier to flow with it Zen-like than to resist the inevitable. All at once Principal Dearest stormed in.

"What's going on in here?" she barked.

As there was clearly art going on in here, her contorted, livid face came as somewhat of a buzzkill. She demanded to meet with me at lunch time. As she charged out the door, I managed to re-set my rolled eyes back just in time to wince at her parting Taser gaze.

Not only was her denigration unfair, but after four years of patronizing treatment, I was taking serious umbrage with these principals who, though in actuality peers (or less), treated me and many others as children. I showed her my lesson plan, which was perfectly fine but she labored to rip apart, saying it required too many class periods. I stood my ground: the three dimensional snowflake sculptures were intricate, and for everyone to be able to take one home, the work was necessary. Principal Dearest refused to listen, my explanation glancing off her crazed eyes. It was clear the "transgression" was nonexistent and I was there just because of her whim—it was simply my bad luck I had been singled out that day. Nevertheless, I had not done anything against the rules, so her crack at infantilizing me was all the satisfaction she would get; Principal Dearest dismissed me with a generic admonishment to not plan such long lessons.

As I digested the rude shock of it, the experience of being hauled into Principal Dearest's office enraged me more and more. Clearly the appeasement of her appetite for degradation was her sole motivation for the event, probably even, for becoming a principal, since she was intimidating other teachers as well. After she had ignored the designs I had done for the auditorium, the disrespect was complete with this newest violation. I now joined several of the other staff members in feeling frankly unsafe. When I came to school I dreaded Principal Dearest more than my worst class, in fact, my nightmare was her ambushing me in my most difficult classes and blaming me for their behavior, which she did several times. Sometimes this incurred another pretentious, inane meeting, but more often just a stab at a tongue-lashing in front of the students, designed to humiliate.

I went to the office regularly, culling parents' telephone numbers from emergency cards and spending every Friday evening calling as many as a couple dozen parents for that week's offenses. Always, about half of the kids' home phone numbers were out of service. Keeping the phone bill paid, or living in a consistent domestic setting, seemed to be real neighborhood challenges. The erratic, unstable home life of our students, especially the disruptive ones I was calling about, really hit home for me when I had such trouble reaching an adult in their lives. Typically, television, in fact, cartoons, was blasting in the background; the parent shouted into the phone rather than turning it down.

For many I relied on a rudimentary Spanish medley of stock phrases like, "He does not behave well," "She gets out of her seat all the time," "He is always playing and never works," "She never stops talking." Many times a truly concerned parent would pour out her heart to me, mourning her inability to get through to her kid, her hard life holding down two jobs, often going to school, raising other children, with no male support in sight. Occasionally, a parent would berate me, in complete denial of their child's behavior. Some refused to accept the idea that little Christian was the most profligate of heathens, since at home, they insisted, Angel was perfectly divine.

There were always parents who screamed at their kids while holding the phone, while I listened to the kid's lame defense, lie or entreaty. These usually ended with the parent assuring me they would "beat they ass" or some such threat. Though I suggested taking something away instead, I must admit the ones who got a smack found religion, at least in my class, and usually for a week or more. So the calls worked, for the most part, but they required repeated strikes, and frequently the effort was an impossible demand on my vanquished Friday psyche.

At least kids whose homes I had called announced in class, "She called my house," and that had its own deterrence value. The worst was when a really heinous rascal did not have a working phone number at all, a very common situation: they knew they had impunity and behaved accordingly. Also, there were always a few whose parents did not respond, and they would taunt, "Go ahead, call my house—my mom don't care" and true, the mother would grunt, "Uh, huh," and indeed, nothing would change.

It always cracked me up when the kids themselves would answer the phone. Sometimes they would fess up to who they were, sometimes they would pretend to be a sibling, or just hang up in my face. All told, though, calling did not help as much as it might because there were just too many calls to make, too much of the time. I could have been on the phone a couple hours every night if I had truly engaged; the energy just was not there to continue fighting them into the evening.

I also reported fights and student misbehavior religiously. We were required to do that, and I comprehended the legal onus for doing so, not just the moral imperative to address bad behavior for the kids' sake as well as ours. The time it took for the witnesses and me to write statements, call the parents of those involved, and fill out accident /injury reports was naturally annoying, yet had to be done. Despite my by-the-book actions a couple other clusters did virtually nothing to enforce the code of conduct. Students often told me of fights in a class in which another cluster simply stood by and later did not even bother to report it.

The underlying reason for this was not just to avoid the ensuing red tape, but to evade the radar of the administration. As clusters we took comfort in a class that was merely loud, considering the alternatives. But Principal Dearest had emerged as a roving kangaroo court of one, capable of instant, simplistic vigilante injustice. Any situation her twisted perception judged out of control, if only a noisy but safe classroom, seemed to suddenly enhance her feelings of vulnerability, as if a switch had turned on her lizard fight-or-flight brain. If cacophony attracted an administrative assault, then acts of violence, reported, truly inspired venomous blame.

Time and again, when following the reporting rules, I incurred one of Principal Dearest's dreaded, erratic, and out-of-the-blue ballistic launches. When a student stabbed another with a pencil in the back of the room, I was at fault because I was conferring with a student in the front of the room. When another student stole clay from me during a sculpture class and I sought his suspension, I was indicted for not having prevented him. The only way I might have avoided these situations would have been to cease art instruction in favor of full-on babysitting, and then only in a lifeguard chair; even then it would be impossible to monitor every student move. But in that case, anyway, I would have been vilified for not teaching.

Indeed, it was a damned-if-you-do, damned-if-you-don't distortion of reality and a confounding conundrum to consider. The absurdity of having to relentlessly weigh this senseless calculation, not to mention the perpetual fear of attack if I erred one way or another, infuriated me. Challenging as my prior years had been, it was the students who were the primary enemy of my blood pressure, hardly a news flash given the poor urban setting. Now, ironically, the one who was supposed to support, indeed *lead* me, was on the contrary, vulture-like, finishing me off at the end of a horrible class.

For Principal Dearest, actual or just possible student injury conjured the potential for what she continued to dread most, parental criticism. As her horror of bad reviews from the parents took on the proportions of a theme, a neurotic ditty to which we had to tap dance on eggshells, you could hardly miss the irony that for Principal Dearest, who thrived on capricious criticism of others, the prospect of it directed at herself was deeply terrifying. The ardor of her anxiety may also have stemmed from an overly-enthusiastic appropriation of the education-as-business, Bloomberg dickdom dictum, "The customer is always right."

In a fourth grade class, when three boys started whipping crayons at one another, a classic disruption in an inner-city art teacher's world, and one nearly ended in an eye injury to an innocent bystander, my report resulted in me getting punished along with the kids. So, after a now-classic over-reaction complete with a volley of vituperation directed at me, for that class's next art period, instead of doing art, Principal Dearest forced me to make the whole class read several pages on art followed by answering written questions which I had prepared. I had to research elementary-level tracts on art, write questions and make thirty copies at my own expense, since the copy machine had taken one of its frequent powders. Instead of the three boys reaping the consequences of their behavior, twenty-eight people including myself had to endure Principal Dearest's perverse inequity, the *coup de grace* being her creepy, neurotic personal appearance in the next class to make sure I was following her orders, complete with a berserk gleam in her eye.

Indeed, as the year went on Principal Dearest's psychotic episodes, not just with teachers but classes, were on the increase. As ever, her Gestapo tactics favored drastic retribution, meted out wholesale instead of to the culpable few. Since this approach never worked due to its enabling of attention-starved instigators, entire classes, for instance, had to repeatedly, day after day, stay inside instead of getting out in the fresh air for recess. It was truly painful to watch dozens of well-behaved, completely innocent kids incarcerated in the stifling auditorium, feckless pawns of the rageaholic "adult in charge."

Indeed, many in the school, from the kids to the head custodian, who ended up transferring to flee her despotism, were finding a reason to hate her. Still, Principal Dearest had her clutch of lackies in fawning attendance—ever the group of suck-ups, most from Guido's tenure—and they scurried around at her beck and call. But though they were never specifically targeted, their obsequiousness did not spare even them from her bipolar apoplexy, luny directives or bar room maledictions.

As ever, my classes of younger kids were the highlight of my day, indeed, I could not have gotten through it without them. Everything about them made me smile: their fresh little faces, their hilarious comments, their wonder, their purity, their unbridled openness. They were simply gorgeous, every one of them. To be in their presence was to be in a sacred space, such was the sense of spirit and grace in the room. Their art was equally miraculous, for each one of them an exuberant splash of *me*. How often I marveled inwardly to see art that could hang next to Miro, de Kooning, Kandinsky, or Motherwell, and no visitor to the Museum of Modern Art would ever be the wiser. The little kids were ever a touchstone for what is real, what is essential and what life is supposed to be.

Meanwhile, downtown at the DOE, business continued as usual. In one of the typical no-bid contracts Klein had awarded since 2003, he had hired consultants the year before to cut back the schools' financial operations. The nearly sixteen million dollar contract was given to a firm which had previously milked millions out of the St. Louis schools prior to that system going bankrupt.[2] Now, at an hourly rate of four hundred fifty dollars, with five hundred dollars billed to expenses every day, the consultants had taken an ax to over one hundred school bus routes, stranding freezing children outside on the coldest days of the year. The wacky changes included such horror stories as six-year-olds using Metro cards to take as many as three different city buses; the necessity for kids to cross six-lane highways; and siblings assigned to bus stops a mile apart, though they went to the same school. Some kids were even given pick-up times that were after school opening times. The chaos took center stage for several days as distraught parents protested and the DOE scrambled to reinstate the bus routes.

Valentine's Day, like every other holiday, required acknowledgment from the art department, and so we made valentines. First I taught them the origins of the celebration, as with many other holidays, a fascinating overlay of Christian characters/ideas onto a conquered, still-cherished pagan tradition. Then I read poems illustrating all the different types of love people have for each other. These drew the expected heckles and shrieks of disgust the word "love" always provoked up through second grade; outside of bodily functions it was the quickest way to a chorus of "Eeewww!" The repulsion amusingly coincided with the vehement separation, at that age, of boys and girls into opposing camps. By third grade, when "love" was mentioned there was at most a muffled hum of awkwardness, then in fourth grade, acceptance, and for the fifth graders, full-on interest.

When it came to holidays, considering the diversity of the students, many of them recent immigrants, it almost felt a patriotic duty to assimilate them into our cultural rituals, the Gods of Hallmark presiding over all. Outside, the stores were in the constant throes of promoting whatever crap accessorized the imminent holiday, while the stuff from the previous one was on sale, then disappeared: desire discarded. The inescapable procession of holidays was beginning to strike me as a cynical cultural conspiracy. In my innocuous projects every year to mark the moment, I was the unwitting bitch of a system designed to breed nothing but consumers;

as such I was complicit in creating more ranks of the tranced and exploited.

Ideally, in the grand scheme of things the kids would grow up to pay taxes and stay off the dole and out of prison, on their path to credit card debt and a mortgage, the American Dream. But notwithstanding my flirtation with my inner Emma Goldman, even as robotic bourgeoisie the kids would live more safe and comfortable lives, a foundation then presenting an opportunity for enlightenment. Only a life free from the grinding imperative of survival grants you the Socratic privilege of realizing "the unexamined life is not worth living." Whenever I would wax philosophic, I reminded myself that my part was to help the kids escape the poverty and limitations into which they had been born, through knowledge, the belief that they deserve better, and most importantly, that better is, in fact, possible. Later they would have the luxury of neuroses.

In April, the DOE transfer website was up. I looked in earnest for a new position but except for high school, no opportunities were available in art. I had noticed I was more qualified than anyone to teach art, at least in my school, and since the whole point was to make a contribution, teaching that subject would best serve that goal. In fact, I enjoyed teaching beginning literacy more.

A lawsuit over class size and state funding for city students had finally been won, recommending elementary classrooms have no more than twenty students (a vast improvement over the union-negotiated limit of thirty-two kids). But the win for parents, teachers and students was a cruel tease: in coming years the funds, three quarters of a billion dollars, were not spent as directed, a situation prompting a lawsuit by the UFT against the DOE.[3] Instead, the money was distributed willy nilly to principals; they only had to report how they had spent it, and did not have to use it specifically to reduce class size, which most of them did not. This embittered parents and teachers alike.

The do-nothing head of the PA, which at that point had three members, was a former drug addict and ex-con named Carmen; her spoiled kid was one of our students. Though Carmen was ostensibly guilty of pocketing the profits from the school pictures, candy sales and any other enterprises the PA sponsored to raise money, Principal Dearest was said to have made these scandals go away, though ultimately Carmen was barred from collecting further monies. In fact, the welfare mom and Principal Dearest were great friends, to the point where she stayed over in Carmen's apartment on occasion. Now in May, teachers received a kooky invitation, a folded, xeroxed paper that spelled "celebration" as "celebratation," to Carmen's wedding reception *in the Teachers Lounge*, of all places.

The amenities of the nine by ten feet catch-all room included a crumbling ceiling, noisy vending machine, rusted white metal cabinets, ripped vinyl love seat with browning foam extrusions, and cracked formica-topped tables from the early forties. This shabby chic, moreover, was accessorized by the carcass of a cockroach here and there, with the rhythmic soundtrack of the dripping faucet finishing the glamorous effect. But the venue was not merely tasteless, the use of a public school for a private affair was blatantly illegal. Incredibly, someone had to mention the inappropriateness of the reception to daffy Principal Dearest, who only then nixed it. However, we were still left to wonder where the bride and groom had registered: the ninety-nine cent store?

The end of the school year came on swiftly as it always did, gaining momentum after Easter. Fortunately, Principal Dearest had other teachers to roast besides me and anyway, was busy with the end of the year paperwork that typically absorbed principals, apparently even the disorganized ones. I got my "S" evaluation paper, and with my five year anniversary, full vestiture in the pension fund. Now, no matter how long I lasted, I would get something later for my DIY indenturehood, though in my case the pension I had accrued would be miniscule. I would have to slog it out for twenty-two years to get the pension's full value; since I had started so late, I could only conceivably retire around sixty-eight. The specter of this induced involuntary shudders, goosebumps and a glistening brow...and not just because we still didn't have air conditioning. Even as my will drove it doggedly forward to school every day, my body had revolted over and over; another seventeen years was not going to happen.

I decided my goal would be, at best, ten years. Even though the pension at that point would still be insufficient, at least I would have given a substantial chunk of my life to something real. That contribution would satisfy the nagging sense of responsibility that plagued me, urging me there in the first place. As difficult as the job was, I was dispatching my debt to society bit by bit, one class at a time.

7

Once again, I had been made an art teacher, a blessing for which I gave a sigh of relief every time. My heart went out to the long-suffering classroom teachers. Ironically, not only did their heroism go unsung, they were tormented by administrators, then endlessly vilified by the right and others looking for a scapegoat for the broken educational system. Despite the far more challenging behavior of the students I faced as a cluster teacher, given my three percent share versus the classroom teacher's eighty-five percent share of their time, the classroom teacher's work load, already daunting, was increasing every year with burgeoning paperwork demands at school and at home. Bloomberg was not just obsessed with bringing a corporate style to the school system; having built his financial empire bringing data to Wall Street, he now perpetuated the heavy use of it in testing and tracking the students.

Not only did they have to learn the city's new computer data program, classroom teachers were increasingly swamped with assessments, to the point where it was debatable which they were doing more, teaching or assessing. The additional work was not limited to the actual activity of it: afterward, the data had to be inputted into the system, then analyzed and acted upon to improve instruction. Moreover, the assessments took place one-on-one during class time while the rest of the students were supposed to be engaged in learning. But these private assessments proved virtually impossible, given the impulse of unsupervised kids to exploit the teacher's distraction for their dastardly devices.

In the kindergarten the testing was particularly demanding, teachers at their wits end in a sea of unsocialized, spirited *enfants terribles*. But the teachers would get no sympathy from the DOE: in the push for statistics the human element had been replaced by the numbers-fueled cult of accountability. Along with the new focus on data, classroom teachers still had the same crammed work schedule as before, outside of the actual teaching day, putting in hours on the still onerous, nonsensical bulletin boards with their mandated trivia, five per room, due monthly; maintaining student portfolios of work; attending meetings and professional development; and planning lessons. Classrooms were regularly patrolled by the administrative Yakuza to judge the "environment," the atmosphere subject to lengthy checklists of trivial objectives.

The torment continued during class time when teachers had to conduct "guided reading," going from group to group of children assessed at the same level, "conferencing" individually and entering that encounter into a log which was then hungrily perused by administrators as a tool for evaluating (all too often, persecuting) the teacher. Errors, omissions, insufficient entries or the worst crime, no entries at all, simply constituted more evidence on which to hang an offending teacher. As with every other measure, these were accorded more or less weight based on the teacher's reputation and position with Principal Dearest. If they were not liked, there was nothing they could do to change that—having their shit in a pile did not make a difference, while being caught unprepared would just add to their daily oppression. By contrast, the teachers who were favored, not just the suck-ups, but those who for no apparent reason were liked, got away with anything short of dating a fourth grader (or other educator offenses gleefully reported in the *Post*).

In the meantime, Bloomberg had given principals even more power to manage their schools, those presiding over the best test scores even eligible for bonuses of as much as twenty-five thousand dollars a year. In return, the city had instituted multiple accountability measures. Yearly Progress Reports issued grades—A through F—for each school on student progress (improvement in test scores, sixty percent), student performance (actual test scores, twenty-five percent) and school environment (fifteen percent).[1] The latter criteria would be determined in school Learning Environment Surveys completed by parents and teachers, concerning academic expectations, student engagement, communication, collegiality, safety and respect, and effectiveness of the administrators.[2] Extra credit was given for remarkably improved performance by students with disabilities, ELLs and kids who had previously scored at the lowest proficiency citywide. As part of the grading the school was scored in relation to forty other peer schools, with like populations, as well as compared to schools citywide. Now, at the beginning of the school year our first Progress Report grade was released: we got a "B."

Another DOE hoop for schools to jump through, the Quality Review was a visit by an expert educator. Going into classrooms and talking to staff, administration, students and parents, the evaluator would employ a rubric to assess the ability of a school to educate its students. The reviewer's feedback would include setting goals and making adjustments, ultimately grading the school "well developed," "proficient," "underdeveloped with proficient features," and "underdeveloped."[3]

The city also launched a computerized data program, Achievement Reporting Information System (ARIS) that brought together all of a student's test scores, grades, past transcript, attendance, and biographical and contact information for the easy perusal of teachers, administrators and parents.[4] Combined with what was detailed in the Progress Report, teachers and administrators could use the data to create strategies and interventions to improve student performance.

On the home front, the DOE had finally gotten around to our school with its asbestos removal program. Trailers of construction workers parked in and around the yard, making nightly forays into the school to make a really big mess of things. They built temporary interior walls which shrank rooms, and all of their scaffolding and equipment diminished the yard for a project which would take two years. With guys in space suits roaming around at night plenty of stuff went missing, including art supplies. The inconvenience and theft were the least of it—of a morning we would discover a pile of dust someone had been too tired to remove. It may as well have been glowing but we would not know for years: we all knew the stats on asbestos lung, which showed up decades later, the infinitesimal glass shards carving away a bit at a time. Anyway, we just crossed our fingers, since we could not do much more than roll with the new added occupational hazard.

I proceeded with the year, as usual starting out with the rules. Over the years I had enlivened the predictable *schtick* by diving further into the most compelling rationale for rules: they make school a safe place to learn, important because just as our parent(s) have jobs, school is our job, we are just not getting paid for it now. Flexing my bicep, I discuss super heros and their physical force (all the boys perk up) versus the greater strength of a brain filled with knowledge. Then I launch shamelessly into flagrant propaganda, repeating again and again, "knowledge is power." Like a fist-pumping evangelist I hammer the point, anvil-like, to convince them they have to take school seriously, or they are toast.

I spell it out in fundamental, unmistakable terms: when you work, you will trade your knowledge for money. The more knowledge you have, the more money you will make. (I wait to be struck down by lightning by this outrageous fib, belied by performers, athletes and Kardashians, but I say it anyway because for most of those without Shaq's height or Beyonce's voice, education is their only hope.) I point out that people who have little or no knowledge to trade, get little or no money for it. People who do not have power from knowledge do not have choices: they can only be poor, or be criminals and end up dealing drugs, in jail or dead (I cite the dropout gang thugs hanging out on the main drag; the kids nod their heads in recognition). When you grow up and go to college and graduate school (*when*, not if) you will have so much knowledge you can trade it to be anybody you want: you can be an astronaut, a doctor, a teacher, a president, an architect, a fashion designer, a scientist, an auto mechanic....anyone you want to be, because you are powerful!

I point out how we teachers went to graduate school and now we trade that knowledge for money. Plus, we get to do something we love: teach. Then I ask the kids what they want to be. By this time they are really pumped and hands shoot up all over the room to share their dream. The really small ones always include lots of firefighters and policemen, but there are also a fair number of super heros and princesses. Although at this point I have delivered this speech a couple hundred times, the energy and passion never fails to build in me, probably because this is the bedrock philosophy that got me into teaching there in the first place. I get especially hyper because the majority of the kids are never going to get this spiel at home.

The side benefit of the pep talk is that every year the first week, when my body literally aches to not be there, I actually get rebooted by my own educational cheerleading. I was going to need it this third year with Principal Dearest. In the fall she strafed me a couple times with her default attack of choice, a drive-by of a loud fifth grade class. In the meantime she persevered at persecuting a clutch of teachers, becoming increasingly demented in her approach. She had one in particular in her sights, Ms. Pallas, a special ed teacher who, having had a baby over the summer, had taken a maternity leave at the beginning of the school year. Freaked out by the subsequent insurrection of Pallas's unruly students, who had been left to a succession of substitutes (as usual, the principal had not planned for the event), Principal Dearest sent DOE inspectors to the teacher's house. She neglected to tell them Pallas was on an approved maternity leave, so when they arrived at the teacher's house they were mystified by the principal's bizarre behavior. The embarrassment of her misstep seemed to only redouble Principal Dearest's torment of Pallas, which continued through the principal's tenure and even beyond.

Just like every other September, Bloomberg called a press conference to exude over the latest test scores triumph, a record which had now won New York City the prestigious Broad Foundation Prize for Urban Education, most improved urban district. *Quelle* surprise: the state tests had become easier than ever. States, beholden by their accountability to the impossible task of achieving "proficiency" levels by 2014, were obviously playing fast and loose with that term. Like a dysfunctional family in which nobody dares speak up to the tyrannical, punitive father, the bullied state education departments, desperate for federal funds, had made a Faustian bargain, with the education of the nation's children teetering in the balance.

By this point the lack of supplies was really getting to me. I had been outraged from the beginning by the teacher's bathrooms, with their chronic shortage of soap and paper towels, when we had them, stubbornly unabsorbent tree bark that evoked the loofah toilet paper of Soviet Cold War outhouses. As usual, classroom teachers had to ask students to bring in basic stuff like paper towels, cleaning products and tissue, plus school materials such as boxes of pencils for the class. I had been shocked by these third world demands even from my own child's public school in a better locale, and during economic boom times, to boot.

For our own specific teaching supplies the New York City Council provided us with a yearly stipend, usually at least one hundred fifty dollars. This came in handy for me because it proved almost impossible to squeeze art supplies out of Principal Dearest. Though she had been given thousands of dollars for the arts, during her time as principal I would only receive two small boxes of colored pencils, a class-size box of markers and one of crayons—to teach hundreds of students, and for years. All else I either bought myself, cadged from around the school or withdrew from resources (from prior principals) I had hidden, squirrel-like, around the school.

Teachers buying their own supplies, anyway, into the hundreds, even thousands of dollars worth, yearly, were typical throughout the system. To not have normal access to things we needed was just a given: even copy paper was a prized commodity. You had to finagle it out of the office secretary or beg the school aide in charge of the supply closet, who nevertheless refused to part with even a ream without the principal's (hard-won) permission. If you had been blessed enough to find a printer that worked in the school, then you would have to make sure you removed the left-over paper: someone else would come along and see it as the treasure trove it was.

At times, copy paper was so scarce we had to buy our own, an insult compounded by having to pay for copies at Staples the frequent times the school copy machine was on the fritz. We had been given a copy machine of our own for the teacher's center, a room dedicated to our use and preparation but instead, as usual, turned into an office for the coaches. After constant repairs that machine was carted away. Years later we finally got another that was shoved into the tiny teachers' lounge where we ate lunch; it, too, broke repeatedly. The inescapable conclusion was, even as we were required to be professional, we would never be provided normal, professional infrastructure. The copy machine dysfunction, it appeared, was simply a Xeroxed metaphor for the broken system.

Bed bugs were in the news, showing up not just in beds but theatre seats and department stores, a phenomenon that was causing alarm for some, hysteria for others. One of our teachers on the 4 train up to the Bronx saw a bedbug hitching a ride on the denim-ed butt of a teenage girl. The fact that, in our profession, we had been around lice for years, meant bedbugs were just another, more challenging, nuisance. A few times a year a child would be sent to the nurse and not allowed to go back to class, the parent charged with Kwelling the pestilence on the kid's scalp before they could return to school. Meanwhile, all the kids in the class got letters home stating that lice had been detected and parents should be attentive to that. The funny part was, whenever the topic of lice was discussed our heads started to itch. Like now.

Early in the year a kindergartner I adored, Kaleem, began crying inconsolably every day at school. It turned out his new foster mother was regularly hitting the little boy, and favoring her own children over him. Our school guidance counselor contacted the city and they removed him from the home. All of a sudden Kaleem moved to a new family, changing schools. Poor Kaleem had been taken away from an abusive birth mother in the first place; I hoped his living situation would stabilize. We had so many more who had been wounded and shunted about.

A beautiful little girl, Aliah, arrived in the middle of one year so traumatized she did not speak at all until two years later, and even then, barely in a whisper. Aliah and her sister had endured abuse from their birth mother, a crack addict, then were put into foster care, then placed back with the mother after she had gotten out of rehab.

A four-year-old, Jacquon, was absent for a week before we found out what had happened to him: he was hospitalized with critical burns sustained when his mother plunged him into a bathtub of scalding water. He never returned to school.

Two brothers, Malik and Rudy, had already been with us for a few years of wilding. Back home in the Caribbean they had witnessed their father chop their mother's leg off with a machete, and the younger one, especially, was understandably disturbed and high-strung.

In terms of sexual abuse, only one fifth grade special ed student, Genesis, ever showed outward signs of that, specifically a very strong odor; the fetid cloud enveloping her provoked banishment to her own table by the other kids. Her classroom teacher was out having surgery so I spoke to the temporary replacement teacher. She contacted the city and the grandfather with whom Genesis and her brother lived; they had been rescued five years before, orphans living on the streets of Santo Domingo. When it came out Genesis had been afraid to be picked up at school by an uncle, the grandfather removed that probable offender from the picture.

Then there was the third grader with the disfigured face, Istenae, who as a toddler had been doused with hot coffee by her mother, but I could go on and on. The guidance counselors knew plenty more, dealing with the toughest kids and their families every day. Still more would never be brought to light, secret hells to be revisited perhaps as adults, upon their own children. This chilling possibility presents yet another rationale for addressing the very biggest elephant in the nation's room, poverty.

Meanwhile, the soft abuse of endlessly plying children with junk food continued as usual. Kids who refused to eat the school lunch brought bags of chips and cookies, chased with any number of lurid, inflammatory drinks. This alarming carbfest made an appearance on field trips, as well, when instead of sensible food, kids' brown bags disgorged a cascade of calories reminiscent of munched-out, late night trips from the dorm to the 7-Eleven. The accompanying maltreatment, as served up daily by the negligent parents, was a lengthy, comatose stretch of passive entertainment in front of one screen or another, the comparatively geriatric exertion involved in a Nintendo Wii game the most exercise a kid might get.

This lethal combination of sugar and stupor had a predictable physical effect on many of the students: at least half of every class was chubby, if not more hefty. By fifth grade man boobs were not uncommon, while girls as well could top two hundred pounds. One of these, Ravielis, since kindergarten almost as wide as she was tall, came from gym where they had done a physical evaluation: her BMI was in the hundredth percentile. The DOE was complicit in the problem, as state law required gym daily for kindergartners through third grade, while higher grades were supposed to get gym three times a week. Instead, all the kids were getting just one gym class per week. Requisite gym classes did not lead to higher test scores, and that was the (ever expanding) bottom line.

That January, furious principals found out about looming budget cuts, not from the DOE but from local newspaper reports. Just the week before Klein had triumphantly released the results of principal satisfaction surveys indicating overwhelming positivity for his programs. But according to the representative of the principals union (the Council of School Supervisors), the survey results were not authentic: given the intimidating nature of the chancellor, many principals taking it were convinced the surveys were not anonymous, and so responded positively.

News of their secret rage was in line with a recent speech by education expert Diane Ravitch to five hundred principals criticizing Bloomberg's educational reforms, a lecture which was met with cacophonous applause. When the speaker asked afterward why, then, the principals had responded so enthusiastically to Klein's survey, she was told they had been afraid to voice their dissatisfaction. The culture of intimidation that enveloped us was squeezing principals too, creating a toxic environment for everybody involved, even the kids. With nobody daring to speak truth to power, Bloomberg and Klein were getting away with murder, of the prospects of a generation.

One day Principal Dearest told three of us clusters she wanted us to "fix" the auditorium with oil paints she would provide, starting Monday afternoon. It had been a year since the auditorium design fiasco and the invasion of do-gooders doing bad; now it turned out even Principal Dearest had a design clue and wanted the murals de-uglied. However, Mondays after dismissal were mandated for professional development, and to oblige us to use the time at her whim was a flagrantly illegal violation of that rule. Indeed, her sense of entitlement was typically in play: in much the same way she had had the security guard get her car inspected and tires changed, on school time. Moreover, to ask me now, after my volunteered design work was neither used nor even acknowledged in the past year, to correct the decorative travesty she had supported instead, was staggeringly rude. Rarely had I encountered such chorrendous chutzpah.

Up till now I had taken hits from Principal Dearest, understanding that to challenge her frangible ego would just increase her aggression. I had never forgotten what she had told me her first week, that she would retire after five years, and I was trying hard to make it till then. My goal of ten years still stood; I was damned if I would let Her Monstrosity push me out.

Principal Dearest told the three of us we could start redoing the murals the next week after we brought work clothes from home. We all felt bitter and exploited, but for me it represented a momentous last straw, forcing me to the very precipice of my self-esteem. I could not face myself in the mirror and do what she was ordering me to do, if I hoped to see any reflection at all. In my psyche, gigantic Cecil B. DeMille letters commanded me to RESIST. I wrote her a letter stating not only would I never work with toxic oil paint, I would not be correcting work which I had not myself designed.

I walked towards the principal's office, not amused by the Sword of Damocles mirage that had suddenly appeared over the door. As I went in, Principal Dearest was just coming out.

"I was going to leave this for you," I said. She snatched the letter from my hand before I could speak. She read half of it and having gotten the gist, tossed it at me angrily.

"Fine, whatever," she hissed.

I was elated: finally, I had taken a stand. The brazen honesty of this was unheard of in the school, the other two painting conscripts gaped when I told them what I had done. They ended up in the auditorium on Monday afternoons and professional development days, illegally, the noxious fumes of the oil paint, an apt symbol for the principal, obliterating designs, brain cells and self-regard.

What I did not count on was the speed and vehemence of Principal Dearest's retaliation for what turned out to be a Pyrrhic victory. The very next day an AP, Mr. Rodriguez, struck in a second grade, asking for my lesson plan. I had it in my plan book, a few yards away in the teacher's lounge across the hall. I told him I would go get it and he said no, I should have had it with me.

"You're going to get written up for this," he said, indicating that a letter would go in my file for not having a lesson plan.

I looked knowingly at him and told him this was about me refusing to clean up the auditorium. He said he did not know anything about that, just that the principal had told him to go look at my lesson plan.

As usual, this amounted to a meeting in her office with my union rep, in which I protested that I had actually had a lesson plan, it just was not on my person at that moment. Of course, the letter made its inexorable march into my file. When I came into the office to sign the official document, Principal Dearest had concocted an apocryphal statement declaring that I had no lesson plan, ending with the tired and trite pedagogical slogan, "When we fail to plan, we plan to fail." I was seething.

"This is not true," I said, "I had a lesson plan, it just was across the hall."

The principal snarled, her face gloating triumphantly, "If you don't sign it, I'll give you a letter for insubordination."

"Insubordination?" I could not mask my incredulity, "What is that?" Principal Dearest had already turned on her heel.

The kindly secretary whispered, "Just sign it. You can attach a statement refuting it," which is all that I could do.

Henceforth, I was the flavor of that year and the one following: no matter how many helpings she got of me, ravenous Principal Dearest needed more. As it turned out I was impressively capable of all sorts of misdemeanors. I was even attacked for a lower grade lesson of paper snowflake cutting—though the intricate process was a boost to motor skills, not to mention an elementary art class winter staple, she judged it "unsophisticated."

Another skirmish took place over an incident in the kindergarten, where I had gone to finish papers started the week before, only to find the classroom teacher had mistakenly thrown the papers out. The teacher enlisted me to do something else she had planned with the kids, but had no time to prepare. Foolishly I agreed, because the materials were not ready and I ended up frantically organizing them as the class descended into mayhem. Two boys began wrestling on the rug but I could not stop them and continue with the class. Though he neither screamed, cried nor even mentioned it at the time, one of them was bitten—I would find that out later.

I was happy to be done with the tumult and go to my next class when I was paged over the PA system to come to the principal's office. Principal Dearest was waiting for me, pacing and virtually foaming at the mouth (I seemed in danger of being bitten myself). It turned out a child was in the nurse's office, bitten because of my lack of supervision. As usual, she needed to see my lesson plan, which I produced, but of course I had not followed it because the classroom teacher had thrown the papers out. So I was in trouble for not teaching the lesson, the teacher was on the hot seat for what she had done, and a child not only had been bitten, but the injury had not been reported. Principal Dearest started the process of putting a letter in my file for the incident, however, several hectic days with postponed meetings and other obstacles followed, throwing her momentarily off my scent; I was granted an uncharacteristic reprieve.

In the meantime Principal Dearest fixated on other teachers, targeting a first year Teaching Fellow with a class so infernal, when entering you did not so much cross the threshold as the River Styx. Inside, Cerberus and other violent boys sauntered around the room provoking fights while gleefully pulling all the marginals into the melee. The result was a daily protracted fistfight during which sporadic bursts of learning erupted. Instead of support, the unfortunate teacher received five letters in her file from Principal Dearest, freaked out as ever by unsafe situations and the criticism from disgruntled parents which could ensue. Even a lame infraction of hair-pulling, because it brought a complaint from a parent, inspired a stentorian rebuke, along with a written one.

The martyred teacher was vindicated the next year when the psychotic ringleaders were exiled to the frozen steppes, a special ed class for mini maniacs in District Seventy-Five. By then, Principal Dearest had shifted her poles again and largely avoided the teacher, making due with a single missile launch at the very end of the year when the teacher got a letter in her file for giving a child a time-out, during which he took it upon himself to staple his own finger—her bad, of course. By her third year the teacher had joined a voluntary academic committee, a politically-astute move which prompted Principal Dearest to permanently train her artillery elsewhere.

This situation highlighted the skewed paradox I had seen since my first week in the school: the toughest classes were always given to the most inexperienced teachers. This absurdity had resulted in teachers leaving not just the school but the profession within the first month or so. This particular year a third grade class had chewed up two teachers in the first weeks and was now on its third.

Though I was still hemorrhaging energy to do it, the actual teaching part of the job was getting better. This was not only due to my mounting experience but the ever-strengthening ties with kids I had known since kindergarten, for the fifth graders, six years worth. Not that it was easy. There still was not a class in which I could teach without disruptions and disrespect—those irritants, persistent in the past, were still there, though in slightly lesser proportion. The shambolic, savage atmosphere which had characterized the place in my early years had given way to a more nuanced dysfunction. There were definitely as many motormouths, impulsive reactionaries and drama queens of both sexes. But in terms of violence, the incidence of hardcores, formerly a few per class, was now just a few per grade. Still, I had to teach at all times as if I were holding the lid, and with all my might, on a Pandora's box of negative potentials clamoring to escape. One hand was always pushing down on the bursting lid, another hand teaching, a recipe for depletion. Hence my chronic energy crisis, relieved only by vacation days with their novel sensation of normal vitality.

For years now we had had a mandated SAVE (Safe Schools Against Violence in Education) room where suspended students did their schoolwork, isolated from their class. However, much like our nation's prison system, the room's door was a revolving one, the same reactionary kids suspended over and over, most of them fatherless boys. The stats are not favorable to these kids: compared to boys in two-parent homes they are more likely to have behavior problems, run away from home, and become teenage parents; five times more likely to be poor adults and commit crimes; nine times more likely to drop out of school; and twenty times more likely to end up in prison.[5]

As teachers we had the right to remove a disruptive student for a single period, a day or up to four days, something which in theory sounded pretty good. In practice, if there had been a fight, for example, we might be able to get the school security guard, or the assistant principal to remove the child on the spot, at least for a few minutes, then suspension resulted when we put the incident in writing. But lower-level, or chronic disruptions, the bane of my existence, were impossible to address. Countless times I just wanted a large hook, vaudeville-style, to stretch into the room and yank away any number of irksome irritants.

Instead, we had to go through a time-consuming system to get a child removed: maintaining an anecdotal record detailing dates and behavior; an account of our interventions, such as phone calls to parents; then if a removal were finally approved, you would have to enter it into the computerized suspension database. All of this could grant me that hook treatment for one child for only up to four art classes—more likely the principal would only approve one period. The dozens of offenders made only pursuing the most egregious worthwhile. Yet the process deterred me from even going after just the hardcores: so much effort was required, with such a small abatement as a reward. I gritted my teeth and attempted to Zen through, usually unsuccessfully, the disruption.

Even the toughest kids, though, were instantly wonderful when I could be with them one-on-one. Gone was the back talk, the showing off, the defensiveness. The psychological armor deliquesced the second I sat down with them. The attention of an adult was, after all, what they really craved and were not getting at home, that is why they were always acting out. The great tragedy was that I could not stay with them, I had a whole class to teach. Clearly programs like Big Brothers and Sisters with their emphasis on individual attention are what is needed most for these sad, angry kids.[6] Plus they fill in for the all-important missing fathers.

The "Song of the Volga Boatmen" was the singular entry on my mental playlist during the late afternoon trudges through the neighborhood, my stunted glucose just sufficient to propel me to the train station. This daily state of stupefaction characterized the virtual out-of-body experience that was my float home. Yet kids—the dreaded, the last thing I wanted to be reminded of at that moment—popped up at me from all directions, like I was in a ghetto street funhouse.

"Ms. Sturt!" they would scream from as much as an entire block behind me, ignoring my ignoring and running closer and closer with their demands to be acknowledged. I was too tired to even turn around, and I did not dare: I needed the momentum to carry me forward. Undaunted, they finally overtook me.

"Didn't you hear me, Ms. Sturt?"

Still others would pant "Hi, Ms. Sturt!" as they ran up to me from a side street.

"It's me, Ms. Sturt—look!" they would yell down from their open apartment windows.

"Up here, Ms. Sturt!" they cried, dangling from fire escapes.

It was flattering to be so popular: it was a rare week that I did not get a picture, loving note or small gift, sometimes in my mailbox in the office. Mostly I got hundreds of hugs. The walk home really distilled the love-hate relationship I had with my job.

All these years the threat of neighborhood violence had been throbbing a steady backbeat to the daylight appearance of a somewhat normal, albeit poor, community. It demarcated the lives of the kids, preventing them from walking on certain blocks, being out safely after five o'clock and in some buildings infested with gang activity and drug dealers, forbidding them to even be out in the hallways and to never, never stand in front of a door.

At least twice a year, the 4 train skipped my station due to a "police action" at that stop. Chillingly, one of these turned out to be a multiple gang stabbing at the very spot on the platform I usually stood, now blood-stained for a couple days. Memorials with pictures of a deceased young male, accompanied by postcards of saints and aromatic candles, sprouted occasionally in front of apartment buildings on the walk to school. A fifth grade student from Ecuador lost her teenage brother to a jealous knife fight over a girl; we took up a collection for the body to be sent to South America. One Monday a seven-year-old spoke of the nauseating blood stain that had materialized on the steps of her building the weekend before, the legacy of a Saturday night stabbing.

Along with our own local busybodies, though the crime page of the *Post* detailed bi-monthly instances of equal horror, the sighting of a cop car was almost a preternatural occurrence. On one of these rare occasions, to my amusement they helpfully stopped to ask me, an itinerant Caucasian, if I were lost. Otherwise, the only obvious police activities were the odd bust of a turnstile jumper by a plain clothes detective, or the sporadic table set up at the train to facilitate random searches of backpacks, a pretentious security ritual since 9/11. (The hated stop-and-frisk craze would start a couple years later.)

Now in the spring, a series of shootings resulting from a gang feud were directly affecting us. The immediacy of the violence was suddenly palpable as the police visited the school, warning teachers staying late in the afternoon to keep away from windows, bullets had been whizzing past nearby buildings. One killing happened in front of a bodega I passed every morning, stopping into often for a cup of coffee; my shot of caffeine might have been one of lead. In the park I hung out in during lunch, a kid had been sitting on a bench when another shot him dead as part of a gang initiation.

On my way home a few days later, there was a crowd in front of a deli: a kid had been shot a few minutes before. As the sirens pierced the distance I veered away, leery of the imminent retribution sure to follow, as soon as right now. With all this unwelcome violence in my face, when the last day of school came I felt more than ever like a spoiled brat. How blessed I was to go home to a place where the greatest tragedy was the loss of a Jimmy Choo heel to a pothole.

In April we had our two-day Quality Review visit, Principal Dearest squiring the "educational expert" around the school, visiting classrooms staffed by Principal Dearest's pet teachers. All schools scrambled to fake ongoing perfection in these largely contrived snapshots of a school. The reviewer was sufficiently persuaded to earn us the top grade of "well developed," appearance vs. reality winning the day, as usual.

In May our last pay raise, as stipulated in the most recent union contract, kicked in. We had made huge concessions, including a longer school day, to get it; little did we know that it would be our last for many years. At the time, though, the pay increase just added to our happy outlook, as the end of June swiftly came upon us and with it, the end of the school year.

That summer I was passing Nello restaurant on Madison Avenue when I saw the familiar Bozo coif of Chancellor Joel Klein. Looking for all intents and purposes like a villainous amalgamation from a Batman movie, he sat at a sidewalk table with his wife, awaiting, apparently with relish, the rape of a fifty dollar order of pasta at the Euro-trash *boite*. Between my outrage at so much I had discovered and my activist penchant for progress, I could not resist introducing myself, though I had not anticipated the impulsive harangue that would follow.

"Hello," I gasped, thrusting my hand out to shake theirs. "I am a teacher."

I told him I was a Teaching Fellow, I was the school's union delegate, I lived in the neighborhood and there were so many things I wanted to tell him. I did not know where to start, I was so excited to have the chance to vent.

"There is no air conditioning!" I blurted out first, as it was the most recent indignity hurled at us at the sultry end of the school year.

"The system is too hierarchical!"

Dozens of thoughts barraged my brain, competing for articulation. It was not just *my* voice, I felt obliged to channel all of my voiceless colleagues at this serendipitous opportunity.

"Principals have too much power! We have a horrible principal!"

I unloaded about Principal Dearest's lack of professionalism, her inability to manage people, her ineptitude at the juggling required of a principal. He asked me her name and the school's name, which I gave. After a couple minutes, he had exhausted his obligatory *politesse* and grew visibly impatient.

"Here, just email me," he said, proffering a gold embossed business card.

I shook both their hands, chuckling a few yards away when I imagined them racing to the restroom to wash the teacher cooties from their rarified paws.

Though Joel Klein had been our tireless adversary and the *New York Post*erchild for epic stands against teachers and our union, when I met him I trusted he was for real. Even though we had innumerable reasons to hate him, I wanted desperately to give him the benefit of the doubt. I did not have any rational reason to wax sanguine really, just blind optimism. Picturing all the good that might come of this chance meeting, surely a message from the universe— air conditioning, the deep-sixing of Principal Dearest and other tyrants like her—I wrote Klein a heartfelt, three-paragraphed e-mail beginning with an apology for interrupting his repast: hopefully my disturbance in the beginning was less alarming than the bill at the end. I went on to say I thought it would be positive for us to communicate because the polarization between the teachers and the city, after all, was not conducive to our mutual goal of educating the kids. Since I was from the union and he from the administration, an ongoing correspondence could be a useful forum to bridge our differences and discuss issues from both our perspectives. Moreover, in contact with someone observant on the inside, he would get to comprehend the reality of the situation in a way otherwise unavailable to him.

Well, the universe had a message for me, all right: Joel Klein is a dick. He did not even have the good grace to respond to my earnest email. Fakely forthcoming in public, his smarmy charm was a just a politically-correct charade. Clearly, when he proffered his card it was simply to minimize his exposure to my pesky teacher vibes. If my opinion of him had been negative before, now he incurred my straight-up contempt. When my wallet was stolen several months later and along with it his grandiose, insincere card, his abandonment was complete.

A couple years after, Klein resigned to take a job, revolving door-like, with Rupert Murdoch's teacher-hating empire. In the 2011 British parliamentary hearings over the phone-tapping slime sprees of the news baron's publications, I recognized Klein's familiar oleaginous pate behind Murdoch. When a pie was launched at the old geezer it might have been better aimed at Joel Klein's dome, and by a New York City teacher.

8

We were now in our fourth year of the reign of Principal Dearest. At least in the real world there was something positive and life-affirming happening: Obama was running for president, and I was obsessed with the election and all of its ramifications. National politics was a welcome diversion, anyway, from the cut-throat power struggles in a Bronx elementary school. The vainglorious, chest-thumping egomania of Sarah Palin, however, did hit rather close to home. She had lurched from college to college: was Bloomberg's Leadership Academy one of them?

Austerity was setting in for everyone and New York was no exception, with budget cuts and a hiring freeze on new teachers. We had fewer school aides to stop fights at lunch and all the other essential, unsung infrastructure they provided, plus even fewer supplies for our classrooms. City parking permits for our teachers were cut in half, a highly stressful situation given the fact that ninety-five percent of our teachers commuted, and necessarily, by car. Moreover, the fact that city employees were not guaranteed a parking place meant our teachers incurred hundreds of dollars a year in parking tickets in a neighborhood where spots were already scarce.

In fact, slashing teachers' parking permits, which Bloomberg rationalized by citing the rights of neighborhood residents to parking, had the unmistakable scent of bullying. By this point, in fact, we could not escape the impression that our mayor actually hated us, as relations between the mayor and the teachers union, never stellar, deteriorated beyond repair. As ever, Rupert Murdoch's *New York*

Post, an equally right wing, reactionary paper version of his Fox News, and the teachers union newspaper duked it out in a relentless onslaught of venomous articles and editorials. Their main beef was that we were all incompetent, while Bloomberg's micromanagement of our instruction, endless piling-on of new mandates and fetish for charter schools was what stuck in our craw.

We probably were not totally justified in taking it personally, though, in the sense that Bloomberg was a control freak with everyone: in the mayor's Nanny State the city had become, bans on smoking, transfats and even large-size sodas (unsuccessful) were enjoined with the same authoritarian relish as his push for unpopular congestion pricing. Anyway, while driving home Bloomberg's antipathy for us, the withholding of parking permits had the added attraction of being just another way to fill the city's shrinking coffers.

Under Bloomberg, finable offenses had mushroomed exponentially, extending to awnings of stores with "excessive lettering" (phone numbers were ticketed); taking up two seats in a subway car, even if it was empty; and feeding pigeons in the park. Indeed, Bloomberg did not even draw the line at ticketing trapped, blizzard-bound cars: giddy with power, he tried, and failed, to force payment of exorbitant tolls on the East River bridges which had been free as long as they had existed. The mayor was not nearly as tough on his own Wall Street brethren, however, refusing to entertain the notion of taxing the rich more even as city revenues were falling. But he still could play king with everybody else, using the same flawed data calculations to brand schools as well as now restaurants, with misleading grades.

By October, true to form, Principal Dearest had continued her forays against me and a few select others. As neurotic as ever about unruly classes (for which, however, she never offered support), Principal Dearest started questioning whether I called parents, indeed ordering me to make the calls, demanding that I keep a phone log. This was weird because she could see me every week in the office before school getting the phone numbers from the blue emergency cards, so clearly I was already making calls. Worse, she was making me keep a phone log subject to her inspection, while no other cluster was required to maintain one. For a while this was Principal Dearest's obsession. I had noticed her behavior was always that way: once she got a bee in her bonnet that was her sole focus. In the same blindered way, she had not seen me in the office getting the phone numbers because that fact did not jibe with her chosen perception of me.

For a couple weeks she wanted to see the phone log and then, poof! it was as if it and her demand for me to keep it, had never existed; she was on to a new obsession involving a different victim. But Principal Dearest still made sure she ambushed me at regular intervals, suddenly entering a class with a lupine grimace, "What's going on in here?" because there had been some noise, and often hurling a jeremiad questioning my "control" in front of the kids, before she skulked back into the netherworld.

My position in the hot seat continued to make following rules a charged proposition. We were supposed to report students leaving a class without permission, yet when an incorrigible student, Nicel, a fourteen-year-old giant famous throughout school for his disdain for decorum, disappeared from his fifth grade class, I had to consider before I reported him. Ultimately taking the required action and calling the office, which then made an announcement over the PA for him to go back to his class, the next thing I knew, just as I had predicted, I was in trouble because he had left and I had neither seen him nor prevented him. When found, all Nicel got was a flaccid "tsk tsk" from the wimpy AP and sent back to class, while later I would get raked over the coals. Probably better to risk not reporting his disappearance, yet if he had been discovered out on his postprandial constitutional that would have only augmented my tribulation. It was still very much a lose/lose scenario.

At one point, Principal Dearest called the cluster teachers into her office regarding the "high" number of suspensions happening during our periods with the kids and during lunch. It was a commonplace that when away from their "home" classroom environment and/or teacher, was when the kids most frequently lost control. This was of vital importance to Principal Dearest's ego because the suspension statistics were on record with the district and indicative of poor discipline. A pretense of order had to be maintained, even as violent children (like the first grade boy who kicked a teacher in the butt as she bent over to pick up her bag, almost breaking her coccyx) reared their ugly heads with regularity throughout the school.

Ms. Alvarez, a fierce, pugilistic teacher and crony vestige of Guido's days, manned (almost literally) the SAVE room, yet the same repeat offenders were showing up there week after week. Now Principal Dearest was faulting the clusters for the lion's share of suspensions, specifically scalding myself and another teacher, Ms. Figueroa, as incompetent. It was not just embarrassing, but frustrating: the fact that Figueroa and I routinely did the right thing and reported discipline issues was now the justification for our public pillorying.

Since I was already the black sheep for so many other acts of willful integrity, I risked nothing now to speak up. I angrily protested, then Figueroa joined me. Neither of us believed the absurd numbers: eighty-five percent of the clusters' suspensions purportedly happened in our classes, and we both asked to see the suspension record book in the office.

When I tried to do this one morning, Alvarez asked me why I was looking in her book. I told her I was counting the number of suspensions incurred during my teaching periods; she grabbed the book away saying she would ask the principal if I could do that. In the doorway, Principal Dearest was listening to this exchange, and as the suspension room teacher went into her office she smiled and closed the door. From inside they both laughed. Alvarez owed her cushy SAVE room job to Guido and thereafter, the good graces of Principal Dearest—her obsequiousness was infinite.

Two years later, an AP who had been in the meeting where I had been lambasted would tell me Principal Dearest had made up all the stats. When I asked why she would do that the AP just shrugged: there had never been rhyme nor reason to her virulence. I never did make a count of the suspensions, because Figueroa would not join me. She expected to retire pretty soon, so why rock the boat out of principle, when you risked a tsunami of tsuffering from the principal? I took a page from her sangfroid. I would just add this latest iniquity to a list I had begun keeping of Principal Dearest's transgressions: now I was planning a union grievance against the principal for harassment. I could have submitted a complaint long before, but I had been loathe to fuel her menopausal mania. Yet I had kept incurring her oppression regardless of my reticence, so now I was collecting ammunition, and steeling myself, for an official inquiry.

At least, this year, there was a wonderful distraction from the persecution that at this juncture, though painful, was verging on the banal. Barack Obama's fist bump with Michelle was a watershed gesture symbolizing a brilliant new era of promise. Since childhood, one hero of mine after another, pretty much anyone whom Ann Coulter would never Friend, had been trumped by war-mongering idiots; now it seemed my side could finally win for a change. Moreover, I was thrilled that youth were finally being roused from an intransigent apathy present since activism Hustled away in the seventies.

The day of the election, I went to the polls early on my way to school. All day it was impossible to concentrate on the dry professional development we had to attend while the kids stayed home, the sensation was just too much like Christmas Eve. Later that night Obama's victory sent me over the moon in terms of what it represented for the evolution of America, humanity even. From now on when I told the kids they could grow up to be whomever they wanted, there was compelling evidence to back that claim! Later, I would not be above invoking Obama to coerce the best from the kids, whether regarding language, "Would President Obama say that?" (the dreaded "mines") or behavior, "Would President Obama do that?"

In the meantime, Bloomberg and Klein were the calendar pin-ups for educational reform, touring the country crowing about their innovations for accountability, teacher and principal test bonuses, and report cards for schools; as Bloomberg testified to a congressional committee, his mayoral control had been sanctified by the halving of the black-white achievement gap, as evidenced in

LAUREL M. STURT

ever-leaping test scores. In fact, the tests had just been getting easier by the year. Their victory lap culminated in November, when Klein travelled around Australia to extoll the virtues of his reforms. As he had been doing the same around the nation, the New York City testing miracle became so well-known, Klein's name was being bandied about for Obama's new secretary of education. The fact that Klein might be rewarded for his chicanery was just plain galling, the prospect of him being in charge, utterly unsettling. Anyway, Klein must have gotten wind that he was not high up on the list, because he made a beeline to saving face, telling reporters he had no interest in leaving the city.

There was a fair amount of concern over our two-day Quality Review in December, even though the typical theatre of much of it, like visiting classrooms that had been heavily coached, gave the lie to its being a genuine evaluation. We were graded "proficient."

For art class the week of the inauguration we did something atypically frivolous, but fun: Barack and Michelle Obama paper dolls with inaugural ball outfits. I made hundreds of copies and the kids colored the clothes, cut them out and dressed them up. It was their first time experiencing paper dolls, a common activity when I was a child (back on the prairie). To her credit, Principal Dearest allowed us to bring classes to the auditorium to watch Obama's historical ceremony.

As an inner city teacher jonesing for justice, those fantastical moments were unspeakably touching. Seldom in my life had I felt so ecstatic, particularly over a political event, but that was exactly its appeal: I had waited so long. For the most part, the blasé kids did not grasp the profundity of it, but that in itself was profound: that a black man had become president was not necessarily something to write home about. Their nonchalant attitude toward the realization of the dream Obama embodied hopefully represented a psychological shift—an African American in the White House was simply the new normal. Whatever. Whatever in a positive, "I can do that" way. I delighted inwardly as I realized for Millennials, the racial divide may be dissolving just as the attitudinal generation gap solidifies. Perhaps my rosy perspective was unduly influenced by the thrilling

161

circumstances, yet everyone had reason to exalt in Obama's success, and fully expect the trend to continue.

The less glamorous day-to-day of the school was boosted by the improved tone of this year's student population. It was our marvelous luck, and the misfortune of our colleagues at other schools, that some of the kids we resorted to calling in sick to avoid, had not been showing up in September. We vastly preferred the ho hum high-maintenance majority of needy and difficult to the select group tasked apparently with the daily extraction of melanin from our hair follicles. One possibility was their parents, often in exasperating denial, were fed up with constant calls and meetings with school administrators and teachers. In fact many had threatened to remove their kid (oh, dread), blaming us. The most logical theory, advanced by a teacher who had taught through the nineties, was the crack epidemic of that time and the decade before had retreated, taking with it the side dish of agonies. Thus, gradually, kids were coming in with fewer and fewer scars from the blight of years before.

Whether born addicted or just an innocent bystander, the cataclysm of crack had wreaked havoc on families in myriad respects, laying waste to innumerable neighborhood kids. As far back as my first week teaching, I had heard kids taunting each other with "crackhead," their random claim to the word manifesting a shocking familiarity. In fact, on the way to school a dilapidated twenties clapboard house, sometimes with a cop car in front of it in the dawn hours, was loudly maligned to be a crack house. A mild-mannered, bright child, Daniel, and his equally promising brother, Xavier, lived there. More than once I heard a child declare, self-righteously, "His mom's a crackhead," while gesturing to Daniel, who said nothing but disappeared into the floor boards, mortified. At one point when I heard that, I did the math and immediately understood why the brothers were late or absent most days: when I looked up their address they indeed lived in the house the police were targeting. But unlike the usual children of messed-up parents they were not troublemakers, just bright, polite anomalies, qualities which made their plight that much more poignant.

I called their mother to extoll their personalities and talents, even gushing, for effect, over her parenting skills in producing such boys. I begged her to bring them not just to school every day but on time so they would not miss any learning. She made the usual excuse of them being sick; all the neglectful parents reverted to that. A few weeks later I saw them with her in front of the house on my way home. This time, in person I introduced myself, again exhorting the at-close-range mostly toothless mother (the less-is-more look a singular junkie approach to dentistry) to get her wonderful sons to school. As I complemented them, now more desperate than ever for their welfare, she smiled graciously, if alarmingly.

I finished my summary on their behalf with a plea for their future success, a potentiality which depends entirely on school. Nevertheless, their sporadic attendance continued until one day I saw the house had a sheriff's notice on the door and the kids stopped coming altogether. The neighborhood grapevine came through with news that the mother had been carted off to jail, while the boys, safe at last, had been sent to Queens to live with an aunt. Phew.

Once the Swine Flu pandemic hit the news, it was on everyone's minds, from the more casual who had simply increased their incidence of hand-washing to the frankly freaked-out, for whom an astronaut suit from the asbestos abatement workers would not have sufficed. These teachers, whose febrile agitation seemed to prefigure a deadly delirium to come, made sure no surface was spared their licentious lust for Lysol. Harkening to the "teachable moment," lessons on germs and cleanliness, usually the purview of the science teachers, were now the talk of the school.

Apparently it took the menace of pestilence to install soap dispensers in the boys' and girls' bathrooms, because all of a sudden the kids could clean their hands. The genesis of the no-soap policy had been years before, when vandals found uses far more entertaining than hygiene for the slippery stuff. The lack of soap was regrettable for the obvious reasons, but also because it sent a rather hypocritical message of us talking, but not walking, the all-important hygiene message. However, there had been sufficient cause for another adjustment to the prehistoric bathrooms: bolt pockmarks in the heaving plaster delineated long-gone mirrors which had once graced the sinks, now exiled to memories of saner times. Also, due to the serial hijinks of kids who locked them, then crawled out, invariably one of the bathroom stalls was closed. But according to the custodians, this eventuality was among the least disconcerting features of the bathrooms. Shit happens, as it happens, even up on the ceiling. Apparently budding Yankees happen, too, because the ceilings are fourteen feet high.

Apart from a direct experience of them, even, the bathrooms broadcast their noxious gestalt in unwelcome ways: the third floor boys,' the door nailed open due to frequent acts of degeneracy behind it, demanded reluctant tribute from your nose when passing by in winter. The olfactory onslaught was due to the cunning wiles of the older boys, who, as amateur physicists, taught those younger how to pee on the radiators, prompting thrilling sizzles of steam and nauseating clouds of our very own aromatherapy to envelop the hallway. St. Trinian's had nothing on us.

The golden days, when little girls with flips used the bathroom mirrors for a mist of Aquanet, as opposed to a canvas for violent performance art, were vividly conjured when a chance conversation at a party revealed an acquaintance had amazingly attended my very school. The woman, in her mid forties, sketched her stolid middle class childhood in the neighborhood, a dream-like reality, try as I might, I could grasp only hypothetically: the ghetto groove, now so deftly etched, defied any attempts at visual reconciliation. Yet the area had incubated many successful people, even celebrities. When the local gangstas sport Calvin Klein or Polo, little do they know they are paying homage to a couple of homies. Now I could imagine rarified Ralph Lifshitz forsaking his limo for a glamorous, armored Humvee to go to reunions at Clinton High, one of the most dangerous schools in the city.

Disappointingly, for secretary of education Obama ended up choosing Arne Duncan, a basketball buddy from Chicago who had run the schools there for seven years.[1] With neither a degree in education nor any experience teaching, aside from supporting early childhood education, Duncan's tenure as head of the nation's third largest school system yielded undistinguished results. Despite championing improved parent input, Duncan strived to eliminate the local school councils, effectively silencing the voice of parents and community in the operation of the schools. Test scores were inflated by easier passing standards from the state, while graduation rates remained dismal, with those who went on to college, unprepared. Duncan's practice of closing failing schools only succeeded in shifting populations of low-performing students into comparable settings, resulting in no gain in academic achievement. Shortly after Duncan took his post in Washington, Chicago students took the National Assessment of Educational Progress (NAEP)—federal tests considered the highest standard in assessments—and his city scored behind several others in progress and performance.[2]

The annual state ELA and math tests were given with the usual accompanying *Sturm und Drang*. Principal Dearest came over the PA system weirdly exhorting the students, on whom her job and bonus depended, "Now go kick some intellectual butt!" which not one understood. As ever, for privacy the kids' desks were separated from their usual grouped tables into rows facing the front; for a couple days grateful teachers got away with leaving them that way, basking in the improved behavior and learning that came from the logical, old-fashioned arrangement of kids facing the teacher and not each other.

Because Easter was approaching, one spring afternoon I taught a first grade about Faberge eggs. I had taken a book out from the public library showing all the intricately jeweled, even mechanical czarist treasures. The kids were enthralled, none more so than William, a wide-eyed Hispanic slip of a child with dark blond hair and almost transparent pale skin. He had just moved to the neighborhood from Alabama and had the southern drawl to prove it. After I taught the lesson, the kids had to draw their own Easter eggs; out of twenty-five kids, William had best absorbed the instruction. The egg he designed opened up with four sections like the czar's most ornate, and he had remembered to include a coat-of-arms: his own, personal version, not the czar's.

William had demonstrated an atypically high level of cognition, synthesis, using the learned information to create something new; I was pleased as punch. From that moment I looked forward to his class, even though it was crammed with uncooperative, squirmy behaviors. Others might be on the rug wrestling, giggling, even sleeping, but William with his spacey expression was nevertheless sitting up straight as a rod, like an antenna pulling it all in. William radiated intelligence and curiosity—it compelled and inspired me. The fact was, those fulfilling moments a teacher craves, the "aha! moment" as it is known in the education business, were what we lived for. Whether the fault of nature or nurture, addicted mom or absent dad in prison, the longed-for satisfaction of coaxing a spark of intellectual combustion sometimes proved an elusive grail. William not only validated my efforts, he singlehandedly reminded me why I was here and affirmed why, despite the difficult students and odious administration, I refused to be defeated.

The third time I came to his class, William asked me if I would like to come to his house for a play date after school! I asked him what kind of snacks his Mom had at home. Of course, I declined but was touched by his sweetness and naivete. William's huge, widely-placed doe eyes announced his dreamy, not-of-this-world personality, an effect only reinforced when he made one of his frequent random comments. Indeed, William's ethereality evoked such purity and vulnerability, he seemed downright angelic.

With Arne Duncan's aggressive cheerleading, mayoral control of schools had become all the rage, several big cities jumping on the reform bandwagon of top-down management, inspired by the shining example of the concept, New York City.[3] Now, with the public showing mixed feelings regarding the tenure of the "Education Mayor," it was time to renew the 2002 law that had given Bloomberg control of the schools. As the expiring law was debated there was plenty of public encouragement to keep the schools in Bloomberg's hands, since, though his critics reviled his autocracy, the prior system had been plagued with inefficiency and patronage.

Backed by a lobbying effort by Bill Gates, along with education concerns who got lucrative city contracts, Bloomberg stoked the support by glorying in the rise in test scores and graduation rates, insisting that interrupting such progress would be devastating. Still, it was clear the pendulum had swung too far the other way: now there were no checks and balances, just Klein and Bloomberg unilaterally ruling their way or the highway.[4] At least the old Board of Education, with seven members, of which two were appointed by the mayor, had been a substantially balanced body. Since Bloomberg's replacement, the Panel for Educational Policy (aka Puppets for Educational Policy), had a majority appointed by the mayor, the sham entity was more a relic of the Cultural Revolution than a valid instrument of educational policy—the panel simply rubber-stamped whatever Bloomberg and Klein ordained. Parent and other community input was completely absent, indeed, the only role parents could take in their children's education would be voting for mayor every four years. The state legislature had never envisioned mayor control to be a monopoly; at a minimum, the teachers union and parent associations supported the appointment of three panel members by city pols to eliminate Bloomberg's certain advantage. That never happened, and Bloomberg was anointed fully autonomous King of Education for the rest of his tenure.[5]

Elections were held for a new union rep. I was encouraged to run, however the attitude of the mostly pusillanimous teachers, the apotheosis of apathy, so turned me off I had no interest in representing them: I left off being the union delegate, even. Graham lost the election to another teacher, Pereira, who would be far more active.

Our Mother's Day card project always brought not only the most engagement, but the best behavior from the kids. The only parent for so many of them, even if she were actually the grandmother, the intense love and gratitude the moms inspired was truly wondrous to behold. Every year we changed the approach. One of the best was one with a pocket that held coupons, filled out with promises to do the dishes, clean their room, walk the dog, whatever they could do to lighten Mom's load.

Father's Day was equally compelling for those who had them at home, and always a time for reconciling the differences in families, for the remainder. When teaching the lesson, I led usually with the disclaimer: there are many kinds of families, and everybody has a dad but not everybody has a dad at home. Usually there was some role model who the kid could make the card for, an uncle, a grandfather, even a big brother. On some occasions no male fit this bill, and so Mom ended up getting another card. The kids with dads in prison often spoke of it at this time; I always encouraged them to make sure the card got to them. A homemade card from their child might not only ease their despair, but that Crayola scribble of purity and love tacked up on their wall could inspire them onto a new, healing path.

No matter what the holiday, I saw the card projects as a mode of cementing the bond with a parent, especially important in a relationship with abuse or neglect. Plus a childish affirmation of love, visually available at all times on the refrigerator, could not help but uplift parents anxious over money, depressed, overworked, or stressed about the future. The bonus of the card-carrying child was the link it encouraged between the school and parent, potentially, if only subtly, involving the parent better in the child's academic life.

Sadly, sometimes kids revealed their parents did not like their art, nor even their cards, which they summarily threw in the garbage (a place more suited to the appalling parents). I was flummoxed by this scenario: the point of the card assignment was for both parent and child to get some TLC. Though the rejection frequently had more to do with paper-eating cockroaches than outright cruelty, the rebuff was devastating to the kid. I stepped in for the parent, requesting the child give the art to me, or make the card for me—could I please put their fabulous art on *my* refrigerator?

Following the 2008 economic crisis, it had become fashionable to demonize middle class unionized state workers, such as teachers with "bloated" benefits and pensions—and not the reckless, criminal greed of those who had cause the world recession, who in fact kept their jobs, bonuses, immunity from prosecution and tax benefits—as the cause of state budget problems. In a deft sleight of hand, the guilty deflected the blame, right wing politicians and media pounding the message that we were poor because of pension-fueled deficits. Unions in general, even those not affiliated with a state, were being persecuted, even though the middle class, the majority of demand in a GDP based on consumer consumption, had been built by union membership and the economy depends on its wellbeing (thirty-four percent of Americans belonged to a union in 1973, compared to just over eleven percent today).[6]

Indeed, organized labor has not just shaped the lives of its own members, but bettered society in ways we now take for granted: Social Security, minimum wage laws, child labor prohibitions, the eight-hour day, weekends off, and more initiatives, are benefits to all that had been fought for by the unions. (In the seventies the teachers union even saved New York City from bankruptcy, guaranteeing loans with its pension fund.) As union members, teachers now had an additional reason to be crucified, with their fat salaries and state pensions rolling in as they apparently continued to do nothing, or so the kids' low test scores implied.

In fact, at forty-four thousand dollars, the average mid-career salary of a public school teacher pegs teaching as the second lowest salaried profession of all. Teachers make less money than comparably educated professionals, plus their wages have been declining in real value for thirty years, making it impossible for teachers to even own a home in most metropolitan areas. About two thirds have second jobs, many, like the teacher in my school who had sold hotdogs part-time in Yankee Stadium, making more than they did as a teacher. Considering over half of the country's three and a quarter million teachers are expected to retire in the next decade, it is hard to imagine who will replace them. The want ads should read, "Seeking selfless, tireless individuals with unbounded idealism, energy, stamina, and a capacity to be abused, maligned, and under-paid."

Indeed, the attrition rate is already huge, in urban districts about twenty percent a year, with about half of teachers nationwide leaving before the end of their fifth year. The instability from that high turnover, destructive to any learning community, but particularly to those in poverty (a change in teachers negatively affects learning outcome), costs in the billions of dollars annually from wasted teacher training, the expense of new training, and the loss of accumulated expertise from teachers who leave.[7]

In a gratuitous exercise, Principal Dearest interviewed teachers who wanted to be clusters the next year, as opposed to the typical application with a cover letter and resume. When it was my turn she was strangely civil, even weird: at one point she proposed the next year I lead fifty field trips to art museums. *Fifty*. In forty weeks of school. I told her I would get the planning materials together, though I well knew her idea was delusional. The next year, in fact, crazy Principal Dearest did not okay even *one* art field trip.

Despite our proximity to world-class museums, in all my years I had only led one field trip, to the Museum of Modern Art. Because my classes back at school would have to be covered by a substitute, and that required paying extra money, I was barred not only from showing the kids the art in Manhattan collections but even masterpieces the kids had studied. This nonsensical state of the art was more than the surface travesty it suggests: incredibly most of the neighborhood kids, as I found out when we discussed our community, never visited Manhattan at all, even though the center of it was a mere thirty minutes away on the train, accessible with a Metrocard. Only a handful of children had been to the Statue of Liberty or Central Park, for example, so attendance at an expensive Broadway show was that much less likely.

Despite their residence in the "Greatest City in the World," with its profusion of beauty, stimuli and inspiration, these kids were confined twenty-four/seven to the Bronx. Fortunately, students were at least fleetingly exposed to Manhattan when their classroom teachers took them to the Museum of Natural History and other city landmarks, in the brief period after the state tests had been administered. Heartbreakingly, kids who had not brought the money from home were unable to go. Several of us had donated money here or there when these cases arose. When negligent parents simply had not signed the permission slip, there was nothing we could do about that. The poignant victims were abandoned in another class, while their classmates enjoyed a day of immeasurable enrichment.

At the late date of June, as if an after thought, Principal Dearest observed me formally doing a lesson on the artist George Seurat and Pointillism. She was in buoyant spirits and her behavior was unprecedentedly pleasant, suspiciously so.

The end of the year came and with it the end of a few teachers, either retiring or leaving to escape the principal. It was always a commentary on the job, that young teachers lucky enough to transfer out, even veterans of thirty plus years with a legacy at the school, never came back to visit and rarely, if at all, stayed in touch. Like trauma victims, best to psychically file the experience away into an It Which Must Not Be Felt repository of buried, unpleasant memories. As usual, I looked in the teacher transfer website for another position, and there being nothing available but utterly lateral moves, decided to stay. Once again, despite everything, Principal Dearest gave me an "S" rating for the year. Other teachers lodged deeper in her bonnet were not so fortunate, and received the dreaded "U."

The last day I floated through the neighborhood, thrilled that I would not be seeing it for the next two months, to the elevated subway station, past the endless hair braiding salons and bodegas that studded the area, two to a block. A kid I knew emerged from a bodega with his mother. With her nine-year-old son next to her, an affable boy in the fourth grade, she groused into her cell phone, "Then he say, "suck my black dick" an' he keep sayin,' 'suck my black dick.'" I tried to drown out the rest of her gripping tale, about calling the cops, an arrest and the dreaded body part being spirited away, by engaging Tyshawn in conversation about his summer plans. That I, a stranger, was more protective than the child's own mother, was ridiculous.

On other occasions I had been privy to this surreal, boundary-free world where oblivious parents cursed or cussed porn as small talk, their kids' innocence regularly violated on a casual, daily basis. On the way home from school, another time, a teen mother remarked to her little kindergartner, and in a patient, loving way, "Why you fucked up yo' hair? I fix yo' hair this mornin' an' look at it now, it's fucked up."

The little girl was wearing a tee shirt emblazoned with the word, "SEXY." In fact, the common custom in the neighborhood of sexualizing little girls was nauseating. Girls as young as first grade had highlighted hair, even acrylic nails made an appearance sometimes. Of course as a child I would have killed for these, as well as the high heels and other teen accoutrements I was banned from wearing; anyway they did not even make those things for little kids then. Now the little girls were decked out in tight, low-rise jeans and leggings, Hugg boots and midriff-grazing tee shirts—five going on eighteen. Like their Bratz and Barbie dolls (who were looking a whole lot whorier, too now: Pole Dancing Barbie), these ethnic Jon Benets were pushing the envelope of taste, safety even, if one considered their come-hither ensembles. Where was West Texas polygamist chic when you needed it?

As I glided towards the train station, Alice Cooper thundered the mental soundtrack to my trippy euphoria: "School's Out" for summer.

But the federal Department of Education was not taking any vacations, choosing late July to mark an initiative called Race to the Top (RTTT), in which states would compete for millions of federal dollars by instituting specific reforms.[8] Winners would work together to create common academic standards and assessments (Common Core Curriculum); address teacher recruitment, education, and retention; change teacher evaluation policies (linking them to test scores and observations); and reward or punish teachers through compensation linked to students' test scores, all in an effort to keep only "effective" teachers. These mandates ignored, as ever, the fact that student success is impacted not only by teachers but intelligence, socioeconomic status, motivation, family support, fluency in English and a host of other variables out of an educator's control.[9]

Regrettably, RTTT actually intensified the focus on high-stakes standardized tests: by 2013 the tests would be considerably harder to pass, while by 2014 there would be far more of them given per year and in every subject, not just the math and reading we had now. "Turning around" failing schools (most of which are already in cash-strapped locales) would be achieved by sanctioning them, starving them of funds if they do not immediately adopt RTTT mandates and demonstrate improvement in test scores. So long to the sense of community the hundred-year-old neighborhood high school represented: rather than help the school, RTTT would provide an excuse to fire teachers and dump the failing kids into other schools which will fail in due time.

Even as public schools were to be punished and financially squeezed, the initiative extended NCLB's obsession with "choice," pressuring states to expand investment in charter schools, typically non-unionized businesses managed by private corporations. Indeed, given this latest round of draconian dictates will guarantee the number of "failing" schools to skyrocket, the bottom-feeding education profiteers will be the sole beneficiaries of the new initiative: not only will the eduvulture industries feed on the dying host, supplying the desperate with every expensive and useless support, but once thus scavenged, the carcass will be expeditiously replaced by a for-profit charter school.

So with RTTT it was beginning to become clear that government edicts were perverting education from a public good and an investment in the future, into a money-making investment for the mercenary few. Between the federal government and the states, after all, a huge education cash cow was ripe for the milking. For example, it would turn out, between 2005 and 2011, ed-venture capital investments in the K-12 education sector would vault from thirteen to three hundred eighty-nine million dollars.[10]

Thus RTTT handily hit all the bases of the educational reform movement, while the underlying themes of union-busting and privatization provided the lilting counterpoint; that our "leaders," Obama and Arne Duncan at the forefront, were whoring educational policy to an obvious corporate agenda, was beyond depressing.[11]

Considering the economic situation, the contest for federal money for education was a contentious one. New York state jumped into the fray, tweaking existing policies and adding new ones to win the desperately-needed money. The incentive worked: we were among the states chosen to fund the misguided principles.

Among the new initiatives was a new cause for teachers to panic: a hefty chunk of a teacher's yearly evaluation would be their students' test scores. As ever, the ludicrous conclusion was a teacher's competence is reflected in these tests, on top of which a teacher alone is responsible for a child's test performance.[12] This bizarre calculation, that teachers are the sole factor determining the outcome of an unreliable assessment, could no longer be dismissed as another moronic idea from clueless policy makers—now the fatuous premise had been given teeth and a teacher's career lay in the balance. Grinding pressure was not new, of course—signs even in charter schools warning, "failure is not an option" were aimed at teachers, not students—now it had merely reached the point of pulverization.

The inevitable upshot would be teachers systematically reduced to dust, replaced by a new tranche of victims. Apparently the loss of expertise would be less grievous to reformers than the happy ending that came with ditching an "ineffective" teacher, the financial savings incurred by continuously hiring newbies at low starting salaries. RTTT's embrace of merit pay as an incentive to "effective" teachers was a distraction from the fact that for state budgets with deficits, young teachers cost less. Moreover, this could be interpreted as racist: urban school districts churned teachers at a higher rate than others, so inevitably the disadvantaged kids who needed more experienced teachers were, in fact, destined to get the cheaper novices.

Given the importance of charter schools to RTTT, Duncan was apparently not discouraged by the fact they have ranged from disastrous to high-performing, but on average they have not proven more successful than public schools.[13] Unfazed by the mediocre record, Duncan saw no problem in forcing state governments to privatize public education by increasing the number of privately-run charter schools, in the process obviously hurting public schools.[14] As ever, many charter schools either select children outright or through lotteries, an indication of parental involvement, thus garnering higher-caliber students from caring families. Many make it known that they do not provide services for ELLs or children with special needs just to keep those expensive, low-scoring students away. Of course, students who do not perform are summarily kicked out, and sent to us.

Not only does the public system have to take in the majority, ninety percent, of the nation's kids, including struggling, under-performing students with disabilities and ELLs, but because of the money drain to charter schools there will be even fewer resources to address these low achievers. This situation gives the lie to the democratic contention behind the reform movement, that every child has a civil right to a decent and equal education. But that is hardly surprising: Duncan's enthusiasm for choice has even extended to that most conservative of disses to the public system, vouchers. Paid for by public funds but to be used at private schools, a voucher campaign driven by Republican governors met with no resistance from Duncan.[15]

Equally destructive was RTTT's emphasis on testing for determining the present and future status of students, teachers and schools, the program continuing NCLB's fixation on accountability through data, at the expense of actual education. As such Duncan has perpetuated the false notion that children are being educated through a steady diet of stultifying test prep and tests which reveal little of a child's achievement.[16] Clearly hypocritical politicians and policymakers behind these reforms have no interest in developing and paying for an authentic, rich educational system such as that offered by the private schools their own children attend. After all, Obama's kids were attending a private school exempt from such negative, anti-intellectual nonsense.

In fact, the top school system in the world, Finland's, only uses testing once, for admission to post-secondary education.[17] Nevertheless, as a champion of accountability, Duncan viewed test scores as the best measure to evaluate, reward and punish teachers and schools, using his bully pulpit as a way to continue a senseless testing mania long since discredited by the results of NCLB. Our future as a country had long ago become collateral damage to the rabid drive for accountability, and there was still no end in sight.

Yet the biggest disappointment of RTTT was its failure to address poverty and insufficient educational funding, the real, longstanding issues behind the achievement gap.[18] Without this reality check, NCLB and its latest iteration would continue as simple pretenses of accountable transformation, with pointless measurements of pointless data.

In a competition more evocative of a Depression dance marathon than a fair contest, recession-famished skeletons of states lunged after Duncan's financial carrot, effectively prostituting themselves while Duncan's command of the purse strings enabled Washington to dictate national educational policy to an extent never seen before. Ironically, given the states' desperation, though RTTT, like NCLB, was supposed to implement foundational, long-term transformation, the seed funding provided would only be sufficient to begin the change, not sustain it. Here we go again.

Ultimately, then, the RTTT incentives extracted huge concessions from states, while the money received would not be destined to shore up budget cuts or prevent layoffs, but to fund the very stipulations, such as evaluations, RTTT mandated. So the winners were nothing of the kind since they couldn't increase educational funding: they simply signed on for more reform agenda with the government footing the initial bill, a clever ruse and a cynical exploitation of the straits of desperate states. Going in, none realized the strings attached would be binding a strait jacket designed by Reform Inc., benefiting not students but zealots and profiteers.

Later in the summer, some NYC Teaching Fellows who had been left high and dry by Joel Klein's hiring freeze ambushed him at an event, demanding jobs. Of the seven hundred recruited that spring, most of whom had left other careers for teaching, only half ended being placed in city schools, the rest left to dangle in the wind. Klein gave them the brush, of course, and being well-acquainted with Klein's indifference, I knew myself their words had fallen on deaf ears.

9

As the next year began, rumors circulated that this might be Principal Dearest's last. True, she had told me she would leave after five years, but that had been a long time ago; given her mercurial nature it was impossible to know her plan. Her bipolar issues had become so pronounced she would vacillate between solicitous and vicious even within a single two-sentenced paragraph of conversation. Because I was planning to pursue my harassment complaint against her, I was awaiting Principal Dearest's next ambush.

Bad news continued as budget cuts announced the year before went into effect, resulting in fewer teachers and fewer resources. This might not have been such a bitter pill to swallow if Bloomberg were not continuing to throw cash at the army of DOE business consultants and no-bid city contractors. The good news was, we had gotten a suspicious A on our Progress Report from the year before; actually, ninety-seven percent of elementary and middle schools had received an A or B on their city-issued report cards. This was because, due to the lowering of the bar for passing the state tests the spring before, reported test results soared, just in time for the mayoral election.[1] Indeed, a political consultant could hardly have scripted better publicity for an election year.

The timing of the fabulous test scores was just the latest development in a Bloomberg reign that was shaping up to be downright monarchical. The mayor had even contorted the system to his personal agenda, muscling through a change to the city's term limit laws by asserting only *he* had the expertise to guide us through the fallout from the 2008 financial crisis. (Once the city had stabilized a couple years later, a reporter asked Bloomberg if he would be stepping down; the question provoked his ire, resulting in a highly-publicized attack on the reporter.)[2] When the debate raged over what many believed to be unprecedented hubris, Bloomberg's money had silenced influential critics, even the normally feisty teachers union. In view of its expiring contract, the UFT was highly diplomatic and remained mum, while Bloomberg's money had galvanized supporters, too, through his personal philanthropic donations to the arts and social services.

In fact, every year, from 2005 to 2009, Bloomberg had called press conferences to exude over the latest test scores triumph. But later in the fall, results of the NAEP tests revealed the flagrant disparity between the consistently low passing bars of the state tests and the more authentic, objective cut-offs on the federal exams. The New York test results proved to be, just like those of other states and cities who had hyped their catapulting scores, a farce.[3]

As vilified as public school educators had become, many of the teachers in my school were in fact accomplished and committed: I would have gladly put my own son in their care. Just like in the rest of the system there were, however, a handful of hacks, protected by favoritism, whose incompetence had never been questioned.

The second week of school, one of this ilk, Sanchez, who had been made an art teacher the year before, slipped on a freshly mopped floor in the cafeteria; I happened to be standing a couple feet away. After she went down she gave an Oscar-worthy performance, a delayed burst into tears timed to the principal's arrival on the scene. I found out later the spontaneous tears were a special talent she employed to manipulate situations in her favor—evidently there was a Method to her madness. Though nothing was broken and her injury could at most have been a sprain, Sanchez hobbled out of the cafeteria on the arms of two people, not to be seen for the next five months. Since the accident had happened on school property and she would receive full disability payment as long as doctors could tearfully be persuaded of her infirmity, Sanchez milked the incident for all it was worth.

Due to budget concerns, substitutes were unavailable and Sanchez's scam resulted in the computer teacher, Ms. Gordon, having to cover her classes. This meant nobody was available to service the school's computers, so much of the year there was no computer access. Gordon, disgusted with endlessly covering Sanchez's classes, ended up retiring that June. When disability payments ran out and Sanchez came back, she roped Principal Dearest into giving her a room that had been used for small group instruction so she would not have to move around. Sanchez, with over thirty years experience as a teacher and a salary to match, had deftly hoodwinked the system, taking a five month vacation on the taxpayer's dime without even so much as a broken bone. Then for the remaining five months of the year, she had been rewarded with her own art room. Sporting a removable boot cast as a prop, sometimes Sanchez would forget her pretense and run down the hall.

The fraud extended to her position teaching art, a job she had been given without education credentials or work experience in the field. Since, moreover, Sanchez had a modicum of art talent, she specialized in easy preschool crafts projects involving glue and paint to hide the fact that she could not draw. With nary a nod to art history nor in fact anything we were required to teach, she had even been getting away with making lanyards as an art class.

It was not just Sanchez's hackery that sickened me, nor that she was getting over. As an art teacher she had a right to share my closet, where she unceremoniously dumped her supplies so I could not access my own. No matter how many times I asked her to clean it, she refused. This was galling, moreover, because Sanchez had her *own* closet. That closet was already disorganized, the floor reportedly strewn with cigarette butts from surreptitious smoking inside; I had seen a few of them at the bottom of her stuff she'd lugged to *my* closet. Students commented on the smell as they came upstairs, getting occasional whiffs of Kools in the stairwell. Meanwhile, AP Moore had been told about it and did nothing: the hazardous behavior, like the feigned art "instruction," was never questioned.

In light of our looming contract negotiation, the UFT continued its delicate dance with the mayor, maintaining a carefully-hedged neutrality in the fall election, endorsing neither candidate. The union gambled that tacit approval for Bloomberg would pay off. He had just given new contracts to other city workers with a four percent raise and four percent increase the next year, implying, through pattern bargaining, to do the same for teachers. Moreover, despite the economic circumstances at the time, Bloomberg had indicated the money for teacher raises was available in the city budget.

By November, much as he had bought the prior two terms with record spending, Wall Street billionaire Bloomberg had spent a national historical high on this campaign. Inundating city televisions with ads for months beforehand, Bloomberg blew one hundred fifty million dollars to win the election with just fifty percent of the vote; a mere fifty thousand votes, a majority of the eighty thousand teachers, would have given a victory to the other candidate, had the teachers union decided to endorse him. Regrettably we did not.

After Bloomberg was elected, seeing no further advantage in keeping his promise of a pay raise to teachers, he blamed the budget crisis and gave us the shaft. In a deft screwing of thousands of teachers who had been unwitting pawns in the renewal of mayoral control, the overturning of term limits and then Bloomberg's re-election, negotiations between the union and city stalled because the mayor no longer needed the teachers' support. Now Bloomberg held all the cards and he flashed them flamboyantly. At one point the debilitated union would even be forced to concede pay raises in exchange for avoiding the layoff of another five thousand teachers.

Early in the year I was teaching sculpture to a kindergarten with individual cans of blue silicone, stuff which was actually blue Silly Putty; I never told the kids because that would have started a bouncefest all over the room. They loved using the "clay" and always clamored for me to bring it. The worst case scenario had been kids stealing it, a frequent occurrence. Now in the middle of the class I noticed a girl, Keilina, with her head down on the table. When I came over she sat up and pulled her two bushy pigtails away from her face. Grotesquely, they were packed with clay. Clearly she had methodically pushed the silicone into her hair, jamming it in till it merged into a solid mass of blue pigtail.

I was terror-struck: I knew her mother would freak out and worse, Principal Dearest would be apoplectic. What is more, I had to go to another class in a few minutes. Expedience suggested the nine inch pigtails be hacked off with scissors—as if. My head swam with remedies for removing gum, which the silicone closely resembled, from hair, involving mayonnaise and peanut butter. Serendipitously, a schedule change meant my next class was in a kindergarten room across the hall, so I took her with me. After giving that class sculpture material and advising them, using her vivid example, not to do what she had done, I got to work.

For just under the next two hours, during that class and through my lunch time, I tortuously pulled the gummy substance out, hair by hair. Fortuitously, I was able to remove the silicone and neither the principal nor Keilina's mother was any the wiser. I could not help noticing the stress the incident provoked in me: the idea that I would be blamed and attacked made an already unpleasant and challenging situation, gratuitously traumatic. The near-disaster highlighted my hatred of Principal Dearest and my anger at myself for being victimized, reinforcing my commitment to launch an official harassment investigation with her very next assault.

I found out from the guidance counselor that William, now in second grade, was living in a homeless shelter and his mother, who came to pick him up everyday in a wheelchair, had multiple sclerosis. Ever since my first week teaching I had had a strong desire to invite especially disadvantaged kids home with me so I could treat them to a day out, even a sleepover. Even though this rescuing impulse was overwhelming, I had never acted on it: there were so many contenders, I did not know how to do it equitably. Moreover, every time there was the opportunity, a weekend or a vacation, I was so exhausted and unwilling to be reminded of Up There, I could not imagine going through with it. But I really liked William, and the staggering negatives in his life pushed me to take action at last. I invited him over after Christmas.

I sent a note home as well as spoke to his mother, and one morning made the trip back up to the Bronx to pick him up at his apartment. It was a pre-war, five-story brick building I passed every day on the train, right next to the elevated tracks, though William said he had gotten used to the noise. Downstairs I was greeted by a filthy, graffiti-scrawled entrance with an intercom that I had been pre-warned did not work, I just pushed the rusty metal door hard and it opened without security. Inside, the dark cinderblock "lobby" was accessorized by a wall of mailboxes behind a locked cage. After a long wait the spray-painted elevator clanged open as a blast of urine hit my nostrils. As the elevator labored heavily up through the building, the oppression was such that I could not wait to get the hell out.

I walked down the garbage-strewn, cement hallway just as William's mother opened the door, supporting herself with a cane. Notwithstanding her severely debilitating illness and circumstances, at thirty years old she had five children. Two teenagers were in Florida, while William, a toddler and an infant (son of her live-in boyfriend, who William identified as his "stepfather") lived with her here. In the gloomy, stuffy living room a sheet shielded the bright eastern sun from the window; I longed to pull it down and fill the room with salutary light and fresh air. A couple dilapidated sofas and a side table with a small forlorn Christmas tree were the only furniture, the sole wall decoration, a dartboard.

Inside the bedroom the twenty-year-old boyfriend lay on a bed cradling the infant while the toddler stood in a playpen, all transfixed by cartoons playing loudly on a corner TV. William's bedroom was tiny, crammed with a set of skewed bunk beds that had collapsed on the bottom; clothes and toys were strewn around the apartment. William's mother was pleasant and said she was glad I had come for him.

"William doesn't get out much," she said.

Considering the suffocating, toxic atmosphere, the thought of him stuck in there was intolerable. As we descended in the lumbering elevator, William was completely oblivious to the squalor, chatting excitedly about his new video game. The blast of fresh air and sunlight outside was vividly welcome.

Though it was bone-chillingly cold, once we got off the subway, we went to the carousel in Central Park for William's first ride on one. Then we went to Border's at Time Warner Center, William snickering at the naked Botero figures in the lobby. We met my son, now in high school, for lunch at Benihana, but the rest of our plans were dashed due to the freezing weather. They both wanted to play video games at home. As soon as we got to my apartment, William put on his Spiderman fire-retardant pajamas, so outgrown a superheroic wedgie seemed imminent.

At one point, he came running into my room where I was lying on my bed, reading.

"Ms. Sturt!" William exclaimed, "Thank you so much for inviting me! I love it here!" and he hugged me and ran out.

Before she went to bed his mother called to say goodnight to him and that was wonderfully reassuring. The next day I took William home in the middle of a blizzard. He had lost his scarf the day before, so I bought him a new one and delivered him, as promised, by late morning.

Though certainly misguided in her endless procreation, particularly imprudent in light of serious health and wealth issues, William's mother clearly loved him very much. Obviously, love could eclipse the negativity of a sordid existence, even one redolent of garbage and urine. After all, William was, blissfully even, unconscious of his circumstances, or any sense of want they might create. As much as I had understood material advantages could never stand in for love, I had never considered the flip side of that equation: that an absence of physical comforts could be mitigated, neutralized even, by the presence of love. I reflected on this on the train back to town; as ever, there was always something to be learned. All you need is love.

My visit to William's building transformed my experience of the neighborhood I had walked through hundreds of times. Now I knew first-hand what was on the inside. Even though William was cherished, there were plenty of kids who were living neglected in that neglect that I had now seen up close. When I pictured our most challenging emotional train wrecks, living brutal existences with abusive parents in these squalid conditions, well, it gave me goose bumps. I could hardly see any way out for them, except through an iron will and education. How they would achieve that, however, was dubious given their lack of support or personal motivation. Enter the teachers. But could our guidance really cancel out the horror at home? I was not so sure any more: there were just too many kids and too many horrors.

Through the rest of the year I stayed close to William, sitting next to him when I came to teach his class. He really needed reinforcement, because he had done the unthinkable in front of the other kids in the afterschool program: he had picked his nose, a heinous act, very high in "Ew!" factor. The timeless kid ostracism that momentary indiscretion had provoked had branded him with a scarlet letter B. Trying to make him feel better, I told him that is something everyone does, just not in front of other people. Still, with a heavy heart, I knew that he would be stigmatized for a long time, at least as long as he would be around these kids. At least his visit to my home had increased his street cred even though it resulted in the expected avalanche of requests from other kids.

My main concern was that William was getting outside, since his mother had mentioned he did not leave the house often. A new playground had opened across the street from school; surely he could be taken there by at least, his stepfather. I sent a couple kid's phone numbers home with William (kids he had known the year before, as zoned out as he, plus they had not heard the booger story) to give his mother, with a note telling her that perhaps the parents of these friends could help by taking him to the playground.

I was also trying to get William a library card. It turned out he could not get one because his mother owed the public library one hundred thirty dollars in late fees, because she dared not go back into a house where she had been a victim of "abuse." I found a solution by taking books out of the school's library for him in my name, which he returned to me as he read them. Since his leisure time consisted only of watching cartoons and playing video games, William was not getting any intellectual stimulation at home. Reading was key, particularly for such an intelligent child. However, this would not work during the summer, and sooner or later they would have to get him a library card.

At the beginning of the year, what we had long suspected was blown wide open for all to see: the Bloomberg education miracle was finally busted when New York state officials announced the test scores of the last several years had been inflated. Not only had the questions become increasingly predictable, the previous state education administration had lowered the bar for achieving the different levels of proficiency.[4] In the spring the kids would take the new, more difficult state tests with their higher passing bar.[5]

Over the course of the year something strange had been happening: Principal Dearest was leaving me alone. In fact, she was more laid back than we had ever seen her, only keeping her hand in, as if not wanting to get out of practice, by casually oppressing two teacher targets already on her list from before. Whatever the cause of her remove, though I was grateful, I was ever-vigilant. The very sight of her smacked my adrenals to attention, as I launched into survival mode. Nothing alarmed my limbic system like the presence of those predatory scales.

So much for the reorganization a few years before from districts into regions; now another new system was instituted by the DOE called Children First Networks. Twenty-five schools were linked together as a network, with a staff of fifteen providing support, technical assistance, and overseeing instruction. The idea was to collaborate, a concept popular with reformers, in training and coaching, sharing instructional materials, budgeting, hiring, managing operations, and using data and technology. The team was also designed to be more effective at delivering services to ELLs and special ed students.

As ever, there was never a dull moment. One afternoon I arrived to teach a large third grade "inclusion" class (consisting of some regular and some special ed students) who were returning from lunch; while I was handing out materials I noticed a faint acrid aroma. I remarked to a couple kids that it smelled kind of like burning leaves. But anyway, it could not be burning leaves because it was not autumn, plus the windows were closed. I did not think any more about it because the kids got to work on a project we had started the previous week.

I was going from desk to desk checking their work when all of a sudden a girl screamed, "Look, doodoo!" She was looking into the wall-length closet with open sliding doors which extended down one side of the room. Inside the closet were hooks with the students' jackets and backpacks hanging from them. Her scream inspired three kids sitting next to the closet to jump up from their seats and peer into the closet as well. "Look, look!" they cried, beside themselves with excitement. The entire class, twenty-eight children, rushed towards the closet.

My heart pounded. This was the scenario from my worst nightmare: a huge, out-of-control class.

"Eeeeeew!" they exclaimed in unison.

Using my best impression of a drill sergeant I boomed, "Sit down!" and half of them did.

The other half required my fist pounding on a table, plus an even louder command, to get back in their seats. I looked in the closet and there, on the floor behind one of the open sliding doors, was a fresh pile of shit.

This was, without a doubt, the most challenging moment of my teaching career. If I were not so panicked, I might have appreciated the metaphor of being dumped on. I had to pretend perfect tranquillity, to not do so risked a bedlam that would reach a new low, as this time any chaos would involve human feces. After banishing the horrified rictus from my face, I warned the students there would be no raffle unless everybody behaved. Then calmly (they bought it), I walked over to the classroom phone and called the assistant principal and the custodian. I told both of them there was an emergency in the classroom, never mind the details, they would just have to see for themselves. Amazingly, the class was perfectly quiet: they seemed intrigued to know how this situation would be handled. Though the kids were anxious to get their coats and book bags out of the infested closet, I succeeded in getting them to remain seated.

While I waited for the cavalry to come, I serenely (they bought it again) stepped into the closet pulling jackets and bags out one-by-one and flinging them on the carpet in a tangled, but shit-free, heap. Then I picked a name out of the raffle envelope and awarded the prize, earlier than usual in an attempt to keep the kids quiet and away from the dreaded closet. As help arrived, all those called insisted in all their years they had never seen such a thing, and between all of us we had almost a hundred years of experience. The closet mopped, we resumed our art.

Grateful beyond gratitude that I had avoided a literally shitty catastrophe that would have most definitely ended in my crucifixion, I moved around the students sitting at the tables near the closet, subtly questioning them. One, Roberto, had always been very immature and might have been the guilty one. He denied the deed, as did the prime suspect, Tysheed, a particularly disabled child. But I did not really think either one of them was guilty, anyway—they would have had to have done it when the class came in from lunch and was sitting down. To step into the closet behind one of the partially-closed sliding doors, still mostly visible to everyone, pull your pants down and let it rip—it was impossible. What third grader would risk discovery and certain social annihilation?

I was convinced that while the class had been at lunch and the door open, one of the fifth grade boys from the floor above (out with permission to go to the bathroom) had come in and left a snarky adolescent calling card. Though that would have been a new low even for them, it was the only explanation, and not totally off the mark considering their wicked ways. At the end of the class the two teachers returned to the room, flabbergasted when the kids swarmed them to tell them what had happened. They, too, were bewildered, powerless to comprehend how such a deed had been perpetrated.

"Function in disaster, finish in style." That was the motto of my alma mater, The Madeira School, as declared by Lucy Madeira at the school's inauguration in 1906. In Room 309 that afternoon, I knew I had made Miss Madeira proud.

A couple hours later I saw Principal Dearest up ahead in the hallway. Without question she had been apprised of the situation which had transpired. I braced for the inevitable tirade of blame, though in fact I had handled the situation to professional perfection. I had made sure no child had been affected, so no parent would be complaining. Safety had been maintained: the shit had not hit the fan.

But I had been blameless before and that had not stopped her. Approaching from several yards away, I stared defiantly, my jaw set, daring her to attack. As I came closer she eyeballed me right back; in the distance I heard the whistle of a Sergio Leone soundtrack. As I passed, her lips parted as she struggled to say something—still we did not take our eyes off each other. I glided by, unmolested, the Spaghetti Western receding into the background. Principal Dearest had not said a word. Boom.

That moment I knew I had survived a five-year rite of initiation. Whatever karma I was balancing through my ongoing clash with Principal Dearest, it was finished. The rest of the year passed delightfully uneventful, at least in terms of interactions with the administration. The kids themselves continued unchanged with their business as usual. But at least their unpredictability, after all, was predictable.

Rubber Rooms were now abolished, an agreement swift after the *Post* published pictures, including our Miss Piggy's. Due to the cheating scandal she, of course, had been paid six hundred thousand dollars during a five-year stint of leisure in the nonsensical holding pen. The UFT, in fact, had long been assailed for the Rubber Room system even though it had always been a DOE program, not the union's. Now teachers alleged with incorrect behavior would ostensibly be assigned to administrative venues to carry out clerical duties while their cases would be adjudicated more quickly.

Though the *Post* that year cited plenty of neighborhood excitement on its crime page, the only one that affected me, albeit indirectly, had been a morning murder on the train platform which forced my train to stop at the next station. The most exciting crimes I witnessed were just the frequent, tame turnstile leaps or Metro card forgings of teenagers. I never saw anyone stop the annoying cadgers who stood in front of the turnstiles in the morning, begging a "swipe" from anyone exiting with an unlimited ride card. After all, for many in the neighborhood, purchasing city transportation was not an obligation but an option. When buses stopped on main thoroughfares, crowds swarmed on illegally in the rear as the back exit door opened for people to leave. On a packed bus there was nothing the exasperated driver could do about it but watch impotently in the rear view mirror.

At one point, some shootings in a house near school prompted the police to erect a temporary tower in front of the gang-besieged deli hangout. I would usually cross the street on my way to the train to avoid passing them as they postured and pimp-walked aimlessly in front of the store, drinking from paper bags, marking their copious amounts of time till prison or death. The deli was on the ground floor of a public housing building, an especially dangerous place considering the stabbings the kids who lived there would describe. The corner was marked by pairs of sneakers dangling from the power lines, decorative code for either a gang's dominion of that corner, drug availability, the demise of a gang member there, or all three features. For the two weeks the police surveilled the block, the sidewalk was free of the gang trash who self-littered the area. The cops left and instantly the thugs returned.

Inside the deli, like others in the area, the man behind the counter was a Yemeni national who had morphed into an Arabian-ghetto hybrid. Many have been here for years and have incongruously entrained with the local culture and patois. It is common to hear one speaking on his cell phone in Arabic, then turn to a customer to unleash a torrent of flawless Ebonics. The Yemeni deli owner then smoothly finishes off the encounter with the latest homey handshake.

Meanwhile, the AP Rodriguez conducted an investigation of the shock and awe downloaded in the closet of room 309. After countless one-on-one interviews with the class, Tysheed, the especially special ed student I had immediately suspected yet could not imagine committing social suicide, fessed up. According to the school psychologist, the deed was symptomatic of abuse at home.

Administrative support was still nonexistent. I was in a fifth grade class when AP Moore came in and went around checking the bulletin boards and meaningless, for-show classroom crap with which classroom teachers were required to cocoon the room. Out of the blue, one of the behaviors referred to me as a "bitch." Several students gasped; I was a few yards away and had not heard it.

Immediately they chorused, "Ms. Sturt, Anthony just called you the B-word!"

Moore, who was nearby, said nothing and continued her "work."

Registering the fact that an assistant principal was in the room, the kids yelled at her excitedly, "Ms. Moore, Anthony just called Ms. Sturt the B-word!"

"Ms. Sturt will handle it," Moore replied curtly, annoyed that she had been forced into participation, and immediately left the room. The problem with this scenario was that the boy's comment *was*, in fact, *her* problem, and she was supposed to suspend the kid.

A couple weeks later, a child had just fainted in a third grade classroom and was lying on the floor when Moore came in. When the frantic science teacher who was in the room at the time told Moore what had happened, she turned on her heel and walked out, leaving the teacher to fend for herself. So much for administrative support. I once asked Moore, who had creative projects outside of school, why she didn't leave to pursue work she admitted was more fulfilling: the mortgage on her summer house was her reason for sticking around.

At last, Principal Dearest made a stunning announcement: she would be leaving at the end of the year. Now it was clear that she had mellowed not because she had matured or relaxed, she simply no longer had skin in the game. Just like the previous principals, Principal Dearest was moving on to better pastures, heading a nice school in the suburbs. Though a *frisson* of relief rippled through the school, one of apprehension soon replaced it. There was jubilation for many of us, but also the familiar dread concerning the next "leader." As ever, the prevailing axiom of long-suffering teachers, preferring the known evil over the unknown, was operative. I reverted to my default stubborn optimism in this increasingly familiar scenario—since I could not contemplate anyone worse than Principal Dearest, I welcomed the new era. I might have remembered I had thought the same when Cruella left, and I had long ago lost the justification for such optimism.

As the end of school neared, I decided to clean my file of negative letters three or more years old, a legal right of teaching staff. I had been trying to do it for the prior two years without success as my written formal request to the principal, part of the process, had been routinely ignored. Now I focused on this task as a ceremonial driving of the stake into the heart of Principal Dearest, a symbolic way to nail the lid on her coffin. Once again, I had to go to her secretary over and over, trying to arrange a time with an administrator to open the file up. During one of these instances, the principal heard me talking about it outside her door.

Incredibly, Principal Dearest looked up from her desk and, dripping with concern in the most gracious, Mayberry-inflected solicitude gushed, "Ms. Sturt, are you leaving us?"

Apparently the fact that I wanted to clean out my file indicated I was looking for new employment.

"No," I stated simply, quite bowled over by her weird and sudden unction.

Subsequently, I sat down with an assistant principal, the legal way of doing it, and perused the huge pile of pages that had mounted up over the years. A couple, like the letter Guido had given me for "corporal punishment," were legally there. However, most of the papers were records of meetings with Principal Dearest or even Cruella years before, illegally placed there as they had not constituted official actions against me. I could not believe the ill will of these "managers," whose carelessness or just sheer hatred of me compelled them to maintain an anthology of their peeves. As I leafed through the years, I revisited the anger stirred by these encounters, most of them with Principal Dearest. In the strange *Twilight Zone* that had become the end of her reign, she now beamed beatifically at me whenever I passed her in the hall. It was a blessed catharsis to give those papers, and her, the proverbial heave-*ho*.

Inevitably, the next ho came on the scene, another anointed Great Leader (Together We Achieve More), getting a tour through the school accompanied by Principal Dearest. Little was known about this one except that she had dabbled in back-up singing, her questionable claim to fame a gig behind a D-list celebrity. In her favor, it was said she had had decades of teaching experience. Also, she had two young children, for whom she'd taken a few years off for mommying: to us professional nurturers this was testimony enough to her menschitude. Notwithstanding the lame eighties R&B reference sadly touted to give her props, her arts connection, as well as maternal focus, evoked a humanity which gave us reason to hope.

Memorial Day weekend I addressed William's problem of not getting out much by taking him home with me. We spent a lot of time in Central Park, where William sailed boats, swung on tire swings and blew gigantic bubbles next to Bethesda Fountain. I introduced him to Peewee Herman movies and the medieval armor gallery of the Metropolitan Museum of Art. He became a fan of lasagna, and after practicing chess at the Marshall Chess Club in Greenwich Village, managed to "fall" into the fountain at Washington Square Park.

Since his wet sneakers were shot anyway, I bought him new ones and some clothes, as well as pajamas that fit for a change. A willing pawn of Pixar's evil plan to rule the collective kid consumer consciousness, William selected ones emblazoned with neon characters from *A Bug's Life*. William was also tempted by the schlock offered by the other two members of the childrenswear coven, Disney and Marvel. Since the entertainment oligarchy holds kids captive to its relentless Kulture of Krap, virtually entire existences are given over to their vapid themes and characters.

I had begun taking serious umbrage with this insidious theft of a generation's childhood, particularly the poor. Beginning with the morning's cereal promotion (Cap'n Tie-In), an existence could be spent wholly in their company: cerebral stupefaction in front of their cartoon spin-offs; zoning out with their themed video games; Happy Mealing or Lunchable-ing with their bane-of-the-landfill, instantly disposable PCBed character; listless attempt at imaginative play with said character; napping under the poly-ed embrace of their licensed comforter; ingesting, for the umpteenth time, the saccharin pablum of their movies; then finally, swaddled in their Dupont-engineered, pilling sleepwear—to the inane strains of a Disney soundtrack, drifting off to the far greater reality of the dream state. If school had only one redeeming value it was its offer of a respite from this tyranny of corporate control, though not completely: at lunch on rainy days, or during "mass preps" (when several classes were combined for a period or two) the kids were grouped in the auditorium and served up more of the same Krap. One could picture the moment, at the end of an unlife, when those in this Generation K, the Kommodified, would succumb to Death by Disney (TM) in a licensed coffin.

In the last weeks of school, the new principal appeared almost every day, trailing Principal Dearest through the halls and, to our dismay, establishing a persona at odds with our idealized impression. In her late forties with a pinched, icy countenance and a mass of wiry hair, she never smiled. This defensiveness, plus her diminutive stature, well under five feet tall, signaled the possibility of a Napoleonic complex, the mathematical ratio of height to ardor for domination, our reluctant conclusion. Most unsettling were her sneaky classroom visits, when she crept into a room unannounced and sat down to jot censorial notes. Indeed, her social awkwardness was such that stories went around of a small, unknown presence appearing and disappearing in the classrooms: was that the new principal?

One of the first reports circulating detailed how in one room she looked at the wall chart sequencing the morning's activities, noted that science was being taught instead of math, and made a note on her clipboard. This story quickly made the rounds, angering everyone. The teacher had her reasons for the switch, and by the way, had she been discovered with her feet up, doing her nails? The new principal's crass comportment, not to mention charm-free mien and precocious officiousness signaled our probable doom at the hands of another card-carrying DOE petty functionary. Cruella's nitpicking obsession with appearances, Guido's micromanaging presence in the classrooms, and Principal Dearest's plasmic power fixes were coming together, now doused in a baptismal splash of the DOE's cologne of choice, Joel Klein's Apparatchik.

Having lived through this before, our desperation was more ridiculous and sickening than ever. Once again, our livelihoods, indeed our lives, considering the economy and the rate with which states were laying off teachers, were at the mercy of someone whose purported superiority was determined only by an easily obtainable master's degree in administration. The actual job requirement, besides having a pulse—a chip on the shoulder the size of a redwood—was bound to emerge over time.

Principal Dearest finished out her tenure in fine fettle, graciously recommending her two favored targets, Ms. Pallas and Ms. Casares, for the new principal's dining pleasure. In this fashion the hallowed torch of torture was passed, probably an ancient rite in the sadistic cult of New York City principalship. Naming the unfortunates was not sufficiently evil: one was actually invited into Principal Dearest's office to meet the new principal, where she was introduced, indeed openly vilified as "the teacher with the worst behavior management in the whole school." My heart went out to the poor teacher. I had only been spared another year of torment by the gods of Principal Dearest's arbitrary whims, perhaps, even, the gods of her prescription meds.

As the staff huddled trying to gauge the level of terror awaiting us with the new principal, a post-mortem of Principal Dearest took place as well. Several teachers were shocked to discover the principal had been plying persecution and vendetta—they had no idea. In fact, there had never been rhyme nor reason to Principal Dearest's campaigns, hell-bent on some, oblivious to others. Kismet had kissed the favored with protection, a benediction which let them do their difficult job without the burden of battling a dragon as well. I hoped against hope I would not need a dose of that the next year.

Our concerns about the new principal were validated further by a study of five thousand New York City teachers who had recently left the profession.[6] Notwithstanding the challenging students and other negative criteria, by overwhelming numbers the most important factor in their decision to leave was dissatisfaction with the principal; in another group of questions less than ten percent found their principals respectful or appreciative of teachers. Obviously, in a city where half of teachers leave their positions before five years, principals have been a big factor in the retention problem. Yet far from making the egomaniacal principals accountable for their terrorism, Bloomberg has himself furnished a bumptious template for them to emulate.

Just once, at outside professional development, I met a teacher who praised her principal; otherwise, only retired principals of long ago are referred to benevolently.[7] The majority of the current ones have not only failed to check their emotional baggage at the school gate, they have conscripted teachers and students alike as baggage handlers. But this principal pestilence hasn't been quarantined to New York City: the nation's school systems are riddled with it. Thousands of anecdotes from union and educator publications, blogs and websites detail the mass, systemic nature of the oppression.[8]

Just like every other initiative in education, there is even a business opportunity here: principals across the country glean tips for bullying teachers from guides published by influential professional development companies.[9] Measures useful in hounding a teacher out of a school include ambushing a classroom when instruction isn't taking place, to assert negligence; requiring lesson plans be done a week in advance for administrative review (fault-finding); interviewing students privately to catch the teacher doing/not doing something; and inundating a teacher with observations, formal and informal, pre-calculated to be unsatisfactory. Books like *Dealing With Difficult Teachers* include chapters such as "Making the Difficult Teacher Feel Uncomfortable."[10] No, really.

We've all encountered teachers we felt to be ineffective, either during the course of our own education or that of our kids; having suffered at their hands myself I am in no way defending these excuses for educators. In the reform era, however, educational hierarchies are typical in which principals, many not even educators, in fact, but business people, wield unprecedented autonomy. Orders are coming down to demonstrate change, most expediently dispatched through the firing or pushing-out of "incompetent" teachers: that means bullying veterans, for example, to save their high salary cost, or persecuting those who don't cooperate when asked to adjust scores or inflate grades. Beyond directives from above, systematic abuse can result from sheer personality issues and office politics. Certainly the questioning of anything, age-old anathema to dictators, invites it; powerlessness to manage behavior problems—in schools with severe discipline issues, unaddressed by a disengaged principal—provoke harassment as well. Moreover, administrators feel compelled to justify their jobs by continuously finding things to criticize.

Serving up an abundance of mortification with a side of incompetence, the neurotic gems chosen to "lead" our schools have become the secret WMD of education: they are important determinants of the success or failure of our system going forward, and as so many excel at nothing more than emptying a school of its staff, we are clearly doomed to the latter.

Even the famed Bronx High School of Science, alma mater of Nobel laureates and Pulitzer Prize winners, has not escaped a martinet principal who turned the school into a prison in the last ten years, causing a stampede of storied teachers into retirement or competing schools, decimating entire departments. Taking a cue from Bloomberg and Klein, the emphasis on testing and data, micromanagement of pedagogy and authoritarian enforcement of her picayune regulations, provoked mass teacher, student, alumni and parent protests. It started when the superintendent of high schools told the principal that "things need to change." When the principal had demurred, indicating the school was so great she had no idea what should change, the superintendent persisted. "That's the question I want you to answer. Let me know, but soon."[11] In an era of reform, something *had* to be found, just the assignment for a micromanaging obsessive.

The oppression was well-chronicled in the media and hit home with me personally: while my son was there, I had my own run-ins with the intransigent principal and her Nurse Diesel-wannabe enforcer, the universally-disliked assistant principal. The *least* retaliation I feared against my kid was the loss of a fruit cup. As a teacher in the same system, I just shook my head: I knew these people already. The DOE seemed to be manufacturing these stock potentates like Chinese Terracotta Warriors by the thousands, then unleashing them on the schools. The two thousand-year-old statues, however, were certainly more humane.

With repression seeping down through the hierarchy, the calcifying system has become suitable only as a home for wayward control freaks. Each school is just a gulag in an archipelago of them, the mission of education subordinated to the principals' drive to act out their power issues. Given the culture of intimidation and angst, it is no wonder teachers, fearing reprisals, never give their names when commenting on principals; considering the volume of rage at them, volumes could be published just on the deeds of the maniacal misfits. The carnage would be that much worse without the teachers union as a supportive, but by no means all-powerful, ally: we would be far more vulnerable to politics and abuse.

Still, an epidemic of Post Traumatic Stress Disorder—with its symptoms of anxiety, depression, insomnia and fatigue—has infected not just the city's but the nation's teaching population, while the systematic harassment has even proven lethal, resulting in suicide. It has been a grievous error to invest principals with so much control under so little oversight, beyond test scores: principals should be subject to evaluations by their own staff, determinations significant enough to remove the incorrigible *bete noirs* from their posts.[12]

Yet in spite of their despotism, principals routinely escape punishment, at most getting a slap on the wrist, while ultimately prospering. Far from being penalized, the three nutcases I had experienced as principals had gone on to lucrative principalships or plush positions at the DOE. According to the union, even our new principal, we would eventually discover, had been fired from that job in another school a few years before, yet without missing a beat had blithely resumed that job *chez nous*. I wondered if parents of our students, indeed *any* city taxpayers, would approve of apparently immortal principals, zombies with connections who refused to die; the secretive DOE made sure the public would never be able to make that call. Even as the corrupt environment which existed before the days of reforms and unions is supposed to be long extinct, Boss Tweed lives on as a fractal in the schools, wielding the erstwhile weapons of cronyism and bullying.

That summer brought bombshell news busting the myth of mayoral control as urban educational panacea: the scores for the recalibrated, harder-to-pass spring 2010 state tests were announced, almost erasing the "gains" students had made since 2007.[13] This was no news flash to us; now it was a relief our concerns were empirically backed and the public finally knew. Admittedly, considering our resentment of a mayor and chancellor who had squelched our input, bullied our instruction, affirmed our inadequacy and cheated us out of even an inflation-level pay raise, the *Schadenfreude* was delicious. The numbers of third through eighth grade students performing at grade level in math and reading plummeted. Charter schools fared even worse, posting a larger drop than public schools, but still maintaining a narrow lead in math and reading scores.

All told, students had only moved up modestly since Bloomberg took over in 2002, the same mediocre gains that had been been par for the course during the reign of the Board of Education prior to mayor control. Despite Bloomberg's frequent boast that he had cut the achievement gap in half, the truth was during his tenure, the achievement gap between advantaged and disadvantaged kids had not moved at all.

But the bad news did not end there. The leitmotif of Klein's tenure had been increasing graduation rates of students prepared for college or careers. In fact, Klein had staked his legacy on this effort, declaring his record on graduation numbers would be the standard for judging his contribution as chancellor.[14] Now it was revealed the advancing high school graduation rates, particularly impressive considering one third of all the city's schools serve students in poverty, had been based on fakery: high school teachers accused principals of forcing them to pass as many as eighty percent of these types of kids, irrespective of attendance or grades.[15]

No wonder the inundation of New York City community colleges with unprepared high school graduates, the majority of whom were found to need remediation, while only twenty-four percent would eventually get a diploma from the two-year program. In fact as it turned out, only one in five students who started high school in 2006 were adequately prepared for college or a job in 2010.[16] Even worse, at more than half the city's high schools, fewer than one out of ten students were considered ready for college or career.[17] These stats for teenagers squared exactly with the deplorable academic performance in my school of the younger kids coming up. Where were the crucial interventions, years earlier, to this obvious crisis?

For two who, from the get-go, parroted the reform movement's concept du jour, "accountability," to the point of parody, Bloomberg and Klein headed for the hills of denial, brushing off the facts and still asserting the "historic gains" of the last five years were authentic.[18] Like other irresponsible megalomaniacs who had run American into the ground in the last decade, they had evidently been taking a page from Goebbels, who famously pointed out, "If you tell a lie big enough and keep repeating it, people will eventually come to believe it." Savvy PR is not merely timeless, it seems—ruthless agendas can make for strange compadres.

10

My ninth year started with my fourth principal, a telling comment on the state of stability in the city school system. Since studies show the negative effects of teacher turnover on a child's learning outcomes, clearly frequent changes in administration would be no less disturbing to the staff, but I could not distinguish between a state of shell-shocked and normal anyway at this point.[1] Our Progress Report grade was announced for our last year with Principal Dearest: we had gotten a "B."

Sanchez and I were to share an art room, alternating months. The first day we were getting it ready, she pretended she needed the room to herself since she had been injured (slightly, an entire year before, and she had taken five months off). The next day Sanchez came in wearing the dirty old boot cast she had used the previous year to scam the administration into giving her a classroom. As usual, forgetting herself sometimes, she ran and even danced around. At other moments, apparently channeling Sarah Bernhardt while gazing at nothing in particular, a stricken expression on her face, Sanchez lamented dramatically, "I'll have a limp the rest of my life." I was waiting for her to say, "I've always depended on the kindness of strangers," but since the principal was not around, her scene was over, for now.

Regardless of my attempts to get Sanchez to be considerate, she had never stopped dumping her stuff into my art closet on the fourth floor, even though she had her own smoking lounge-cum-closet. I had taken to hiding my materials in teacher's rooms all over the school, not only because she had monopolized my space, but because she helped herself to my supplies. Sanchez had gotten away with fraud as an art teacher (her students strung beads) and as a handsomely-paid "disabled" victim rewarded with an obscene amount of time off and her own private art room afterward. The injustice of the situation, that she was trying for fraud again, and directly at my expense, was too much. I girded my loins (since I always wanted to say that—do they sell those at Macy's?) for a fight.

Since Sanchez had the art room for the first month, the last week of September I put up a sign in the office notifying teachers my art classes would be in the art room for October, intuitively anticipating some kind of drama. Sure enough, as I was sitting in the teacher's lounge just half an hour later, the new principal burst in and attacked me. How dare I put up a sign without asking her! How dare I think I would be sharing the art room, when Ms. Sanchez was injured! Beyond frustrated and convinced I had to seize that particular moment, I asked to see her in her office. Once inside, I let it rip. On Sanchez, then on Principal Dearest. With my lower back out and a welcome-back sinus infection, I was all doped up on pain killers and respiratory meds, and the combination was creating my own private (or not so) party.

The principal must have thought I was some wild woman, though she avoided eye contact most of the time, looking coldly at her Blackberry while I fulminated, only interjecting a comment now and then. I was not only fending off the injustice that Sanchez was sending my way, I found myself unloading years-worth of pent-up rancor with Principal Dearest. My emotional torrent was so passionate, not to mention medicated, at times my dry Mojaved mouth fought to extrude the words. Nevertheless, I apparently made my point. The principal said she would figure out the art room situation. I knew I had won the right to share it.

Sanchez responded to the loss of her art room dominion with histrionics, though I personally steered clear of the Wagnerian fallout. Moreover, having lost her selfish battle, apparently she had spent lunch hour in Lourdes, because her foot had spontaneously healed and she openly walked without a limp, or the trusty boot cast prop. I had told the principal that I wanted my art closet to myself, that Sanchez already had her own, so I would need her to surrender the key.

But after school, the principal came upon Sanchez outside the closet. She immediately collapsed in the hallway and wept hysterically that she could not move her mountain of stuff out. Mission accomplished, Sanchez was awarded the second-best thing to the Tony she deserved: she was allowed to leave her towering pillars of junk in my closet.

As I lacked the dexterity of a Collyer brother to navigate the miscellany, my supplies remained obstructed and inaccessible. Fortunately, I had moved much of the important stuff out when she had been taking her five month cure on the city's dime. But clearly, Marienbad had done nothing for her etiquette.

In a faculty meeting the first week of school, when asked to tell us about herself, instead of delivering a generic, *comme il faut* introduction, the new principal had launched into an inarticulate ramble about how she loved singing. She had been doing it "as far back as in the womb." This irrelevant pronouncement, expanded with the news flash that she had sung back-up (our rumor mill was so beyond this) segued clunkily into a discussion of school issues. What we deemed important to know, her education, teaching experience, why she had become a principal, boilerplate introductory spiel, was conspicuously absent. The weird dodge only added to the strange impression she had made from the beginning, when she had snuck into classes without identifying herself or even making eye contact. Now as then, the principal came off as distant, all the while acting cloyingly cute with the kids: in the mornings the PA system oozed her daily aural serving of treacle.

In Extended Time, I tutored a French-speaking boy from Togo, as well as an Arabic kid from Yemen, teaching them English. The language instruction exempted me from the enervating ennui of test prep, a more frenetic endeavor than ever given the low scores from the 2010 state math and ELA tests. Later that year I orally translated the state math test for the African kid, who was exempted from taking the ELA. However, the next year, just like all the other ELLs who had recently come ashore, after a mere year of school in English he would take an exam that necessitated years of fluency to master. Given this shockingly clueless federal requirement, it was no wonder our multitude of immigrant children drove the school's test scores into the basement.

Meanwhile, the level of rage at teachers and teachers unions, as the primary obstacles to the nation's educational progress, was ratcheting up. Yet all the statistics were on the side of the unions: states without teachers' unions had the lowest achieving public schools, while non-unionized charter schools nationwide only outperformed public schools seventeen percent of the time, underperforming them significantly thirty-seven percent of the time.[2] Teachers at those same charter schools were one hundred thirty percent more likely to leave than their unionized counterparts at public schools, already a group with high turnover.[3] Moreover, states and even countries with strong teachers unions were at the forefront of educational prowess and progress: nobody dared mention that teachers in Finland were not only unionized, but had a contract two hundred pages longer than the UFT's.[4] Still, the anti-union blitzkrieg rolled on with the overwrought documentaries *Waiting For Superman* and *The Lottery* joining the increased presence of lobbying groups like Wall Street's Democrats for Education Reform.

Jumping on the bipartisan witch hunt, NBC launched *Education Nation*, a three-day televised summit, much of which was a teacher-bashing free-for-all, even on liberal MSNBC's *Morning Joe*. A show I normally listened to while getting ready for school, the facile, unapologetic lynching en masse, of hard-working, underpaid and under-valued teachers, masquerading as information/entertainment, disgusted me. As part of the Nielsen Helper ratings fodder, I half expected the live town hall audience to break into choreographed chants of "Death to Teachers!" After a few minutes I rushed to change the channel to Fox News for some relief.

One October morning I was in the art room for my hard-won first month, when the principal swooped in with a quizzical look on her face: what was I teaching? The older kids were painting their watercolor scenes of New York City, while the younger ones were doing Halloween. What did I mean by that? I showed her patterns of bats, jack o'lanterns, black cats and ghosts I had made for the kids to trace on large sheets of paper, with the concept of composition at the core of the lesson. Where is the rigor? she wanted to know, using a buzzword of the moment. The principal made me explain this further, her brows knitted in an accusatory expression, telegraphing not only her conviction of my utter incompetence, but her intent to catch me being so. Her witchy features only added to the impression of invasion during the encounter, less a conversation than an interrogation.

There was an ineffable quality of desperation in the air, a veritable compulsion to make me wrong. Thwarted by my ready defense, she saved face by promising to come back to watch me teach the lesson so she could "understand better." Of course she did not return. The encounter had just been administrative theatre, the Kabuki posturing meant solely to intimidate. The hoped-for bonus of the harpy's ambush, exposing inadequacy and the opportunity to criticize and diminish, never materialized.

I exhaled a sigh so exaggerated I could not believe it was spontaneous: *deja vu*. The principal's aggression radiated her appetite for power, the derisive tone and expression, the urge to shame, that had been predicted months before by her lack of charm and physical stature. From now on she was no longer, neutrally, "the new principal"—the tiny tyrant had earned her own special moniker: Rosemary's Baby.

It was timely, then, that bullying was in the news. The media was publicizing the consequences of being bullied, including anxiety, post-traumatic stress, depression, absenteeism, poor health, alienation, lowered achievement, lack of self-esteem and self-confidence. These were all symptoms teachers had been having for years, whether brought on by bullying from the reformers and media; the micromanaging DOE; or the everyday, in-your-face garden variety we were used to from a principal! The state had just passed a Dignity For All Students Act meant to give kids a "safe and supportive environment free from discrimination, intimidation,

LAUREL M. STURT

taunting, harassment, and bullying on school property..." but could the teachers get one passed for them?[5]

Now Rosemary's Baby began baring her little incisors in the direction of the ill-fated, scapegoated teachers Principal Dearest had so graciously separated out before she had left. If there had been a honeymoon period with such a socially-awkward, remote administrator, well, it was now over: Pallas and Casares were now hounded relentlessly. First they were given several "U"s for informal observations, so every week they had to spend hours at home typing up elaborate weekly lesson plans made purposely time-consuming to further harass, then were forced to meet with the administration to review them. No other teachers were harnessed with this additional burden on top of an already back-breaking workload. Moreover, Rosemary's Baby's sidekick, Moore, was sent into their rooms sometimes several times a day to monitor them and write negative entries regarding what she saw in their classroom logbooks.

These books, placed next to the door in all the classrooms, were supposedly informal "support" notes from visiting administrators. However, they were actually a tool of systematic intimidation, not to mention simply a validation for assistant principals and coaches to justify their ridiculous pencil-pushing positions. Since the comments inscribed were invariably negative, whether deserved or not, the logbooks served also as an effective paper trail establishing evidence to fire a teacher.

Obviously, notes left in the logbooks of the targeted teachers were only derogatory. Frequently, Rosemary's Baby herself ambushed them, and the extent of her interest in the two, who had been after all, haplessly served up by Principal Dearest for her persecutory pleasure, without incurring it on her own watch, even recalled the laser focus which Principal Dearest brought to any issue, like punishing me for not painting the auditorium.

Pallas was a fourteen-year veteran struggling to cope with the worst class in the school, a special ed class I referred to as "The Victorian Asylum," a room of students she had taught up through the grades where daily imbroglios, often spilling cacophonously into the hallway, were accompanied by a contrapuntal chorus of shrieks and moans. On entering, one expected to see white-nightgowned, straitjacketed urchins with matted hair ricocheting off padded walls. Indeed, for some of these kids just waking up on the wrong side of the bed could spark a forty-five minute spasm of rage, resulting in a morning of turmoil and the concomitant loss of instruction time for the rest of the class (those remaining, slated to freak out in the afternoon). The class, designed, ideally, like all those in the general special ed universe, for slow learners, nevertheless included psychotic, even schizophrenic children with severe mental and emotional issues.

Those kids belonged in the specific special ed program, District Seventy-Five, catering to particular issues such as autism or violent disorders, for example, that had been set up citywide. But for Pallas and others, placing extreme students in it was an arduous task based on mountains of anecdotal records as well as observations by teams of psychologists and social workers. If a child were ultimately diagnosed with a particular issue and required placement in a District Seventy-Five program, then parents still had to agree to bussing the child to that specific school. More often than not parents refused, saddling unlucky teachers like Pallas with their kid, wrecking their own child's education as well as the others' in the class.

I could well comprehend the difficulty, as I had experienced it myself when teaching an especially special ed class. This year I dreaded Mondays because that day I taught a special ed first grade that was host to five fractious boys. Not only did it take place last period, when even regular classes, tired and bored, were prone to catastrophe, but the male paraprofessional who solely commanded their respect had left early to go home, leaving me illegally in the classroom by myself.

One of the boys, Joshua, had the most severe case of ADHD I had ever chased around a room for fifty minutes; at times like this I envied the skills of cowboys, or at least defensive ends. On his own, Joshua required such extensive babysitting it was impossible to attend to anyone else, but there were twelve students, including the four other difficult ones. The other really challenging one, Samiel, was actually mentally ill, hearing voices, talking to himself and instigating fights by slap and run. Two others were just followers who happily engaged in and expanded upon whatever mayhem Joshua and Samiel were creating.

The last of the gang of five, Jashawn, had ADHD but had been placed on meds so when he was using, he was cooperative. Though cooperation is necessary for learning, their own and other students,' that word had always made me squirm, for what it implies: that a child's personality has to be molded, almost fascistically, into a compliant, manageable presence. Yet, the year before, Jashawn had been an obese kindergartner short on attention and long on trouble. After a month on Ritalin, not only was his prediabetic predisposition a thing of the past, he was now amenable to learning.

My opposition to pharmaceutical interference with a child's brain had vanished my first year. Though I favored dealing with ADD and ADHD, the twin scourges of the school, through diet and behavior modification, it seemed the parents of these children, possibly Cheeto-ed and grape soda-ed themselves, were hardly going to liberate their children from neon food coloring, multisyllabic preservatives or Chicken McTumors. It guilts me to condone shackling the spirit of a child—I cannot escape the idea that it is a form of soul murder, in fact, especially when I see glazed, over-medicated kids who are for all intents and purposes, stoned. But truly healing them would require expensive, intensive behavior modification training, as well as equally elusive parental commitment and education.

Though I am loathe to congratulate Big Daddy Pharma, with its penchant for pathologizing any condition for profit, notwithstanding the laundry list of side effects (my favorite: death), I have come to believe that medicating these cases, in the smallest dose and short-term, for their own benefit and the good of those around them, is a necessary evil. It is just a fact I cannot run away from, regardless of my Restless Leg Syndrome.

In October, we were assaulted anew when Joel Klein, Michelle Rhee and fourteen other schools czars from cities published "How to Fix Our Schools: A Manifesto" in the *Washington Post*, a recitation of the reform agenda with its typical adulation for testing, data, charter schools, etc., and requisite vilification of teachers, unions, seniority, etc.,.[6] The statement, clearly meant to ride the coattails of the highly-publicized, Bill Gates' sponsored reformist propaganda vehicle *Waiting for Superman,* was textbook reactionary, an obvious parry to the recent release of dismal city test scores, an embarrassment which Klein simply could not brook with any hint of grace. Despite their professed allegiance to accountability, none of the superintendents had the cojones to take the blame for anything. Instead the old reliable default scapegoat, teachers, once again made an appearance. In one part the statement declared, "As President Obama has emphasized, the single most important factor determining whether students succeed in school is not the color of their skin or their ZIP code or even their parents' income—it is the quality of their teacher."

In fact, Obama meant, rightly, that teachers have been proven to be the most important factor *in a school* in influencing a child's education.[7] But research demonstrates that at most a teacher can have a twenty percent influence on a student's achievement. That is because, obviously, in a child's life the most important school is the home, while the most important teacher is the parent. Moreover, even as findings point to teachers as the most important in-school factor to a child's education, while at the same time class size, administration, supplies, programs, etc., are impactive variables, obviously the teacher cannot make up for a child's life outside of school. In fact, family SES has double the importance of all in-school aspects put together. Since the first research in 1966 found student achievement to be founded on "one-third in-school factors, two-thirds family characteristics," no additional analysis has changed this fundamental equation.[8]

But Klein & Co. were not about to let facts get in the way of their rigid ideology: desperate for a distraction, the superintendents doctored the quote about a teacher's importance among school factors, to validate further teacher-bashing, particularly necessary given Klein's dishonor, Rhee's secret shame (a test cheating investigation involving her was underway), and skeletons in the closets of the rest of the manifesto's signatories. With perfect timing, a two-year study came out a couple days later detailing the results of mayoral control in nine of the nation's cities: notwithstanding the sweeping declaration, the system had failed to yield improvements in student achievement, even as it stifled the invaluable contributions of parents and educators.[9]

In November, we got the news: after eight years Chancellor Klein had resigned, an understandable retreat given the recent reality check his inflated claims and test scores had received. At a press conference, Klein took a stab at saving face by praising Bloomberg for making education his number one priority as mayor, while shamelessly gushing over his own legacy: sixty percent more city kids were graduating and going to college than when he started in 2002. Later that assertion would be demolished, too, when the actual numbers of college-ready kids came out.[10]

Mercenary Klein immediately jumped ship for News Corporation and a salary of four and a half million dollars a year. A teacher and union-bashing right wing assault weapon with media holdings like the *New York Post* and the *Wall Street Journal*, Rupert Murdoch's company could not have found a better fit than the opportunistic corporate apparatchik Klein. With bald-faced indifference to conflict of interest, he became the chief of the company's new education division, immediately purchasing a company he had used during his DOE tenure to consult on the problem-riddled, money pit ARIS program which tracked students' academic achievement.[11] Klein's subsequent twenty-seven million dollar no-bid proposal to the state to purchase consulting on the same system was tentatively awarded, then withdrawn, officials slamming the contract's conflict of interest as well as unsavory provenance from the phone-hacking News Corp.

Undeterred, in early 2012 Klein got the DOE to assign his company the last month on a five-year, eighty-three million dollar contract the department had with IBM. The legal, though slimy gesture, meant Klein would now be heir to IBM's option to another two-year contract, worth ten million dollars. Since the computer system itself was already seen by many as incompetent and inefficient, not only was Klein's deal not kosher, it represented a waste of precious taxpayer dollars. The cozy connection between the

DOE and News Corp. continued to prosper as both the DOE's chief operating officer and later the DOE's communications director joined Klein's company, peddling its services back to the city and state, to the tune of millions of dollars, in the ensuing years.[12]

As fall progressed, three-day simulations of the state math and ELA tests arrived. Just like every other aspect of NCLB (aka NPLB, "No Profit Left Behind"), the testing fever had spawned a parasitic behemoth, this one peddling preparation materials, simulations, predictors and actual tests, along with armies of experts to evaluate the results, an industry worth tens of billions of dollars a year. After all, Joel Klein had readily forsaken his daily hand-to-hand combat with the UFT to jump onto the testing data gravy train.

Indeed, there is so much money to be made pigeon-holing children as they progress or regress into other pigeon holes, it is no longer clear whether government testing mandates support the educational measurement/materials bonanza, or the mammoth industry itself perpetuates the dash-for-data delirium. Like so many areas where massive sums of money are at stake, the boundaries are blurred between governance and exploitation in ours, the greatest democracy money can buy. Nevertheless, later in the school year a panel of heavy-hitting education experts published findings of a ten-year study on standardized testing. Their research, ignored this time by the reformers entranced by the phrase "research-backed," demonstrated testing does not improve educational outcomes, something we already knew.

Since the economic crisis of 2008, the number of homeless kids in the city's schools had quadrupled, rising by over thirty-two thousand. Still homeless, during the summer William had been unable to attend the usual free day camp for shelter kids since bussing had been cut, and his stepfather could not afford the Metrocards to take him. While I was away the weather had been blistering, and the thought of him stuck inside that execrable building without so much as a single beach outing was really disturbing. When I saw William at the start of school, though, he was as cheerful as ever and said he had had a great time. He was in third grade now in a class taught by pregnant Ms. Martinez. This meant, as it always did, that the stability of the class was compromised while a six-week maternity leave was accommodated.

A ditzy, forty-year veteran, Ms. Smith, was brought in from her out-of-classroom position as an intervention teacher, to substitute. Smith's temporary position ended up being prolonged as Martinez, back from having her baby, was assigned to another classroom. This was unfortunate for the children who had stopped receiving Smith's tutoring services, as well as for William and others in his class: not only had Smith not had sufficient recent experience in the classroom, her extreme ADD, as played out in her lack of organization and predilection for procrastination, doomed the kids to a lost year. Moreover, Smith was planning on retiring that June, so her burned-out state combined with a lackadaisical "I'm outta here" attitude.

The class became one of the most chaotic in the school while Smith phoned it in. When passing by, I would see boys crawling on the floor from desk to desk, holding giggling *tête-à-têtes* in their impromptu below-desks fort, as Smith stood at the blackboard broadcasting her discombobulation over the pandemonium. Under ordinary circumstances a principal would have eaten Smith alive. But considering her seniority, not only was she doing the administration a favor, it was known her retirement was imminent (and she would take her high salary with her), so regardless of the detriment to the kids, innocent hostages to a simple pregnancy situation, she was left alone. The collateral damage wreaked on the students' intellectual development was unconscionable and completely avoidable.

But such professional administrative foresight, *de riguer* in the real world, had always seemed more hard to come by in our school. Though "accountability" had figured in the *Call of Duty: NYC School* live version game hunt for teachers to terminate, the concept never applied to any level of the administration, all the way up to the mayor. Nobody would pay for the fact that William's class had lost most of a year—only the kids themselves would pick up the tab.

Rosemary's Baby spent long periods behind the closed door of her office with AP Moore. It seemed after five years of suffering at the hands of Principal Dearest, a state of torture she had freely shared with the teaching staff, Moore was at last in a position of strength, if not power. She had spent the previous summer showing the new principal the ropes, and it was obvious that Rosemary's Baby leaned on Moore's greater experience, even if technically she was her boss. Rosemary's Baby's pronounced reliance on Moore gave the AP a new calling: she relished the role of Rosemary's Baby Whisperer. By contrast, the principal had little time for the other AP, Rodriguez, who had been a favorite of Principal Dearest but was now left out in the cold. In fact, it was suspected that Moore had been trashing him with five years of accrued resentment.

Adding to the intrigue was the aggressive self-promotion of Ms. Gonzalez, a crony of Guido's empowered as a coach years before, who was rumored to be intent on pushing Rodriguez out as assistant principal so she could assume that position. Though the teachers despised her, an unabashed control freak, armed with her judgmental clipboard to enforce the administration's lust for irrelevant minutiae, every principal found her an obliging sycophant. The pathetic jockeying for position was dreadful to watch, and just another discouraging indication that, as ever, there were no adults in charge.

The wretched power machinations of an inner city school now provided the backdrop to a new systemwide campaign against bullying. Classroom discussions and writing appeared, while posters went up among other places, outside the rooms where Rosemary's Baby was apparently pursuing a professional degree in bullying. On the wall next to Pallas's door there was a red lettered sign with the word BULLYING on it with a diagonal slash mark across it, virtually an international interdiction. Despite this bold graphic, inside the teacher languished from the stress of being, well, bullied. The crushing additional weekly paperwork, never approved by the administration, despite its thoroughness, was the least of it: the plague of nitpicking administrators, sometimes several times per day, were an undisguised hit squad which never failed to write a negative comment in the "support" log.

Despite the year's draconian school budget cuts, Rosemary's Baby had contracted Columbia University Teacher's College to provide weekly professional development, as opposed to replacing the retired computer teacher, so the kids lost computer class and our school computers were unusable, choked with viruses. Since the professional development was taking place during class time, the teacher's schedules had to be covered, resulting in crowds of raucous students in the auditorium in the cattle calls known as mass preps. Always a disturbing waste of educational time, this group babysitting was little more than callous, impersonal warehousing with expediency the only imperative. Students were condemned to hours of animation blasting at levels designed to counter the decibels of talking/fighting which naturally erupted, given the stultifying prospect of an umpteenth viewing of some movie. As ever, I was not about to tilt at windmills in a fruitless attempt to get them to shut the hell up: I needed to save my disciplinary voice for my own class. A couple of male teachers, always equal to a wrangle for control, stormed the perimeter, booming endless instructions and admonitions to kids who, seconds later, would blithely resume their defiant blabbing.

Michelle Rhee had been the autocratic schools chancellor of Washington, D.C. from 2007 to 2010, when the local electorate voiced its displeasure with her arrogant, take-no-prisoners zealotry and voted out her protector, the mayor, a situation which forced her resignation. The most prominent and egotistical of the reform mafia, puppet-stringed ideologue Rhee now made an announcement on *Oprah*: to the thunderous applause of a simple audience pathetically brainwashed by an ostentatious preamble, as well as Oprah's excess of effervesce, Rhee trumpeted modestly, "I am going to start a revolution. I am going to start a movement in this country on behalf of the nation's children!" With cringe-worthy color purple prose— "I'm not gonna cry but I could. You know, the little hairs on my head are raising"—Oprah conferred sainthood on Rhee, while exhorting one million of her viewers to participate in the billion dollar fund drive for Rhee's latest, self-aggrandizing mission. [13]

Thus Rhee debuted Students First, a national political organization with mainly anonymous donors (Bill Gates, who has labeled American public schools "obsolete," is one of her major funders) created to muscle privatization through with tenets such as vouchers ("opportunity scholarships"), charter schools and teacher evaluations using test scores, while raging against tenure and other union-backed issues. In other words, the generic reform toolkit. Naturally, Students First is allied with the insidious American Legislative Exchange Council (ALEC), providing conservative politicians with talking points and fully-written bills to submit to a vote.

Rhee, an unabashed, soulless propagandist whose boasted achievements in her brief stints as a teacher and chancellor constitute flagrant dissembling if not outright lies, had become the poster child for convulsive educational reform, quite literally, making the cover of *Time* in December 2008. This accolade had been bestowed for illegally firing hundreds of teachers (most of them with senior salaries) according to a flawed, experimental data system of test results. At the same time Rhee presided over literally fantastic test performance gains: later, an investigation would find the trajectory of those vaunted test scores to be, in fact, no arc of triumph.[14]

More disturbing even than the benediction conveyed by a hug from gushing Oprah (who failed to grasp the impostor's true character, even as she clasped her to a well-meaning bosom), Rhee had been invoked in heroic terms during the election by both McCain and Obama, while Arne Duncan showered her with praise as well.[15] But educators knew better: as Number One on the Most Wanted list of War (on teachers) Criminals, Rhee's position in the crosshairs of thousands of haters would even prompt her own dedicated website, rheefirst.com, hosted by the American Federation of Teachers.

After all, Rhee was a person who tyrannized all with an even hand, even as a teacher taping closed the mouths of her first grade class when she couldn't get them to walk to lunch quietly; in a later fond remembrance of the moment Rhee actually laughed when recounting how some of their mouths bled when the tape was ripped off.[16] An ambitious narcissist whose M.O., "You're fired" echoed another successful snake oiler, Donald Trump, instead of being fired herself for abuse, sociopath Rhee had been exalted, basking in the dangerous, irresponsible glow of political and media consensus.

As Christmas approached the kids began getting pumped for a day they only knew involved Santa Claus, candy canes and hopefully a deluge of new video games to play on their new, promised game systems. I always read *The Night Before Christmas* to the younger ones in an attempt to give them a foothold on traditional American culture. It was new to most of them so I knew they were not getting it at home—it could not be ingested through a video game. I gave the little kids large gingerbread men I had sketched out of paper for them to decorate, while the older ones always had a more sophisticated card to make, a new design every year.

Though there was sometimes a show during the rest of the year, the Christmas spectacular was the only dependable one, especially as budgets shrank and with them the money to provide afterschool performance practice. This celebration of the Baby Jesus (or was it the Baby Santa?), challenged us as at no other time to manifest qualities of Christian love, compassion, mercy, and most of all patience, as we strained every charitable cell of our being to survive, and then applaud, a performance only a loving parent or teacher could cheerfully endure.

The ordeal began with us bringing the little kids, kindergarten and first grade, down to the front of the auditorium where they could ostensibly best see the action. But this meant, alas, that the most easily bored, the youngest ones, would be exposed to the deadly entertainment at the closest, most pitiless range. This was not a calibration conducive to a satisfied, cooperative audience. Also, the little ones could not see over the seats/heads in front of them, so whatever snatches of entertainment they might glean when springing up illegally were hardly sufficient to palliate the boredom of staring at the back of a chair. This, then, was a moment ripe for getting up, or punching the boy to the left of you, or pulling the hair of the girl to the right of you, or loudly expressing your ennui, or suddenly requiring an emergency visit to the bathroom. Indeed, *anything* other than being held captive to this mandated merriment.

The performance constituted an indictment of Bloomberg's recent evisceration of afterschool funds which had, even in the flush times, been ridiculously skeletal. The current result was a barebones afterschool program impossibly starved of funds and therefore, sufficient direction or rehearsal time. As wrung with difficulty, then, out of a group of predominantly ill-prepared kids, the show featured voice-accompanied dance numbers choreographed to recorded music. As dozens of them came down the aisles toward the stage, the blare of a familiar song was enough to bring the audience on board, everybody clapping to the beat.

Since I had known all of them for years, seeing them in this new guise was always fun, and nerve-wracking in a motherly way: I prayed they would hit it out of the park. But once on stage a sort of simmering chaos set in as the dancers, most of them not only wracked with shyness but painfully unclear about their moves, unsuccessfully fudged their routine. Looking frantically at each other in search of steps they should have learned by now, typically only a couple actually performed, serving up the correct words and steps while facing the audience.

Between the regrettable dancing and the unpracticed, off-pitch singing, a tone-deaf condition which remarkably seemed to afflict many of them, the theatrical effect was audiovisual waterboarding. But the recorded music turned out to be a godsend, considering other points in the show when the afterschool music class put in *its* two cents with a dissonant din of keyboards and drums. This racket was mitigated only by the three-chorded, sometimes just three-noted funeral dirge repeating on the star student's keyboard, as background accompaniment to the merciful reprieve of actual music from the teacher's electric guitar.

But the part that always induced the greatest insurrection from the kindergartners was the awkward skits with their stilted, poorly-read dialogue, the actors as unprepared as the dancers had been. What is more, their words were always inaudible because the kids did not properly engage the mike. What we *did* hear was the chafing, deafening sound-effects of wind, mouth-breathing (and was that cars crashing?) punctuated by frequent ear-stabbing screeches of feedback.

For the audience this was the *coup de grace*. At this point the young kids—most of whose politesse (if there had ever been any), being just an abstract principle, had long ago seized its freedom and fled the scene—literally had their hands over their ears. The poor things were fairly bursting out of their skins, chomping at the bit for physical release, a catharsis which came just in time with the end of the show and their chance to leap up and jump, clap and stamp not in thunderous applause, but relief that the torture was finished.

For the second show for the upper grades, the performers had usually gotten better, so the ghastly meter registered one or two less involuntary sound effects on the microphone. Anyway, the older kids, though an even tougher sell, were just thrilled to get a respite from writing and math.

Though all the first graders wanted for Christmas was their two front teeth, the rest of us prayed for afterschool funds, and lots of them.

Now, with Rosemary's Baby in charge, all of a sudden a *staff* Christmas show was organized, an obvious platform for the back-up singer to, well, back up her claims to an irrelevant eighties musical lineage. To pop music, teachers who had volunteered, dressed in reindeer antlers, red turtlenecks and leggings, boogied up the aisle to the stage, their surprising incarnation as entertainers causing the kids to explode with delight. The music teacher performed, as well as a beloved veteran para who brought the house down with his stunning James Brown spins and splits, accompanied percussively by the Rice Krispies apparently residing in his joints. Even Rosemary's Baby was great at her soulful rendition of "Silent Night." Though a command-ed performance and we were forced to be there, the amazing entertainment brought the house down. It was a rare moment of community, in fact, the most impressive I had experienced in all my time there. Yet it was fated to be not just the first, but the last staff Christmas show: the staff would never again have the spirit or the energy. Rosemary's Baby would see to that.

Early in the year, Bloomberg announced the appointment to schools chancellor of Cathleen Black, an Upper East Side neighbor without a shred of educational experience, like other corporate executives he had brought in for his third term. Flaunting his disdain for meritocracy, the mayor's gushing praise was apparently meant to deflect criticism of his flagrant recruitment of an unqualified crony, a magazine executive he had met at a dinner party. Nevertheless, he designated Black a "world class manager," as ever to Bloomberg a more important qualification than actual education experience. Completely clueless about running the schools, and equally challenged at dealing with the public, for even the smallest issues Black deferred to the opinions of two aides, whom the rest of the staff began referring to as "chancellor." The DOE drifted, unmanned, mounting one instance of incompetence after the next, for example, failing to apply for millions in federal funds available to turn around struggling schools. So lackadaisical had the DOE become, emails and phone calls were routinely unreturned.[17]

Through the winter we had had snow, though as usual Bloomberg did not close the schools, even as all the Catholic schools, and those in surrounding areas, were closed. Most of the students, who lived nearby, showed up, while most of the teachers, who commuted from a distance, did not, leaving, as ever, a monumental job for the few teachers who made it in. This was emphatically the case the day of the biggest of the blizzards, when I trudged through banks of pristine snow (the only time the Bronx ever looked clean) larger than we had ever experienced. The city was completely shut down by it. I had gotten up early expecting the schools to be closed, and on television Bloomberg was making a statement exhorting everyone to stay home. Then he added, bizarrely, and sadistically, "The schools are open!"

I arrived to find a frantic Rosemary's Baby at the office counter, two teachers helping her assign classes to the few who were straggling in; the two assistant principals had not shown up. I was struck by the precipitous drop in her composure—she was on the verge of panic—though we later found out there had been a contingency plan in place which she had ignored. As students and a few more teachers trickled in, my assignment was changed repeatedly until it was determined I would sub a first grade class, combining the students from two classes. I improvising activities in literacy, math and art I had learned to call on my first year when I frequently subbed. Snow days never amounted to much educationally, which was ironic considering Bloomberg was so dead-set on avoiding a loss of instructional time. The day turned out to be a scandalous one in his administration as systems were mismanaged, workers mutinied and it took weeks to plow out and even pick up garbage from many neighborhoods, including the Bronx.

Though the trip to school the next several days required parsing an icy obstacle course, things returned to normal. I was teaching a kindergarten special ed class about the approaching Valentine's Day, and I had sketched half hearts on folded paper for them to cut out. Many had never used scissors and this was one of my favorite lessons to enhance their motor skill development. As I was stooped over, guiding a kid's hand in a literal hands-on engagement, Rosemary's Baby burst into the class. "What's going on here?" I heard from behind me. I glanced back, exasperated at the interruption. I was met with an expression of condescending incredulity, like in October, the same manufactured look and voice designed to wordlessly communicate my utter ineptitude. WTF! I was in the act of teaching a child how to cut with a scissors.

I felt engulfed in gloom as I emptily stated the obvious, what I was doing, knowing that in fact she did not have any interest in that at all. By now I was a pro at evaluating that expression and tone from Rosemary's Baby and her three predecessors: having lost her sense of control the day before, she simply needed a transfusion. As she continued to cast her gimlet eye around the room, I went back to helping the child, ignoring her. Rosemary's Baby's abrupt jones for power, and the fact that she was trying to get her fix at the expense of the student's learning, was maddening. My nonchalance exacerbated her aggression and she demanded my lesson plan, which I had left in my cabinet (outside the room) during the snowstorm the day before. I told her that it was there and I would get it out at lunch time. Rosemary's Baby seethed, her tiny fists clenched, on the verge of stamping her little foot like a toddler. Then, emphatically sucking her teeth, she left the room in a huff. Later I found out Rosemary's Baby had been in the kindergarten classrooms just before mine, pouncing on several petty issues resulting in teachers getting letters to their file; I was merely the finale of a productive morning's shock and awe.

Two hours later during the bedlam of clean-up, Rosemary's Baby, clearly now obsessed (Principal Dearest 2.0), snuck in during my fourth grade class and quietly asked two students what I had taught them. They had been given the history of Valentine's Day as well as read love poetry, and they were now making an abstract collage of pink and red scraps I had saved from years of valentines projects, a great call considering we had no money for that paper now. In terms of lessons, mine was unimpeachable as it involved social studies, literacy and art. Rosemary's Baby slipped out without addressing me, at which point the kids ran over and told me about the encounter. I expected she would come by later to see the lesson plan I had retrieved from the cabinet, but she never showed up.

Since I had a dental root canal emergency, I asked AP Rodriguez to leave school a half hour early and he wrote it in the log book in the office. After dismissal, everyone headed upstairs to correct the results of test simulations; we clusters had been assigned classroom teachers to help. As I was leaving I ran into Rosemary's Baby in the hall. Though my excuse was legitimate she was livid. Had I asked an administrator for permission? Where was my lesson plan she wanted to see? Her need to infantilize was breathtaking. I was in a rush and as I was walking spoke quickly about Rodriguez's permission, then said about the lesson plan, "Can we do this tomorrow?" Rosemary's Baby sucked her teeth for the second time that day and stormed off.

As I was one of a handful of teachers who had come in during the snow storm the day before, Rosemary's Baby's thank you message was especially uncouth. Evidently Mrs. John L. Strong had left the building, if indeed she had ever been there. In Guido's years, at least, he had been so gracious to the ones who showed up, he would order us pizza for lunch, then wait a couple days for a bout of rudeness. In fact, how much had the snow storm of the previous day, when Rosemary's Baby's virtual hysteria broadcast her inability to deal, to do with the blitz she waged the next day? This was textbook over-compensation; Kim Jong Il caught with his pants down (or without his ladies' sunglasses) went on rampages as well.

The next day, Rosemary's Baby never stopped by the art room to see the lesson plan, so I figured she had found sanity, or maybe gotten laid, and let it go. But then I got a call from the office: I was to come and sign a letter—I would be having a meeting regarding my missing lesson plan from the previous Thursday. Since even the spring before, the omens pointing to it had been too plentiful: now it was clear, the school was to be the Stygian minefield it had been under Principal Dearest. Nothing had changed, except as somebody noted, "This is just a new kind of crazy."

In the subsequent meeting, a senseless squandering of time and energy, Rosemary's Baby had concocted an elaborate prevarication to justify calling me on the carpet, the most absurd being her insistence that I was not teaching anything. I countered that I was modeling and developing their motor skills through the use of scissors. As I sat across from her while her pathetic emotional issues, clothed as words of criticism, paraded in front of me, I had to marvel once again at the cockeyed nonsense that passed for management and worse, leadership. This desperate little creature, whose ridiculous effect was rendered more so by the fact that her feet did not touch the floor, was my boss.

At her whim she could make my existence a living hell, choosing to express her cruelty in a slow burn of injustice or ramped up in an all-cylinders-firing blast to the apocalyptic *denouement* of termination. My co-op maintenance, my kid's college, my welfare in old age—were all vulnerable to the caprice of this grandiose speck of consciousness. Merely by virtue of a crony at the DOE and the possession of an easily obtainable administrator's license, this smidgen was my "superior." In fact, there was no substantiation for that rank, nor for a term which declared she was better than I. In what way did she surpass me or any of the teachers? Admittedly, as a power-starved douche bag, she beat us hands-down.

I left Rosemary's Baby's office glad to be done with it, but it appeared I was not. The meeting turned out to be a less-than-amusing *amuse-bouche* for a letter she had spent a great deal of time writing, served the next day. The letter was not only titled "Informal Observation," said observation was rated "Unsatisfactory." Nothing had hinted that our encounter had been anything more than a casual meeting, so I now read with interest what was to take up residence in the airport novel that had become my file. Rosemary's Baby detailed her ambush of my kindergarten class, noting the children using "sharp" scissors, the absence of crayons on the tables (a meaningless observation, we did not need them that day), and the fact that my lesson was missing. Later, she continued, she had seen a fourth grade class "cutting and coloring hearts," even though they had been making a collage without coloring materials, and in truth she had only witnessed the clean up.

Then, bringing up something which evidently irked her but had nothing to do with my teaching, Rosemary's Baby mentioned that I had gone to the dentist instead of going to my assigned test-scoring that day. She also noted that I had never brought her my lesson plan though I had promised to. In closing, Rosemary's Baby wrote, "While I came into your classroom to observe a lesson, I did not observe anything because you did not teach during the time I was in the classroom." But what was stooping over a child, while guiding his hand with a scissors, instructing him on how to use the new tool, if not teaching? Not only instructing, but doing it actively in the most in-your-face way. The charge was downright obscene.

I was taken back to my first year when I had been teaching SFA, yet Cruella accused me of applying makeup. At least Bill Murray experienced some contentment in *Groundhog Day*—this existential loop I was marooned in was a dimensional downer. Anyway, obviously the trifling vacuity and malevolent dishonesty of her screed was an attempt to rationalize her power-lust, so at least I hoped its placement in my file engendered a shudder of pleasure. I pictured Rosemary's Baby in her office, laying back rapturously, savoring the sadism: *The Ecstacy of Saint Rosemary's Baby*. Bernini himself would have found marble exactly the medium for her frosty intransigence.

When I was called to sign the letter, proof that I knew it was going into my file, per the union contract I was allowed to attach a rebuttal. Considering what I had discovered in Rosemary's Baby's personality, I declined: I was loathe to provoke a pogrom. I was in my ninth year and a forced march out of education was not on my itinerary, at least for now. Instead, I gave my refutation to the union rep, whom I discovered had been deluged with similar cases from other teachers.

Shortly after this travesty of a mockery of a sham (thank you, Woody), Pallas spoke of a hair-raising face-to-face she had had with the principal. Rosemary's Baby had declared, "If I go down, I'm taking you with me." By this time several of us had experienced Rosemary's Baby's fascist intensity when she felt out of control, but this was chilling: you had to marvel at the cold-bloodedness of it. After all, not only did Pallas's family rely on her salary and health insurance, one of her two small children was actually in our kindergarten. Rosemary's Baby had a son the same age yet did not shrink from crucifying another mother. By now Pallas was showing the strain of the torment, visibly wasting away from the stress of the principal's ruthless campaign against her. She soldiered on in her special ed Dickensian asylum, trying to teach amid the grab-bag of issues that shrieked and clawed their way through the day. Meanwhile, the administration charged with supporting her did nothing of the kind.

Bloomberg had been trying to get a law passed against LIFO— Last In, First Out union rules that protected seniority, using the arm-twisting of budget cuts and thousands of imminent teacher lay-offs as a blackmailing ploy. Even though I had never completely agreed with the seniority rules, since I noticed the younger teachers were often as good or better than the veterans, I could not condone the mayor's embrace of tactics more befitting Tony Soprano. Fortunately by June, between money Bloomberg found in an obscure city fund and money-saving concessions pitched in by the UFT, one of which was not to replace the twenty-six hundred retiring or resigning teachers in June, the teachers lay-offs were averted.

William visited me in the art room, when I had it, during lunch. Now his mother had decided to move to Florida; they were to leave on the bus the next week. There was no time to have him over to my apartment one last time so I put together a package of activities for the trip and a letter to his mother with all my contact info in it. I wanted to give him more money but I felt it unwise, so I enclosed just a $20 bill in an envelope that said "For William's Savings

Account" asking his mother to open one. The money may simply have ended up paying for the family's Slurpees at a truck stop, who knows: despite my email address and everything else, I never heard from William again. He was always losing everything anyway, and I could not be sure that the handicapped mother, moving an infant, toddler, William and the boyfriend on a Greyhound bus,-would be able to keep track of it.

One thing he better not lose is my parting advice. As I hugged him goodbye, I just kept saying, "Go to college...make sure you go to college!" over and over, trying to seer it mantra-like into his brain, deep enough so it would never be forgotten. Some day I hope to get a phone call from the homeless, Yu-Gi-Oh card-collecting kid who pointed at the eighty thousand dollar statue in an antiques store window, cackling delightedly, "Look, it's Shiva!"

The teacher-bashing frenzy had been drawing increasing criticism from those who comprehended academic advancement to be a more convoluted issue than merely firing teachers could resolve. Finally the cavalry was coming, though its voice in the media was still being drowned out by the pervasive, simplistic views of the one-celled organisms. At least discerning people were finally shifting the onus off of teachers and considering the behavior of parents for their children's dismal achievement. Given parents are a child's first teacher, as well as the one they spend the most time with, it would not be out of line to judge their involvement in the child's education; attendance, lateness, homework and respect, all in their purview, affect academic performance.

After all, high-performing students at good schools come from homes with parents involved in their children's education, whether reading to them as toddlers, enforcing homework or participating in the PTA.[18] Since legislating teaching had not produced significant results, maybe legislating parenting could work. In various states, laws were being proposed to require parent involvement and criminalize "educational neglect," such as nonattendance.[19] One idea even recommended grading parents on involvement, then putting that mark on a child's report card.

But our hallelujah moment was not to be. Since parents could be called "failing" but not fired like teachers, in the end there could be no real accountability. Some comfort could be taken in the few laws that had made it on the books like fining parents for truancy (Alaska), and charging them with a misdemeanor for a child's excessive absences, or mandating parenting classes for those with a child in a gang (California). For years I had dreamed of laws forcing parents to come and babysit their misbehaving children in school; making welfare payments contingent upon adult education and children's school attendance would also be beneficial.

In March, I was formally observed by Moore, whose sudden interest in completing my observation, though it was a yearly occurrence, struck me as connected with my recent infelicitous exchange with Rosemary's Baby. It concerned my unit on Egyptian art, for which I had been lugging around an inflatable mummy I had gotten at the Metropolitan Museum gift shop, defending it from frequent assaults from boys who found it a ptempting ptolemaic punching bag. Like all my yearly formal observations it went well; without them I would not have gotten my satisfactory yearly ratings. A few other teachers, though, were not passing them and had to do their observations over, mostly teachers on the administration's hit list. At the same time, the age-old situation of favoritism persisted— a couple teachers never once made the principal's radar, succeeding in doing, or appearing to be doing, just enough.

In April, after several elitist gaffes and public appearances in which she trembled like a deer in the headlights, Chancellor Cathy Black resigned after a mere ninety-five days "on the job." Afterward, she admitted she was woefully ill-prepared to lead the largest school system in the nation. Vilified for months as unqualified and incompetent, the ever-insensitive Black moaned the worse part of the experience was the unflattering photos of her in the media; the pathetic TMI somehow seemed an apt nail in her Park Avenue coffin. Dennis Walcott, a deputy chancellor with, amazingly, some teaching experience, was named chancellor.

Embarrassments to Bloomberg and the DOE continued for the next three months. In a no-show job ring scam, a consultant was indicted for stealing almost four million dollars from the DOE. Then a DOE honcho in the financial operations division resigned after she was busted for corruption. She had secured millions in city contracts for her lover, as well as tipped him off to fraud investigations. By the time the scam was discovered, the boyfriend had received almost one hundred million dollars, primarily to service the DOE computer system, charging exorbitant rates.

Another investigation revealed the DOE's former chief financial officer (salary just under two hundred thousand dollars) and several cronies he had brought on, at one hundred dollars per hour—all former employees of Bear Stearns hired just when that company went under in October 2008—were not engaged in DOE business, but instead planning their next securities company! Eleven months later, the CFO left when the cloud of scandal began to descend, he and his band of "consultants" transitioning seamlessly to the securities company they had set up on the taxpayer's dime. By early June, indictments came in against corporate and city employees for fraud in the CityTime computer system scandal. Twelve years long, eleven times the original estimate and a billion dollars in cost over-runs, the project installed a computerized time-keeping and payroll system for city employees. While these expensive scandals were making news, among other massive budget cuts, the city laid off a thousand workers.[20] And it goes without saying, we did not have enough money for afterschool.

By early spring, complaints of Rosemary's Baby's nastiness had crescendoed and the union rep, Pereira, sent out emails noting issues teachers had been bringing to her all year. Many of us agreed we should stop this one in her tracks before she became another Principal Dearest. An afterschool meeting was called, led by an expert from the district union office, to discuss actions we might take. Everyone was interested to see who had the balls to come, as Rosemary's Baby's spies, though unidentified, were certain. A small crowd of brave teachers showed up, and the union guy, who had been involved in actions against principals for many years, addressed us. He gave a rousing speech; in view of our demoralization his words hit the mark. When he got to discussing Rosemary's Baby's tyrannical and disrespectful behavior, a point he made really resonated with us: speaking as a teacher he declared, "When you come after me, you're coming after my family (pushing up his sleeves and taking a meaningful pause)—it's on." This was so true.

As the weeks passed and Rosemary's Baby's behavior continued unabated, our union rep brought up the teacher's issues to the principal. Rosemary's Baby responded innocently that no teachers ever complained to her (nobody was dumb enough to provoke her ire). The *coup de grace* came in June. Miller Time after a grueling year of test prep and tests, the traditionally festive, most relaxed last month of school was usually devoted to field trips and less-onerous teaching/learning. Since we still did not have air conditioning, this slower pace was due as much to the looming vacation as to the sweltering classrooms, which discouraged energetic output in favor of instruction delivered in Tai Chi mode.

In the past principals had been as played as everyone else and throttled back along with the rest of us. However, incredibly, Rosemary's Baby seemed to have sucked in a second wind and went about tormenting the staff with renewed vigor. Gratuitous initiatives, diminishing at any time but now, at the end of the year, blatantly perverse, bombarded the classroom teachers. The hated bulletin boards, never, for obvious reasons, required to be renewed the last month of school, were suddenly mandated, though they would only be up for a couple weeks, and as ever, nobody would look at them, except for nitpicking administrators who orgasmed when a cause to criticize arose.

An "Environmental Walk Through," the similarly absurd ritual of robotic petty functionaries with clipboards pouncing on the classroom teachers, was announced, just to remind everyone who's boss. It reminded us of how for teachers the "aha moment" we longed for was the split second of a student's realization; for administrators the "aha!" was the voiced delight at incriminating teachers for some puny, superficial mistake.

As I pointed out at the next union meeting, there was not any justification for these unprecedented late-year directives, Rosemary's Baby was imposing them capriciously, just because she could.

Moreover, if Rosemary's Baby was this emboldened her first year in our school, one could only imagine the horrors awaiting us the next year, once she hit her stride. Everyone remembered our mistake in letting Principal Dearest impugn with impunity, and in this biggest gathering of teachers to date, many had responded because they had been abused in some way. Others came because they were no fools: with a principal like this, they knew they could be next. The union guy spoke to us again, this time outlining a tiered set of actions.

First, we would all wear black in solidarity on the upcoming Chancellor's Day, a day every June when the kids stayed home while teachers had professional development. We would band with the parents, who according to the head and only member of the PA, had their own beefs with the principal, through informal breakfasts in the morning before school started. The culminating event would be a protest outside of school by parents and teachers, apparently an occurrence at Rosemary's Baby's prior school, the one that had kicked her out. Many of the teachers who attended the meeting spoke out, including a well-known brown-noser assumed to be an informer.

On the specified day, word had spread and most of the teachers were wearing a black tee shirt. We were basking in our unity until we saw that Rosemary's Baby and her minion, the hated coach Gonzalez, were wearing black tee shirts, too. As Rosemary's Baby addressed all of us with studied indifference at a school breakfast, her clothes mocking our attempt at solidarity, we could hardly believe her gall. Later that week, out of nowhere, she started breakfasts for parents, insidiously usurping our idea for that as well, continuing to dilute our subversive impact. Then out of the blue, the hated Environmental Walk Through was cancelled. Clearly an informer had been at the union meeting a few days before: the most likely rat, the unctious one who, as a weasel all the way back to Guido's time, might as well be a rodent, too.

The union rep Pereira called another meeting, though it was last-minute as well as poorly publicized. She asked if anyone would join her in protesting outside the school, if it came to it. Besides the two most harassed teachers, I was the only one to volunteer, and vocally. By now, though my loud enthusiasm for a coup against Rosemary's

Baby was surely getting back to her, I had reached critical mass repugnance with the decade of invidious principals she embodied. Yet because Pereira had begun the offensive late in the year instead of months before, our *Norma Rae* moment was not to be, there was not time.

During the year Pallas had incurred an incredible fourteen "U"s for formal and informal lesson observations from Moore. Considering the rest of us had been given, at most, only two of these observations, this was a testament to the ferocity of the administration's harassment of her. Three teachers received their expected, rigged "U" ratings while the rest of us got our "S" for "Satisfactory."

Thwarted in his attempts to end LIFO seniority rules, now Bloomberg was on a tear in the media, blasting the average ninety percent rate of teachers getting tenured after three years. The DOE ordered principals to change tenure recommendations to deferrals, such that the 2011 award of tenures had suddenly dropped to fifty-eight percent, a statistic Bloomberg triumphantly touted, even though the number had been contrived through his interference. In the same way principals were commanded to arbitrarily decrease the granting of tenure, we had the distinct impression they were secretly pressured to get rid of teachers, if simply to send an intimidating signal to the rest. If test scores and graduation rates could not validate education reform, at least a pile of teachers' scalps, justified or not, might convey some kind of constructive change.

Indeed, you could understand Bloomberg's increasing desperation: the mayor's record, the Cathy Black debacle and the DOE scandals had certainly influenced public opinion, as illustrated by a June poll indicating Bloomberg's plummeting popularity when it came to education. By wide margins voters disapproved of his handling of the schools, sixty-four to twenty-five percent. Parents were even more negative, blasting his management of the schools, seventy-eight to twenty percent. All told, the "Education Mayor's" control of the schools was seen as a failure by a ratio of fifty-seven to twenty-three percent.[21]

I had made it through another hard year, with the added novelty of a new principal—regrettably on an old mission. Speaking of which, Principal Dearest's school mission statement was still in play: "Through equity, respect and empowerment we will create a community of learners both big and small," with the annoying, mawkish school slogan from Guido's time prominent at the bottom, Together Everyone Achieves More (TEAM—anvil clang). Since so many of us had, on the contrary, been dissed: disrespected and disempowered, while notably excluded from Rosemary's Baby's "equitable" TEAM, the palliative platitude was the same insulting window dressing we had come to expect. As if these posted maxims were not creepy enough, we were aurally subjected to the same gooey bathos whenever Rosemary's Baby referred to us as "Our School Family."

That summer, the year-long investigation of Michelle Rhee's prior term as chancellor in the Washington, D.C. system (she had successfully headed off investigations while she was there) found rampant test cheating through a high rate of erasures, plus dubious increases in performance at forty-one schools (by early 2013 it would come out Rhee had hired a famous defense attorney specializing in corruption and fraud).[22] Moreover, Rhee's decimation of half the teaching force had cost the D.C. schools millions of dollars in teacher training and litigation; now with the new teachers, test scores had either decreased or were flat, whether due to the change in staff or the inflated, cheated data of prior years.

As in Atlanta, where erasures at forty-four schools prompted a similar inquiry, discovering no less than one hundred seventy-eight teachers and administrators to be guilty of cheating to raise test scores (resulting in the indictment in March 2013 of thirty-five officials, including the lavishly test score-bonused superintendent), Rhee had depended on a culture of fear in the drive for data. The Atlanta superintendent had threatened teachers with firing if test scores did not go up, while as chancellor Rhee had enthused, "We want educators to feel the pressure."[23] With these cheating scandals getting nationwide coverage, now both tyrants had been served their just desserts: a nice plate of tiramigiu.[24]

11

When September came we shuffled back into school with the lissome gait of a chain gang; regardless of the time off, the job was just too arduous. This was to be a year less momentous for me personally than the millions of teachers as a whole. Because unlike the incremental changes of past years, sweeping transformation, driven from the federal level on down, would further shake the very foundations of the teaching profession. For the classroom teachers in my school it would be an *annus horribilis,* as Rosemary's Baby drove them further into enslavement to her personal agenda.

As I started my tenth year, I reflected on the teaching commonplace that teachers achieve their highest proficiency at five years, then hold that peak performance level for the next five. After ten years, then, for many, but not all, burn-out can set in, and teaching enthusiasm and quality, wane. I could readily believe the ten year construct: if I had felt burned-out years before, in hindsight, I had been comparatively smoldering. Now my roasting ten-year tenure was sending up smoke signals announcing my last lap towards the inevitable finish-ed line, the DOE ash heap. Viewed this way, an inner-city teaching career is actually an isolated interval, the pursuit representing less a profession than a protracted incineration. Despite this new-found discernment, however, once again I gritted my teeth and vainly attempted to ready my psyche and body for the high stress, middling salary, lowered immunity and zero social life that lay in store in the forty school weeks ahead.

A total of six thousand city teachers and support staff had left of their own volition or retired the previous June. Though the exodus of all new teachers, forty percent within their first five years, was less than the pre-recession rate (fifty percent, still applicable to high-needs schools), the training, expertise and stability these teachers brought to their schools had been lost. Among those hired exactly five years ago, over half of ESL and science teachers had left, fifty percent of English teachers, forty-five percent of math teachers and thirty-five percent of elementary and special ed teachers.[1] Considering it takes five years to hit your stride as a teacher, the loss of experience was nothing less than tragic.

The statistics indicated the DOE would do well to change its focus from firing teachers to retaining them. Though Bloomberg asserted merit pay would attract and retain good teachers, there was no evidence that this is true. Indeed, a trial of merit pay in several city schools, as well as in a number of states, had neither improved teacher retention nor student test scores.[2] What research showed keeps good teachers, particularly in high-needs schools, are good working conditions including smaller class sizes, extra time to teach struggling students, encouraging principals and opportunities to creatively adapt curriculum.[3]

With the theft of my backpack the prior spring, I had lost my key to the upstairs closet. Sanchez had lied, saying she did not have the key, but the custodian came to my rescue and I got in, only to find Sanchez had predictably pushed even more of her stuff in there. Unfortunately, now I would have to share the equally jammed art room with Sanchez again, navigating my way through the towers of tchotchkes and gallons of Elmer's glue she used to facilitate the infantile crafts projects she passed off as art curriculum.

The first day of school brought the usual contingent of wailing kindergartners wrenched from equally codependent moms. Like every first day, it was awesome to see the kids again. While we just had more free radicals to show for the summer, the kids had added inches and at least for now, considerable charm. Reconnecting with all of them the first week, newly installed in their next grade classes, was lovely, for them as much as for us. Like every other year, that ambrosial interlude necessarily gave way, bit by bit, till by Thanksgiving many were the same marauding malefactors we had longed to escape from the June before.

Because of the high attrition and fewer teachers from budget cuts, elementary schools started the year with the largest class sizes in decades. The two hundred fifty-six thousand students crammed into about seven thousand over-sized classes was an irksome reminder that the DOE was not honoring the seven hundred fifty million dollar settlement won from the state in 2007 to lower class size.[4] While contractual class size limits for kindergarten are twenty-five with the rest of elementary grades thirty-two, the city had allowed elementary school classes to increase the most, thus putting them at a disadvantage to achieve.

Cleverly keeping the older kids in smaller classes could increase upcoming graduation rates, the imminent ones people would connect with Bloomberg's legacy as mayor. He would be serving his last year in 2013, may as well do all he could to leave a good taste in people's mouths. More recent bad news from his DOE revealed middle school test scores showed barely one in three kids performing at grade level in reading, while just over half were scoring at grade level in math. Lack of proficiency in middle school had been an ongoing problem given the numbers of elementary school graduates entering them who lack even basic skills, among them, our former fifth graders.

For years we had had maddeningly limited, sporadic access to functioning computers, copy machines and printers, since Bloomberg's corporate approach nevertheless did not include professional infrastructure. Now our school librarian, a super-veteran, fed up with the nonsensical directives, retired and was not replaced. The library was supposed to be staffed, then, part-time, but that teacher was used to sub. Since the computers and printer for staff use were in there, they were left to collect viruses and malfunction all year, no librarian to tell the vanished computer teacher, still not replaced, to fix them. The upshot of this was teachers could no longer get any work done or printed on the library computers, while, though they had some books in their classrooms, the kids could never get into the school library to check out books.

Most elementary schools were not replacing their librarians, in fact, since the position was not mandated. Even as the DOE punished schools with low reading scores, it had dollars to give its plethora of highly-paid consultants but none for librarians for those schools; the hypocrisy was dazzling.

In late September NBC's *Education Nation* came back for its second year, accompanied by the *de rigeur* preponderance of reformspeak that had characterized investigations of public education in the past decade. At least there was again a *Teacher Town Hall* in which teachers were given a rare opportunity for input—normally teachers were notably absent from discussions on education, much as they had been barred from participation in local, state and federal agencies making educational policy. Also, the film *American Teacher*, narrated by Matt Damon, had its premiere, a voice for the difficult lives of teachers with second jobs struggling with the challenges of a high-needs school. But the over-all tone had not changed as the rest of the program unfolded, the hysterical cries for teachers' scalps directed at the teachers unions, the go-to doormat on which to wipe the problems of the nation's public schools.

Despite its competitive nature, merit pay for test scores got its typical endorsements from the reformers, ironic given the powers that be were always pushing collaboration. Teachers were amenable, in fact, to working together, even as federal directives required them to compete for bonuses and higher test scores in order to keep their jobs. But how much, in fact, could financial incentives motivate already committed teachers? The good ones got into the profession because they loved kids and wanted to make a difference, characteristics that cannot be bought. Anyway, the premise of paying teachers for increased student test scores, already a suspect measurement of achievement, was an impossible pipe dream: doing so equitably would involve distributing students into classes in a fair way, a proposition undermined by principals who rewarded cronies when assigning students.

In my school we could identify, according to the principal's preferences, which teacher would be given a class unlikely to improve while another perhaps worse teacher could shine with a class of motivated, or simply on-the-cusp-of-moving, kids. The only just way of allocating students would be at random, however it still would not be fair to reward the lucky teachers while penalizing those less fortunate. Indeed, the sole incentive plan which verged on equitable, distributing performance pay among the staff of a school, regardless of who was involved, had been tried in the city without yielding measurable results. The most successful school systems in the world do not use merit pay, anyway: given the myriad variables impacting a student's performance that day, test scores are not deemed sufficient to measure a teacher's input.[5]

Another darling of the education deformers (and no, that was not a typo), the concept of choice as represented by charter schools, was given its expected glowing appraisal. The head cheerleader for them, Harlem Children's Zone (assets, two hundred million dollars) founder Geoffrey Canada (salary, half a million dollars), aggressively declared when his students do not succeed, all the adults get fired. He neglected to mention it was the kids he fired when the low test scores of his first middle school class (at the school since kindergarten) got them booted out, thus upping his "success rate." Indeed, it is the public schools who by law then, have to take the charter's cast-offs, which is just what happened with Canada's rejects.

Also off the table for discussion were charter schools' cherry-picking application process, virtual blockade of under-achieving kids with disabilities and ELLs, and sky-high rate of teacher turnover in the non-unionized pressure mills. Charter supporters also failed to mention how the majority of American kids would attend a public system increasingly starved of funds because of the drain of money to charters, even as charter academic outcomes have often been mediocre, many of them trumped by the results of public schools.[6]

Through the early fall, the older kids studied Van Gogh and copied his "Starry Night" in oil pastel. There was a great deal of complaining over the difficulty of the assignment, nevertheless they came through with stellar pictures. With Candide at my side in my own resource-rich classroom, I would have begun the unit showing a movie about Van Gogh's life on a Smartboard (my part-time room did not have one), subsequently using it to enhance our hands-on project (with quality oil pastels, not the truncated powdery stumps I had horded from years before) with lessons including geography, slide shows of his *oeuvre*, homages (they would love the "Starry Night" in bacon) and the famous song by Don McLean. At a minimum we would take a field trip to the Museum of Modern Art to see the original; in our harsh reality, of course, even that was not possible. Not only were there not funds for the electronic gadgets and decent supplies, there was not even money for a sub to cover my schedule back at school—Bloomberg had spent it on a fraudulent consultant with an inflated invoice. Private schools took their kids on trips to see Van Gogh's work as far away as Amsterdam, yet we could not even conjure a twenty-five minute trip on the subway.

By October the classroom teachers, already reeling from the mountain of paperwork piled on in recent years, were unbelievably deluged with more. Though the teachers only judged about fifty percent of it to be actually useful, the Bloombergian fascination with data, a commodity which after all had made him a billionaire, was just another aspect of the mayor's business model. To procure the data, along with everyone else, the kindergarten teachers were required to perform one-on-one tests of kids while simultaneously managing the other twenty-five plus children. To add to this daunting obligation, teachers were now criticized if they gave the little kids anything absorbing to do like coloring pictures. One had been vilified the year before when Rosemary's Baby had burst in and discovered the dastardly coloring sheets, as opposed to a "rigorous" assignment. But any unsupervised group of small kids is unlikely to behave if given something difficult to do; with something challenging our unruly urchins were especially prone to mutiny. Nobody dared point this out to Rosemary's Baby. As ever, principals were never questioned, except with "How high?" when they commanded teachers to jump.

To compound the outrage, the one-on-one assessments were scheduled to resurface several times during the year, each session requiring weeks to complete while full class instruction time was sacrificed on the altar of the mighty business statistic. With teachers in the grades above, often equally flummoxed in juggling the rest of the class, also testing individually on a regular basis, assessment was increasingly taking the place of instruction. Regular group test simulations for the state tests just increased the inundata. Adding to the absurdity, the DOE's poorly-reasoned, shoot-from-the-hip directives meant that insufficient time was allotted to even interpret the data generated.

This latest ramp-up in assessment was expected to enhance the oppressive directives of recent years regarding "differentiated instruction," the latest trend in educational policy. We were supposed to design instruction for each student according to the results of these ceaseless masses of data, yet another impossible, nay hilarious, demand: tailored teaching à la private tutor. For every lesson in every subject students at grade level would receive specific instruction, while "strugglers," as the slow ones are called, would receive their own added teaching; "enrichment" students, the handful of kids above grade level, would be required to be serviced as well. What's more, within these separate groups, individual kids were to be written their *own* individualized lesson plans. This painstaking differentiated instruction continued even to the realm of homework, the culmination of a preposterous and unavoidably pretentious day of individual catering. Naturally, personal teacher comments were expected on those homework pages that few, if any of the parents would bother to look at. In fact, Rosemary's Baby demanded teachers write regular comments even in the kids' class notebooks.

Another theft of instructional time, a current education darling from the business model, "goals," had to be conferenced, created, individually updated every marking period and supported by attached evidence. Also new, "data talks," in which the teachers discussed the results of the many assessments with the principal, led to "chalk talk," a new prop to literacy in which the lower third of kids grouped to hone their understanding before moving on. Meanwhile the demands of conferencing, frequent evaluative meetings with students in as many as six differentiated reading groups, recorded by jotting notes in the conference log, continued as the practice had for years.

Besides report cards three times a year, parents also received detailed progress reports at intervals, yet another obligation to dispatch.

For the classroom teachers the addition of these recent tasks, on top of an already crushing workload, really accentuated the delusional attitude of the administration. For example, the "chalk talk" not just required teacher preparation and supervision, but notes on yet another conference log. Though some were admirable, all of these ideas were tenable only with the presence of another adult in the class to carry them out; as long as DOE money was directed at consultants and not schools there would be no reprieve. As it was, there just were not enough hours in the day to discharge the ever-soaring demands, much less focus on the area arguably more important than any other: the planning and teaching of lessons, the bedrock of a teacher's DNA.

But it did not stop there: as the year went on almost every week brought new paperwork. Stacks were morphing at warp speed into paper towers, necessitating time-consuming organization into logs for no other reason than the infamous "they" might attack. Rosemary's Baby ordered teachers in the lower grades to take notes on kids in virtually every situation; in all grades teachers were required to jot them for each student, in each taught subject, at least once a week. The demand was farcical: not only impractical because of time, but it ignored the teachers' natural intelligence and observational ability. There was not a single comment a teacher wrote, jotted, logged, or noted—in their slavery to datamania—they had not already filed in their highly capable brains. We all knew our students inside and out; the extra task of recording that insight was a gratuitous waste of time. It was just the latest wretched attempt to *project* competency, the triumph of style over content, and just like the other showy measures of "accountability" to be checked off some clipboard in the sky, destructive on a multitude of levels. Bloomberg's initiative Children First only made sense if you considered they were being measured "first;" in fact, they were "last" when it came to receiving an authentic education.

Not even the posh private schools of Manhattan made these frivolous, laborious adjustments to instruction or demands on teachers' time, yet the mayor blithely dictated them to seventy thousand teachers educating over a million students. Bloomberg generated endless mandates, and with an increasing vehemence proportionate not only to diminishing test scores, but to his time left in office. For the victims of his whims, the results of Bloomberg's dabbling were devastating: added to the recent surge in the micromanagement of instruction, the paperwork vise crushed the very will-to-teach of the teachers—that is, if there were any spirit left after the empty stares of indifference/incomprehension from so many of the kids, lack of empathy from a never-satisfied administration and frankly sadistic demands of the mayor, transparently represented by the DOE. The tyranny of monthly rounds of bulletin boards, the vapid requirement never more resented than now amidst the increased paper-pushing, continued.

To complete the mountain of work meant weeknights with four hours of sleep and weekends devoted to more of the same; much of it was actually redundant. As the work load vaulted the threshold of impossible, Rosemary's Baby slipped a juicy Freudian when she emailed everyone: "Deadlines are to be adhered to. If deadlines are not met you may be *subjected* to a Letter for File." Indeed. The *coup de grace* was, despite their colossal effort, teachers continued to be blamed by the powers that be: the mayor, the government and the media.

Small wonder that by October, two teachers had been hospitalized with heart issues doctors determined were caused by stress, while another two had miscarriages, one of them Pallas, after receiving her first "U" observation of the year, driving up the already-high schoolwide statistics for that tragic occurrence in recent years. One of the hospitalized teachers, a veteran who had been hounded by Principal Dearest, was now getting daily bouts of bullying from Rosemary's Baby's henchman Gonzalez; playing right into their hands she screamed "uncle" and took an early retirement.

The day before school started I had made a pact with another teacher to go to the gym and meditate every day in the upcoming year. We had made the agreement in prior years when, refreshed and optimistic, "normal" even after a summer's vacation, we committed to a mental and physical regimen to fortify us against the tribulations of the next ten months. Once again, despite our noble intentions, we bailed on our plan early on, too depleted to see it through. Only in the summers could we give ourselves the nurturance people with regular jobs took for granted.

We were really feeling the money pinch. Rosemary's Baby illegally excessed one of our guidance counselors, the better-paid one with seniority, replacing her with a part-time rookie who cost her a quarter of what she had paid the other. Since the counselors had already been overwhelmed when there were two full-time, their jobs were now impossible: budget cuts certainly had not cut the number of student fights. Teachers who had retired had not been replaced, while even boxes of pencils were not distributed but opened and divided up, eighteen to a teacher. Schools reported widespread instances of insufficient instructional supplies and texts, burgeoning class sizes, cut programs, reduced support staff and other factors in a quality education. The City Council had stopped giving us the small allotment to be spent on supplies, so now almost all came from our own pockets. Nationally, the majority of public school systems had incurred an equal or worse beating from the recession. In some locales school buses sported bank ads on the sides, while the lower two inches on students' report cards had been sold for ad space.

Meanwhile, many other wealthy countries, regardless of the economic hit they were taking, had either maintained their funding of education or even increased it. Schools and universities were being supported, while many were contributing financial aid to students to surmount the limitations that had crippled their unemployed families. Despite the doomsday scenarios in Greece and Ireland, for example, those countries were investing as much or more in education, since it is obviously the only choice for growth.[7] Here in America, neither federal nor state governments were willing to raise taxes on the rich to provide an education for the generation charged, in fact, with paying the social security costs of the future.

Once again, the perennial focus on the state tests enforced the impression of kids stuffed like Strasbourg geese full of numbers, words and strategies, fattened for slaughter on the altar of educational reform. Since their foie gras of test scores was designed more for phony teacher accountability than actual education, the real sacrifice would be their individual futures as well as our collective national one. Regrettably, as the round of test simulations began, their results only provided Rosemary's Baby justification to turn up the pressure. In the fifth grade class I was placed in for small group test prep at the end of the day, the disastrous scores on the ELA simulation were such that half the class scored a 1 (failing) while only one kid in the class of thirty students got a 3 (proficient, at grade level). A grade of 4, beyond grade level, was equally beyond this entire group.

Though no surprise to me given the constellation of strugglers I was charged with preparing, the stepped-up classroom visits these scores prompted from the administration only served to harry the teacher, already at her wits end. Passing another class that had bombed on the predictor, I overheard a burned-out teacher in a rambling rant to the kids: "I don't care anymore, do whatever you want. I can't make you want to learn. You're not my children—I go home to them every day. I'm gonna finish the year and go home in the summer. You'll be here. That's not my problem." If the principal had heard her she would have gotten a letter in her file since her lament fit the parameters of "verbal abuse." She was simply verbalizing the fed-up exhaustion everyone felt; other teachers were smoldering, too, and it was still early in the year.

As ever, test scores would be a huge component on the school's Progress Report, especially significant this year because last year's pathetic math results had contributed to this year's grade of a "C." The mediocre grade also came from a low score on the school Environment Survey in which we teachers eviscerated Rosemary's Baby, especially for her bad communications skills, giving her an "F." Extra credit was given for having moved special ed students into "inclusion" classes: no wonder Rosemary's Baby had created more of these.

The "Environmental Walk Through," which Rosemary's Baby had threatened the June before now made its inevitable, distasteful appearance. In service to that modish policy term "print-rich environment," a forest of trees gave their lives to the pulpy mass of bulletin boards, charts, "word walls," "data walls," number lines, alphabets, and other righteous scrip of the educational moment, much of it flapping from clothespins on laundry lines strung across the rooms. More evocative of a Neapolitan alley than a classroom, the paradox of the paroxysm of paper was that students still never looked at any of it. Yet the administration circulated complex checklists regarding its sacred construction, partaking in a greedy slurp of teachers' time, energy and dignity, to emphasize the semblance of education over actual learning. If teachers were not on board with the Epcot Center fake educational sets, then they risked a take-down by the clipboard vigilante squad. Yes, the dreaded Letter to File. When Dad gets home you're gonna get it...

Like every other pretense staged in the school, the blanket of paper was conspicuously absent in better-performing public schools downtown, not to mention suburban schools. Wherever true learning was taking place there was no necessity for the distracting flutter of clutter.

Election Day was always a holiday for the kids but teachers had to come in for professional development. As usual I had the option of going to another school for art training, but those sessions were too sophisticated projects I could never replicate, given my students' level, behavior, and the dearth of materials. So I attended the literacy workshops offered to the classroom teachers.

At this point mandated professional development, an ideological pillar of NCLB, was nine years old and a hoary, moss-covered conceit which by historical educational precedent should have by now been exalted and discredited. Instead, the research-backed, expert-touted training was hanging on by its venal institutionalized tentacles, arrayed as ever in its Emperor's New Clothes, unassailable and oh, so lucrative. An entire industry had been parlayed from the notion that teaching elementary school is not only rocket science but a profession morphing at the speed of light, and therefore, in need of constant expert cultivation. Unlike other standard occupations in which education and apprenticeship give way to mastery, we were marooned in a limbo of perpetual preparation.

The actual professional development—usually a dry, repetitive barrage of stale Powerpointed bullets squeezed off by an equally fusty facilitator—provided little improvement to anyone save the salutary salve of a discrete nap for those who could get away with it. The presentation was often sandwiched in between the dreaded, stock professional development lead-in, the "ice breaker," and the equally mechanical conclusion of "breaking out into groups" and finally, "evaluation" of the facilitator—all little more than Professional Development Helper transparently designed to kill time. Whether led by our own well-remunerated school coaches or by extravagantly paid outside contractors (twelve to fifteen hundred dollars per day), all feasting on the increasingly dear taxpayer dime, the malodorous presence of bullshit was unmistakable: usually half or more of the information had already been given at other professional development sessions. On rare occasions, actually beneficial knowledge would be imparted, but usually, just like so many other requirements, the unquestioned, shallow professional development diverted time and energy from relevant pursuits like instructional planning, and money away from badly-needed resources.[8]

Rosemary's Baby's introduction of more inclusion classes was just the prelude to a distinct new trend in reform education. Now kids with severe disabilities, who in the past would have required a self-contained classroom of twelve students, would be placed in large inclusion classes with mainstream students, with two teachers. Though they now received less individual attention, they were still taught curriculum designed around state tests, with a focus on passing commensurate with the pressure on the regular students around them. Yet there was no proof that mixing special ed with general ed students yielded improvement in student achievement, or decreased challenging behavior. Instead, research indicated special ed students working several years below grade level need explicit, intensive instruction, not team teaching or a few sessions a week with a special tutor. Still, going forward starting September 2012, the new approach would be used throughout the system, phasing out the traditional self-contained classes. No matter how emotionally or cognitively disturbed, these disabled kids would no longer get the slower-paced, individual guidance so necessary to their development.[9]

Paraprofessionals, instrumental in one-on-one help plus periodic removal of disruptive behaviors from the special ed classes, would also be diminished, except to help the most extreme cases. Many of the seriously unbalanced ones, previously bussed to District Seventy-Five settings around town designed specifically for them, would stay in our school, merely receiving counseling during lunch or in class a couple times a week.

I pictured Davonte, a fifth grade child who had regular psychotic tantrums where he would overturn shelves, desks and anything else he could move. Even though he was not more than eighty pounds, usually two people had to carry him, head and feet, out of the room, sometimes to a waiting ambulance, since he was a threat to others and himself. Now, profoundly disturbed Davonte would be in the same class with those who, in general, could sit still, their primary transgression being their obnoxious talking. Clearly this wholesale replacement of self-contained special ed classes was not going to benefit the mainstream kids any more than it would Davonte: the fact that he would be behind the rest of the class guaranteed he would be in crisis academically, only aggravating his meltdowns. Moreover, teaching these classes would be a nightmare, like the fifth grade class of this kind I currently dreaded every week. Now, essentially, our Victorian Asylum would be opening franchises around the school. Too bad they would not be drive-thru.

Despite no information backing the claim, these changes to teaching "students with disabilities"—all, coincidentally, tremendous money-saving endeavors—were absurdly fobbed off as benefiting the low performers. Sure, by sharing classes with higher-achievers, special ed kids, who tended to perform at a consistently low level, staying in special ed classes up through high school, might rise to the occasion. But in my own experience, in ten years I had only seen two kids leave special ed, mainstreaming into general ed in fifth or sixth grade after five years in the lower-achieving environment. Yet the rest of the special ed kids were frankly slow, unmotivated or both, and they would drown in a regularly-paced class. To envision them thriving on harder curriculum, with less attention, in bigger classes, was unimaginable.

But I knew reformers were too self-serving to be having a Kumbaya moment over the special ed population. Instead, the feel-good initiative was a cover to save money, public funds that could be spent on...privatized charter schools? Moreover, regular schools would thus be overwhelmed with the impossible task of educating disabled students; with all students further weakened, they would be ripe for the failure, closure and replacement by yes, a privatized charter school.

Apparently the powers that be were not too upbeat about the special ed reform either. By spring, the deputy chancellor who crafted the reform announced her retirement, while two days later the DOE's director of special education quit. Better to leave well before the special ed *Titanic* launched the next fall.

The changes in overseeing the special ed students had entailed administrative adjustments as well. All fall, the school staff who administered services struggled with a new computer system the DOE had installed to streamline documentation and efficiency.[10] Instead, the abstruse, dysfunctional Special Education Student Information System (SESIS) proved so slow and problematic, guidance counselors, speech therapists, social workers and others involved found themselves giving up regular work time with students and parents, lunch and dozens of hours at home performing the redundant, overwhelming task. Though the union had repeatedly brought the problem up with the DOE and tried in vain to get the staff compensated for the extra time, the situation became so untenable the union asked members to keep track of hours worked and file their own grievances with the DOE. Naturally, nobody had the courage to do this since complaining, even justifiably, might result in retribution. We were well-versed in the high maintenance demanded by principals' egos—it was paramount to be seen as a loyal party member. Later, the union sued the DOE and won staff their compensation for five and a half million logged-on hours, a total of thirty-eight million dollars.

When confronted with a child who would be better off with a special ed designation, teachers had customarily relied on their grades, scores and anecdotal records detailing their behavior; then evaluators would weigh in and convene to move the child to the smaller setting. But recently a new system, Response to Intervention (RTI), had been put in place whereby a teacher was now required to intervene, writing detailed individual lessons (when?) and providing one-on-one remediation (when?), in incremental tiers as necessary, to the child at risk.[11] A crowning touch of ludicrous to the paperwork situation, the initiative was doubly resented because teachers knew the first week which child would be better off in special ed—the painstaking tailoring of weeks of personal lessons was a waste of scant time. Moreover, it was insultingly transparent that RTI was a ploy to spend less by keeping children out of expensive small classes; best to wring free resources out of a teacher, while conserving dollars for the profiteers.

As during the year before, the martyrdom of Pallas continued, and she was still required to furnish Moore with a weekly action plan of lessons. She received relentless classroom visits from the AP who, as the principal's nun-shoed version of Luca Brasi, carried out her strong-arming orders, sans Vitalis. Some days Moore perched like a gargoyle in Pallas's asylum for hours at a time, a blatant gambit to collar the well-meaning teacher for some infraction, whether real or invented. Not only did these visits result in several new unfounded "U" rated informal observations that went into Pallas's record, but at one point she was accused of verbal abuse when she yelled at a child. Later the kid was interviewed for the case and denied the event entirely, yet the trumped up fabrication went into the teacher's file anyway as a formal letter.

A week later, I yelled at a fourth grade kid to sit down while Moore was in the room jotting a note in the "support" log. I wondered momentarily whether *I* would be in trouble, then banished the thought: unlike Pallas, I was not, after all, on the hit list. The idea that raising one's voice, officially verbal abuse, was punishable, anyway, was absurd, as there had never been a teacher in the school who *didn't* yell; indeed there was a handful of terrifying Ninja teachers whose bellicose bellows registered as downright grotesque. In a typical occurrence, I had seen a particularly unconscious teacher, with zero emotional intelligence, thunder invective at a child having a fit, one of the sensitive, high-strung kids. This ham-handed approach not only fanned the flames of the boy's tantrum, but the bovine bumpkin had the temerity to deliver a final blast, "You've got *issues!*" even as her outlandish behavior broadcast her own.

New York's 2011 NAEP national assessment test scores had just come out, revealing proficiency rates for fourth graders in reading were a mere thirty-five percent, while in math just thirty-six percent were deemed proficient, a four point drop from two years before. The 2011 state standardized test results showed the scores up by a small percentage, though the achievement gap continued to widen. The city kids did best in math, an indirect accolade to teachers: while the ELA scores reflect the influence of a child's literacy environment, home and school, math skills tend to be the result of school alone. Despite almost a thousand allegations of teachers or administrators cheating to help New York kids pass in the last six years, the standardized testing juggernaut continued to lumber forward, now taking the last innocents out of the equation: the state education department announced upcoming plans for testing *kindergartners.*[12]

Incredibly, still no connection had been made between the lack of readiness for college of four out of five New York high school graduates, and the all-consuming test prep and testing which crowded out a real education. Whether swept forward by the daft suits in education departments or the mega-rich industry it fed, the testing behemoth was still swallowing everything in its path, unchecked. "McGraw-Hill" had become cuss words to students and teachers alike.

Except for a brief visit to look at my lesson plans, Rosemary's Baby left me alone through the first half of the year, only asking me to design a daily attendance board celebrating classes with one hundred percent attendance. These classes had been hitherto listed every afternoon by the soporific tones of the cherished office secretary, Linda, over an endless broadcast message blaring into classrooms and interrupting instruction. The cadence of her Central Casting New Yawk accent, an exaggerated Bowery Boy that would haunt Henry Higgins, did little to elevate the plodding monotone of a recitation which did not so much instill pride in the classes honored, as cue the first graders to insurrection. We clusters taught them last period when they were tired and punchy, and the eye-crossingly boring interruption was all the fed-up, precariously-managed group needed to move into meltdown mode.

One afternoon, while in the middle of a miraculously riveting read-aloud to a bilingual class, Linda's regularly scheduled dirge deftly removed the kids from their absorption. Worse, this time her ritual was followed by a gratuitous medley of lengthy announcements regarding testing for other grades. Unable to continue the story and driven to fidgety madness like the kids on the rug around me, I risked the certain loss of control and for once, expressed the irreverence that always played in the back of my mind, the default soundtrack to my life. Since we were silent during announcements, I broadly pantomimed various hilarious expressions of extreme boredom and irritation. The six-year-olds on the rug, having never seen me so drop my teacherly demeanor, squealed with delight and then, just as predicted, dissolved into mayhem.

The consequent difficulty in getting them back on task made little difference—the announcements had already wreaked havoc on the routine. The refreshing, once-in-a-decade interlude of sustained silliness, as an indulgence of my inner child, could only be fleeting, or I would be doomed to bad behavior every time they would see me again. So I immediately resumed Miss Grundy mode, and the kids soon forgot the kidding around I had found momentarily irresistible. Regrettably, I could not show that side of myself more often.

Now, having received complaints from teachers regarding Linda's daily PA interruptions, Rosemary's Baby asked me to create a new, less invasive mode of acknowledging attendance: a showy attendance bulletin board outside the office.

Parent-teacher conferences took place in November and March. Despite their ridiculously dismal participation in the PA (this year there were two members, a president and vice president), at least one half to two thirds of parents usually showed up to discuss their kids and report cards. Unfortunately for us, these events meant afternoon meetings as well as evening marathons which went until eight o'clock. Not only was the hour late enough to give the impression the next morning that we had never left, but for those of us who did not drive, the journey home in the dark was fraught with trepidation. I had gotten used to these walks in recent years, just hitting my hyper-vigilance switch till I got to the well-lit business street where the train station stood. The most threatening types I encountered were the pimpesque old guys, tipsy fugitives from a blaxploitation movie, swaying to R & B in front of the armored liquor store near the elevated train tracks. With their gray fros and burgundy patent leather shoes, I yelled as I passed, "Yo, the seventies called...they want their Curtis Mayfield back!" They loved it when I said stuff like that to them, and they gave as good as they got.

As some parents rarely cared about their child's grades, let alone their marks in art, music, or gym, we second class citizens in the teacher hierarchy were posted, during the conferences, wherever there was a gap. In previous years I had been assigned to the library, where parents of students with attendance/lateness issues had to come before meeting the child's classroom teacher. One of the red flags of delinquent parenting, low attendance is the bane of poor urban schools, and nothing irritated me more. Any fool could see education was the only sure ticket out of that neighborhood.

Yet as many as one quarter of rural students, and one third of urban students, are chronically absent from school in high-poverty communities. A study showed the obvious: kids with five days or less of absence have double the chance of passing that kids out twenty or more days have. Indeed, the obvious importance of attendance, at all levels, is clear. Research affirms chronic low attendance in kindergarten translates to impeded performance in first grade, while attendance in sixth grade proves to be strongly connected to graduating from high school on time.[13]

So getting just shy of up in their grill, I pointed out to the grandmother, mother's boyfriend, aunt or whoever had made it in, they were sentencing their child to a life of failure. The ones who were consistently late, like kindergartners held back a year just to make up the daily letter and word practice they had missed in the first hour of school, were hardly treated more sympathetically.

"You are crippling your child by not letting them learn what the rest of the kids are learning. Plus you are teaching them it is okay to be late," I said, practically jabbing my finger in their face (I wanted to grab them by the collar and shake them silly, I mean, more silly). "You are training your child to get fired from jobs later!"

I laid it on easy or hard, depending on the situation and what I figured I could get away with. By the end of the year in a fifth grade special ed class, one girl would be absent thirty times, while a boy would be out forty-eight times, missing nearly ten weeks of instruction. Even as I yelled at those kids, it seemed a better idea just to jail their parents.

The attendance board came out well, big bracketing titles with the words, "100% ATTENDANCE" and "KNOWLEDGE IS POWER" as bright yellow thunderbolts, while distinguished classes lettered onto individual thunderbolts were attached to a cluster of dark grey clouds. One of the clouds had a face, truly twee if not for the environment, with a speech bubble at the eye level of the kids, "Come to school every day!" I flagged Rosemary's Baby out in the hall to show her; we discussed how the attendance would be printed out every day, then I would put the honored classes up the next morning.

But the aim of it, to instill the kids with the desire to come to school through acclaiming those who did, was missed, being outside the office in a place the kids didn't usually pass by. Though the board saved the school from Linda's daily proclamatory interruption, it did not reach the kids and the teachers never looked at it. Like so much artifice in the system, it was obviously not a paean to the kids but an elaborate prop to impress the honchos that be: after all, attendance was an important factor in a school's annual report card from the DOE. Now, like the classroom teachers, I too had a meaningless bulletin board, complete with an absurd existential job every day maintaining it. When I mentioned this to classroom teachers they high-fived me. Ultimately, after all these years, I too had been conscripted as a window dresser. Did I just catch a whiff of Rod Serling's cigarette?

Curriculum Night, an opportunity for parents to learn about their children's course of study, did nothing to dispel Rosemary's Baby's dark mood. To get parents to come she offered a twenty-five dollar raffled prize for each grade, most likely the only reason even seven parents showed up. Rosemary's Baby angrily complained the refreshments she had provided had hardly been worth the turnout. As apathetic as the parents were, the school's parent coordinator had not come through, again.

In a position that had been created citywide during Guido's time, the parent coordinator had the job of liaising with the administration and teachers, and was also expected to bring parents into school. With research indicating students in high-performing schools had involved parents, schools had been allotted money for parent events and programs.[14] Unfortunately, our parent coordinator used the excuse of neighborhood lassitude to justify her own transparent lethargy; milking the taxpayers for a salary of fifty thousand dollars, her position garnered the same salary as young teachers with a few years under their belt, without the added inconvenience of higher education or actual work. The malingerer was finally fired, this year, after years of doing as little as possible. Parent coordinators in other schools were busy with activities, newsletters and emails—hopefully the new one would inspire involvement at last.

Back in my first year teaching, I had become very friendly with a kid named Jeremiah in the class I was assigned to for Extended Time, the infamous one in which boys had lobbed text books out the window unbeknownst to three overwhelmed teachers. As the years passed, I saw him every couple weeks on my way to the train, hanging out near his decrepit building or on the main street. He always called out to me in a familiar way, purposely muddling my name one way or another in a jovial, affectionate manner. Now, just before Thanksgiving, not far from his home a corner had been taped off by the police and was swarming with television news vans and reporters. The night before, a young man walking with his little girl had been jumped by an armed guy and his friends. His jacket appeared to be one stolen a few weeks before: the muggers wanted it back. There was a tussle and the gun went off, shooting the child. The gun fell to the ground as everyone turned and ran, the kid's father then shooting the assailant in the back. It was painful to see Jeremiah's name in the paper, arrested as one of the perpetrators.

I had believed all this time Jeremiah had been in school. By now he should have been a sophomore in college. This wholesome scenario was suddenly unlikely, given his situation at the far less collegial Riker's Island. I did not just feel bad for him, but a sense of guilt that I might have, if ever so slightly, impacted him onto a different course. That was because the common occurrence of reconnecting with kids who had graduated, whether on the way to the train, in the supermarket, passing the basketball court or during parent conference days when the kids came to visit, inevitably ended with a pep talk encouraging them to stay on track to higher education.   As my stretch in the neighborhood went on, my former students were adding into the hundreds, and though I could not always recall their name, the faces were indelible.

Gratifyingly, many of the kids from my first years were in college (community, for the most part) already. My conversations with the younger ones in middle and high school were filled with hugs and enthusiasm on both sides, as I had known them longer as a teacher, most for six years. It was fascinating to see them morphing into adults. With the boys, when an unfamiliar bass voice called me, I could at least descry the child's face under the spray of acne and the downy goatee. Often the girls' childhood visage was now so obscured, the name Maybelline jumped to mind before their own. Sometimes a fourteen-year-old sported a mortifying baby bump, or those just a tad older, a baby in their arms. For these a lecture was pointless, though I could not resist a tempered sigh of disappointment and a falsely jocular grimace, followed by advice to stay in school (for you and your baby!). Since I had actually fought the urge to throttle them, I was quite pleased with my restraint.

Anyway, my encounters with Jeremiah were different. Though engaging to a point, he only knew me from a year's worth of acquaintance, and his standoffish manner kept me at arm's length. So the pang of guilt I felt was essentially silly, but nevertheless, I felt it. There were others like him who we would hear of later, in prison for dealing drugs, robberies, gang initiations. But Jeremiah had never actually been difficult, just a wise ass. Since I never saw him again he could well be in jail; rarely did anyone emerge from that brutal environment changed for the better.

Since the kids I had taught my first year were now as old as twenty-two, some had already achieved the doomed potential their behavior predicted. Delvin, a hold-back with braids who had been the ruination of my first year SFA class, had never had a chance to achieve literacy: his drug-addled mother kept taking him to Santo Domingo for months at a time, then bringing him back. Kids who disappeared into the Dominican Republic always came back less educated, just as those emigrating from there, no matter what their age, appeared in our classes knowing absolutely nothing. Though school attendance there was mandatory, there was no money to enforce the law. Delvin, a victim of this careless scholastic approach, ended up dropping out and was last known to be incarcerated for drug dealing.

Another graduate from our school had stolen a car, and in the high-speed car chase with the police that followed, smashed it into an elevated train support. Not only were he and two friends killed, the kid was decapitated.

Trevawn was a kid so troubled it was just a matter of time until his face would be tacked up as "wanted" in the neighborhood post office. Involved in a drug deal gone bad, just a block from school, Trevawn moved upstate to lay low for awhile. Foolishly returning, he resumed dealing drugs and was gunned down by the promised hit in that very same spot.

I hoped that Jeremiah would not end up dead, too.

Meanwhile, the appalling record of deplorable test scores and graduation rates and readiness seemed to be making the "Education Mayor" increasingly belligerent. In a speech, the megalomaniac not only referred to the NYPD as his own army, but declared that in a perfect world he would fire half the city's teachers, paying the rest double salaries to teach double the class size.[15] Not only did

Bloomberg just assume that half of teachers are bad, obviously he was clueless about teaching: a high school double class of eighty students would be an unthinkable nightmare. When asked later about his comments, Bloomberg noted his generation had been educated in classes of forty or more, receiving an education as good as could be gotten today. Hypocritical Bloomberg had not only been elected on a platform of reducing class sizes, but his own daughters had attended the private Spence School with its classes of twelve students.

As the year went on, the frantic Keystone Cops flavor that characterized the administration's frequent disorganization was in full force. Adjustments were made to teacher's schedules, then not corrected on the office's master one, resulting sometimes in dominoed screw-ups. Spontaneous changes were likewise not always recorded nor conveyed to those affected by them. A typical glitch was the time the kindergarten teachers were scheduled for a meeting during their class photo shoots, thus unable to appear in their own group pictures. Weirdly, my picture was taken with the class I had at at that time for art: I would henceforth reside in yearbooks through time as Milagros Calderon, the bilingual kindergarten teacher. Fortunately, Rosemary's Baby recalled the classes to the photographer at another time, so my sentence on a stranger's refrigerator was commuted.

But Rosemary's Baby had her own gaffe to gift: the Monday before report cards were due to the office for the subsequent parent-teacher conference day, Rosemary's Baby abruptly recalled them, declaring she preferred another version. This spur-of-the-moment edict negated the entire weekend teachers had spent marking the old report cards. Too often, a few minutes before dismissal, a harried announcement crackled over the PA system calling for a monitor to race to the office to pick up papers that absolutely, positively had to go home that day. The kids were already packed up, many even lined up to go, so the rushed imperative only succeeded in discombobulating everyone and delaying dismissal, which then angered parents.

We had to marvel at the double standard: had one of us made a far lesser mistake, we would be in deep trouble, yet nobody suffered consequences nor even apologized. Yet, even as its antics broadcast its lack of professionalism, the administration stayed beyond reproach. After all, *we* were the crux of NCLB's accountability frenzy, even as those invested with greater power and financial reward were, unlike the scrutinized teachers, immune to examination. Yes, the school's report card gave teachers a perfunctory nod by according a scant percentage of its value to our review of a principal. Of that portion, however, just a tiny fraction referenced, say, a principal's organizational skills.

We wanted the same scorched earth capability the administration employed with our records, to apply to them: it was high time they were subjected to Letters to File. Moreover, even as Rosemary's Baby was accountable, if inadequately, through our say on the school's report card, the assistant principals inexplicably got off scot free. We had certainly seen less than professional moments from them: they needed to be held responsible for their actions, just as we were.

I continued tutoring at the end of the day in my fifth grade test prep assignment. As ever, the reading comprehension passages were often prosaic, a drudgery unassuaged by the mid-afternoon biorhythmic plunge affecting the entire room. Nothing had changed since my first summer school assignment ten years before: these nascent teenagers read haltingly, wrote incoherently and spelled drunkenly. Punctuation: what, me worry? No need for periods here. Common words were greeted as exotic constructs from outer space. One kid would be reading to me, then make a mistake and be corrected, only to keep reading the same word incorrectly when it was encountered again....and again...and again.

Then, of course, on the days we studied math, they did not know their times tables, still. Every single child required energetic, committed one-on-one teaching, but my group had eight of them. Our time together spurred unspeakable frustration, not from the kids' dysfunction so much as the consummate dysfunction of the overwhelming situation. I was powerless to achieve anything with them in that insufficient window of time, I would have to enter their lives full-time to put them where their age demanded they be. If I could turn their televisions off, throw their video games away, read to them, read with them, converse, listen to music; take them to plays, good movies, museums and foreign countries...in other words, if only I could parent them.

Not that this chagrin that consumed me was novel—it had happened daily for the previous decade. But now, given the national discussion on education with its pervasive, asinine conclusion that the remedy lay in more testing, firing teachers, and charter schools, I was seeing the problem with greater lucidity. The reformers had it wrong: they should be training their guns at least equally, if not primarily, on the parents. But then again, failing teachers generate profitable situations, not failing parents. Parents could not be fired.

Principals were evaluated annually by the DOE based on a system including the school Progress Report grade; movement toward student achievement goals (test scores) set by the principal and supervisors; the Quality Review (QR—with a good school grade, now given only once every three years); and compliance with district mandates, for example, the provision of services to special ed kids. The QR would count for twenty-two percent of Rosemary's Baby's grade as a principal, every point especially crucial since she was already in the hole with our mediocre Progress Report grade of a "C."

Though a school accountability measure, most of the teachers did not know the Quality Review's result did not impact a school's status like the test scores-based Progress Report or AYP (Adequate Yearly Progress), used by the feds to evaluate and close failing schools; rather, the QR took a closer look at elements of a school, like instructional practice, management and communication. But as the most significant factor in *her own* evaluation Rosemary's Baby could personally control, the QR provided an opportunity, on the shoulders of the teachers, to elevate herself.

With the announcement that the Quality Review would be given in May, thus commenced our Great Leap Forward as Rosemary's Baby forced the agenda of the entire school in service to these looming two days. Even as she told one of them not to concern themselves about the QR saying, "It's my worry, not yours,"

LAUREL M. STURT

Rosemary Baby's shamelessly enslaved the classroom teachers to her effort to save her own skin. Every nitpicking directive she issued, and they were relentless, served, either blatantly or surreptitiously, the purpose of scoring high on this ultimate Bloombergian assessment.

Rosemary's Baby's obsession was no more than a terrified lunge at expanding and perpetuating her power, such that a circular behavioral axiom was beginning to emerge: Rosemary's Baby tormented the teachers to pass the Quality Review so she could keep her job and torment the teachers to pass the Quality Review so she could keep her job...*ad nauseum*. The kids had been guinea pigs to educational reform for the past decade; by the same token we teachers were hamsters, never more than now, with our wheels a blur of frantic activity.

The frenzy began with a "Mock Quality Review," however it was hardly a true trial run, given it was administered by crony principals from Rosemary's Baby's network of schools. Rosemary's Baby mostly used the occasion to bolster her ongoing scheme: their sole group visit to one specific classroom, instead of the many they would ordinarily look in on, was Pallas's, of course, where they uniformly found no indication of learning. Clearly, prior to the tour of the school Rosemary's Baby had told them there was a teacher she wanted to terminate, so she unleashed the Furies upon Pallas.

Unfortunately there was not, in fact, evidence of learning for two of Pallas's special ed students, though their blank notebooks did not testify so much to the dearth of teaching as to their lack of motivation. Given the absence of parental support and discipline which characterized the home life of some kids, there was, in fact, no way we could make some students do anything.

A kid a few years before in a fifth grade special ed class copied words from the board without knowing the alphabet sounds, let alone being able to read, even bragging that the letters were just pictures to him. I discovered the twelve-year-old had avoided learning to read for the previous six years because, as he gloated to my stricken face, his mother "didn't care." Though that struck me as big time "educational neglect," the parent was never held accountable and the child "graduated" to middle school; his teacher had not been able to force the kid to learn, nor the parent, to parent. Neither the teacher nor Principal Dearest had addressed the situation. The current data system would probably red-flag the student/parent now, though that still would not necessarily mean any consequences would follow—there aren't any.

In Pallas's class, nevertheless, the lack of evidence of the two students learning was used against her: she got another bad notice put in her file over that "impromptu" visit. Pallas was now offered participation in a Peer Intervention Program (PIP) in which an "expert" is sent from the DOE to watch the teacher, then reports back their recommendations. A refusal to take part in this process, Rosemary's Baby insisted, would speed termination and even a court case to seek revocation of Pallas's state teaching license, if the principal were to seek that.

Rosemary's Baby's neurotic compulsion to drive the hapless teacher out had reached fanatical dimensions: it had become her own personal *jihad*, pure and simple. It was bad enough to fire a teacher from a school, and the resulting expulsion from the system, even worse. But the gratuitous and cruel step of taking her license would strip Pallas of a career. A fourteen-year veteran with three years elsewhere in the system, as a teacher in our school alone she had received eleven consecutive ratings of "Satisfactory." If she were so incompetent, why hadn't it been caught in any of those years? Even Principal Dearest, for all of her harassment, had given Pallas an "S" rating every year.

In the meantime, Pallas discovered a website on the Internet of a former teacher advocate indicting the Peer Intervention Program as a sham independent entity: the "expert" was in fact nothing of the kind, simply a mechanism for the city to deep-six teachers.[16] Several blog comments echoed troubling agreement from dismissed teachers who testified to the sinister arrangement between the DOE and the PIP evaluators. Pallas, pressured to make a decision within ten days regarding the PIP, arrived at school the tenth day in nervous-breakdown mode; the melodrama of a year's conflict with Rosemary's Baby reached Douglas Sirk magnitude when Pallas had an anxiety attack, collapsed and was whisked away in an ambulance. Tests conducted at the hospital indicated, what else, high levels of stress.

Pallas returned to school a couple days later to agree to the PIP. Despite the condemnations of the blog, her lawyer had advised that she appear cooperative: if the case went to state court that effort at cooperation could help her keep her license. Later, the expert turned out to indeed work for the DOE, subsequently towing the company line in her boilerplate negative evaluation of Pallas.

As a beloved school aide of fifteen years, on moving away, pronounced, "Satan is in the building." Though, besides Pallas, only a few staff members had attracted Rosemary's Baby's perverse stalking, nobody was free from her harsh, micromanaging scrutiny. With her sadistic noodgery, Rosemary's Baby was equal parts Simon Legree and stock Jewish Mother on steroids. She had been getting ideas from her sons' school in the suburbs and was intent on carrying them out at our school, notwithstanding the vast differences between the population we taught and that of the upscale suburbs. But Rosemary's Baby's dominant obsession, the drive to score points on the Quality Review, remained at the forefront, in a bid to wring ever more out of teachers who had nothing left to give.

Around this time, DOE officials presented impressive statistics indicating rising high school graduation rates as well as college enrollment during Bloomberg's reign, notwithstanding the recent report from the City Universities of New York (CUNY) that eighty percent of city students who enter the city's community college system needed remediation in basic skills.[17] The head of the UFT noted Bloomberg had shifted from "social promotion" to "social graduation." In fact, rising city graduation rates—while the percentage of college students requiring remediation remained virtually flat—had tipped off the state education commissioner the pressure was on to graduate students. High schools relied on "credit recovery," whereby students who failed a class simply completed some minimal work instead of retaking the failed class, an increasing practice which had prompted an inquiry by the state the year before. Erasures evidenced widespread "scrubbing," in which high school teachers generously rescored just-below-passing Regents exams of kids in their own schools, to raise graduation stats.[18] Despite his stagecraft, Bloomberg's phony triumph was busted once the incompetents proved unequipped to handle even the minimal requirements of community college.

Two French-speaking, eight-year-old girls from the Ivory Coast arrived in school and were placed in the second grade; they apparently had not had any prior education. I was redeemed from my onerous fifth grade test prep to teach the girls English at the end of the day. They were a gift, cute and effervescent, instant Americans by way of their little Jonas Brothers and *Dora the Explorer* backpacks.

Encouragingly, Obama gave kudos to teachers in his State of the Union speech, then subsequently announced a new initiative: "Teachers matter, so instead of bashing them, or defending the status quo, let's offer schools a deal."[19] But the five billion dollar competitive grant program was, much like Race to the Top, comprised of many stock reform ideas. The stand-out breakthroughs were the push to put teaching on a par with other professions by making teacher education programs more rigorous and selective, while career ladders and autonomy for teachers would be established in exchange for greater responsibility. Since teachers in urban schools agree they were not adequately prepared for the job, as I felt, the better teacher preparation outlined was significant. Sadly, Obama's exhortation that educators should teach with "creativity and passion...to stop teaching to the test..." was a flippantly hypocritical platitude. When forced test prep, testing, mandated instruction and data collection took up so much classroom time, those inspirational words rang hollow.

The controversy over teachers' evaluations, an ongoing wrangle for the past couple years, was now in the news every day. Two years before, RTTT federal money had been awarded to states based on conditions, including a new evaluation system be put in place. Up to now annual observations, one formal and the other informal, plus attendance stats, were the criteria for our evaluation. Now the education reformers endorsed a ludicrous proposition which included annual multiple observations by administration, plus as much as half of the evaluation be determined by test scores.

This was impossibly unfair. Despite the lamentably misguided premise that a child's growth could necessarily be measured with scores, results moreover believed to prove a teacher's effectiveness, a teacher could not be blamed, with any degree of justice, for the performance of so many maladjusted children: kids born prematurely, with fetal-alcohol syndrome, or addicted to crack; kids mesmerized by electronic babysitters blasting cartoons or video games, who never did their homework, not to mention read books for pleasure; kids with uneducated, impoverished parents, neglectful from depression, stress or the impossibility of being present when working three minimum wage jobs; kids who moved several times a year, or went back and forth between relatives and foster families; kids living with single mothers, the passel of siblings all with the different last names of disappeared dads; kids emotionally, sexually, physically abused, brought up around alcoholism, drug abuse, domestic abuse; kids who could never feel safe, living in a neighborhood where violence was the norm, muggings and shootings weekly occurrences.

The number of potential negative variables affecting test scores was simply staggering, even incalculable; parking these students' performance at a teacher's door was not only unjust, it was just plain stupid. The reform movement had made teachers the bullseye in its compulsion to shoot a silver bullet at a tortuous target. The only variable in the parent/teacher/child equation reformers had any power to control, teachers could nevertheless provide only cathartic—albeit impotent—target practice.

Like others who taught subjects outside of the classroom, it was unclear how, going forward, I would be evaluated. Though tests were purportedly being designed for our subjects, specifically to glean scores with which to evaluate us, it would take a unified curriculum for all these areas to be tested. Though years before I had been given benchmarks to hit by second and fifth grades, I had created my own curriculum to address those. Given the preponderance of behaviors, the lack of an art room for the greater part of that time, plus the dearth of resources—this year I had gotten eighteen number two pencils, that was the extent of my supplies for six hundred fifty kids—I had been stymied with obstacles in meeting all of the benchmarks.

I could not regularly teach painting not only because of the lack of materials, but the limited time for an activity and its cleanup in a classroom I visited; then there was the problem drying the work in that same crowded classroom. I faced incalculable logistic and supply problems teaching a subject starved of funding, whether from the DOE or the current principal's decisions on spending; even in past economic boom times, the generous arts funding had been discretionary. Limitations sprang not only from the personal expense of the materials, but the fact that some lessons necessitated another adult assisting, the case when teaching printmaking. Granted my dream, my own, permanent room with a sink, a Smartboard and the thousands of dollars of art materials the DOE's art program had listed several years before as "basic," which I had never received, I could accomplish so much more. It seemed to me, if I were to be evaluated as a professional than I should first be treated and resourced as one, otherwise the evaluation initiative would just be more empty posturing.

Anyway, the notion of assessing hands-on art skills in a state test conjured impossibly complicated, chaotic scenarios involving at the very least, multiple staff. In fact, the recent push to evaluate teachers would require a plethora of ancillary personnel dedicated just to the evaluative process. The expense would not be limited to the expanding purview of testing—now teachers would be subjected to far more yearly observations, an impossibility given the already harried state of school administrators. Moreover, the craze for evaluation had the uncomedic timing of arriving at a moment when school districts lacked the money to implement the changes. Federal RTTT funds would dry up, then what? If history offered any wisdom, just as my cynical professors in graduate school affirmed, the program would ultimately be abandoned. In the meantime, at least the cast of thousands of parasites: curriculum experts; trainers; evaluators; and test designers, marketers, facilitators and graders, would ride the doomed cash cow of educational reform till its legs gave out. In that sense, the evaluation initiative was at least au courant as a jobs creator.

Finland and other countries judged high on the education scale spent neither money nor time on evaluating teachers.[20] Over years of teacher education, the best and most committed teachers had been efficiently culled, and once in the profession the well-paid and respected professionals didn't need any gratuitous hectoring. Resources were plugged instead into school materials, curriculum, teachers' salaries, diminishing class sizes, afterschool programs, tutoring and all the other supports known to sustain good academic outcomes.

American education reformers lacked such perspicacity, fixating on raising test scores and punishing teachers as the answer to our pathetic academic rankings in the world. The goal seemed to be to castrate the teachers union, destroy the teachers, then reap the profits of privatizing the school system, worth over a staggering six hundred billion dollars a year, while sacrificing the nation. We could only cling to the teachers' union, as well as informed parents who know up-close the quality of their children's teachers, as the last bastion of protection from the trampling of the reform stampede.

Though Bloomberg had asserted the union only cares about protecting bad teachers, the union's stance on evaluations had always been that they must be fair, rational, and used to bolster teachers and help them improve rather than be punitive instruments. Evaluations should be positive supports, not a "gotcha" form of intimidation. Those teachers who, given the opportunity to improve, fail to do so, must leave the profession. After all, fourth grade teachers have a reason to care about the competency of third grade teachers, since they inherit their well- or ill-prepared students.

The component the union most objected to was the reliance on test scores, since tests are not designed to evaluate teachers but students, and their capacity to even do that is in doubt. Testing is just one facet of a teacher's duties in a complex job involving many aspects that are difficult to measure empirically. In fact, results from a study by the Gates Foundation of what makes teachers effective showed the two most important components of a great teacher are caring, "social support;" and challenging, "academic press;" neither a quality which can be easily quantified.[21] Gates should have given the millions for that study to teachers directly, since we could have told him that information without any gratuitous "research."

The teacher evaluation negotiations between the DOE and the UFT had heated up to the point where the governor had to intervene; the union wanted to be sure principals could not blithely fire a teacher without justification. Bloomberg argued it was up to the principals to make the call, saying it was their "judgment, that's their job."[22] We knew about the expertise of the principals, alright. When we won an important safeguard, Bloomberg retaliated by announcing the closing of a couple dozen schools, making good on a threat he had been using as blackmail during the negotiations. Many of the schools were small schools created since 2005 with Gates money— so much for that innovation.

Bloomberg channeled his fury at not bending the union to his will, by firing the teachers in the closed schools, then making them reapply, a method of circumventing union seniority rules. But obviously closing schools, over one hundred since he had taken office, was not just destructive to teachers, the greater damage was to the kids and the community. The following summer a judge would rule in favor of the UFT, denying the closures as illegal without community input, reinstating the fired teachers and ticking up Bloomberg's hatred of us yet another notch.

In the meantime, Rosemary's Baby circulated a memo, then a hard copy, of the grading rubric for the Quality Review, so we could sleep with it under our pillow as she did. She sent out another memo highlighting the areas which scored double points, her glaringly mercenary agenda conspicuous in conclusions she had drawn from the Mock Quality Review. For example, when asked about their reading goals, some kids had not been able to answer, so Rosemary's Baby commanded that teachers "continue to discuss individual goals with students so that they become more familiar with their goals and are able to share when asked." The setting of goals was not important so much as the ability of the kids to testify they had made them.

Checking off boxes was what counted, not the actual value of any of it; Rosemary's Baby formed a committee of teachers to meet twice a week, charged with conjuring the illusion which would pass for "quality" with the DOE.

In an email from Rosemary's Baby we had been informed the school had been placed under an NCLB designation, School In Need of Improvement (SINI) due to the fact we did not make Adequate Yearly Progress. Later that designation was expanded to the entire district, which was declared DINI. The number of city schools with the embarrassing status had increased by eight hundred percent since the year before, due to the recent plunge in test scores. When we had learned the tests would be more difficult, we could not fail but see the writing on the wall, in our case, even if it was illiterate and riddled with spelling mistakes. At least our SINI status meant government money was coming in for afterschool tutoring (though restricted to the poorest kids) plus professional development, a bonus in a year when budget cuts had axed afterschool programs.

Yet because of Rosemary's Baby's botched administration, countless children were turned away from the tutoring because sign-up protocol was not followed. With typical disregard, form letters written in inscrutable federal education legalese had been rushed home to barely literate parents to decode on their own. Moreover, parents were not told cross-outs of mistakes would disqualify the applicants; given our high population of uneducated and Spanish speaking families, countless forms were turned in that way, only to be denied. Rosemary's Baby's bungling of the application process ended up barring needy kids from valuable and free remediation. Instead of managing the process effectively, she was probably in her office typing up another trivia-filled report for Pallas's file.

At this point, NCLB had been up for renewal for five years, stalled in a recalcitrant Congress despite the belief it needed to be fixed, traversing party lines. In the meantime, the rigid, bullying law that forced states to increase the number of proficient kids every year had become increasing unpopular. Administrators could not handle the insane demands and draconian consequences, while parents and teachers hated the emphasis on test scores and the shame of being connected to a "failing" school. Now Obama announced waivers freeing states from the worst of NCLB's mandates, specifically the absurd 2014 deadline for all American students to reach proficiency in math and reading, a target which no state could meet.[23]

States could now create a flexible yet rigorous methodology for accountability, though this would still require federal approval. The waivers assured that states would continue to focus on closing the achievement gap for struggling impoverished, disabled and ELL students. Rewards and punishments, prized aspects of educational reform trends, were included in the federal requirements. On the surface, the waivers appeared to be a welcome reality-check that one hundred percent proficiency by 2014 was a quixotic fantasy.

In actuality, the so-called "flexible" waivers forced on states Arne Duncan's plan to evaluate teachers primarily through test scores, punish low-performing schools by closing them and axing teachers, and implement national standards, and more tests, in reading and math. Again, the approach relied on extortion: states unable to meet the severe requirements of NCLB by 2014 were being strong-armed into playing by Duncan's rules, victimization cleverly masked as "flexibility." The arrogance behind the authoritarian patronization was breathtaking, all too reminiscent of the top-down educational dick-tation mayoral control had inflicted on many of the nation's cities.

As the year progressed, even as an art teacher I could not escape the sentence of "I Quality Review, therefore I am." Like the classroom teachers, I was expected to bow to the concept du jour of creating and monitoring individual goals with students, though it was not clear how I was to do this with so many. Since "differentiated instruction" was all the rage, I had to address that as well, though I had already been tweaking instruction for different levels for years: the top kids were exhorted to more complexity and detail, while the strugglers were given repeated instruction, conferencing and more time. There were so many of the latter, the gifted ones got short shrift.

No matter the subject, we all mourned the neglect of the higher-performing students in the shuffle. We were so busy repeating instructions and attending to the rampant neediness, the few stars just could not get the attention they deserved. Indeed, the year before we had seen that our level 4's, the highest performing on the state tests, were nevertheless staying at the low end of that level and not progressing. These isolated students had few peers to inspire them upward, and the sticky vibe of the critical mass of lower level kids to pull them down.

Most alarmingly for me and other cluster teachers, Rosemary's Baby was panting hard for the double points the school would earn on the Quality Review if we cohered our lessons to those in literacy and math. Since these were the primary tested subjects, the stats of which were a school's *raison d'etre*, there could never be enough reinforcement, even at the expense of bastardizing other subjects. But though art is not foundational, that does not mean it does not merit its own integrity. After all, almost the entire academic thrust involves the rational left brain; the creative right side deserves more than the cursory attention it has received in recent years.

The value judgement implicit in the sidelining of the arts is a generational bomb ticking off the impending demise of art, books, film, music, dance—indeed all expressions of the spirit. Anyway, right brain activity brings a fresh approach to work again on the left side, ultimately improving the function of that lobe as well. Considering the formidable problems facing the planet, anyway, thinking outside of the box isn't a luxury, but a necessity.

I simply did not see why I had to whore my beloved art lessons to the state tests. For years, the part of the job that sucked the least was my freedom to design my own curriculum, the only constraints, the broad objectives which Project Arts, Bloomberg's arts initiative, mandated. Now I found my creativity strangled while I was forced to obstruct that of the kids. There was no way, for example, we could have done the Van Gogh study we did early in the year: it took too long and would not necessarily coincide with the math and literacy units taking place in the classroom. The kids had created gorgeous versions of the "Starry Night" over a few periods, learning not just about art and technique but developing a patient, determined work ethic. Surely my emphasis on quality, achieved by diligently revisiting a piece, could not but strengthen the kids' approach to other school work. Moreover, I did not just sling lessons in art but served up geography, history and many other aspects of social studies the kids were not otherwise getting. Math and literacy references were always present anyway, as well.

I told Rosemary's Baby I could not reconcile the scheduling of my lessons with grade math and literacy units. The hours of weekly time needed to sync with individual grade and teachers' plans were not there, plus the abrupt switching of gears every period to give each grade a catered lesson with its own specific materials would be impossible. The best way I could observe the directive would be to continue doing something I had already been doing, using math and literacy concepts and terms in my teaching, as they naturally arose.

Since the aim was to enhance the kids' math and ELA test scores, I researched the yearly literacy and math units, extracting more vocabulary and principles I could reiterate in art. Though for now I could get away with a desultory nod to the concept by tweaking existing lessons, down the road I would be forced to get more specific. I guess it was inevitable that at last I would collide with the hateful tests. For years I had escaped their farcical tyranny. Now, just like everything and everybody else in the public school system, I'd become their little bitch, too.

The Teacher Data Reports (TDR) rating more than twelve thousand of the city's teachers for the school year 2008-2009, were statistics ranking ELA and math teachers, grades four through eight, based on their students' test scores. In compiling them, the DOE had ludicrously forced teachers to search for records they had never been asked to maintain, rummaging through school basements, calling former principals and wasting hours with the school secretary reconstructing classes from years before. Because the initiative was experimental, then-Chancellor Klein had assured educators the results would only be available to teachers and principals. Not only were there thousands of mistakes—students missing or listed in the wrong class, teachers in the wrong school, teachers who had been on maternity leave counted as present, teachers ranked on subjects they did not teach—but the untried "value-added" formula, designed to link a student's progress to a specific teacher using a scale of zero to ninety-nine, had spectacularly wide margins of error, as high as fifty-four.

Eccentric scoring added to the lack of credibility, for example, high-achieving students counted against teachers because they did not show improvement. Long since discredited as incompetent, while many, including Bill Gates and Chancellor Dennis Walcott, had noted the error-riddled statistics should not be used to judge teachers, the reports had been discontinued by the DOE.[24] Moreover, their stats were for test scores incurred during the invalidated, dumbed-down state tests prior to 2010.

Despite his written vow to the teachers union to keep the skewed data private, Klein later pushed the media to file a successful Freedom of Information suit. The DOE readily complied, providing the reports instead of fighting the request in court, as the deputy chancellor at the time had promised to do. Eighteen months prior, teachers in LA had already been pilloried when similar flawed rankings had begun to be publicized in the *Los Angeles Times*. One of them had subsequently committed suicide. Arne Duncan had not only approved the public flogging— "What's there to hide?" he asked—but encouraged other cities do the same.[25]

Now, in the last days of February, the Teacher Data Reports were made public in a week-long binge of teacher-bashing headlines, front pages and lengthy articles in the *New York Post* and other right-wing newspapers screaming for teachers' heads.[26] The foolish assumption—that a test a child takes on one day of the school year can quantify the quality of a teacher—had nevertheless become scripture, thanks in no small part to champions of testing all the way up to Obama. What is more, equating test scores with teacher quality constituted an unmitigated diss at the teaching profession itself. Education experts across the nation lambasted the data as preposterously flawed and its release, a destructive sideshow. Indeed, the brouhaha furnished Bloomberg with a welcome distraction from the DOE's battle over teacher evaluations, as well as unpopular bid to close struggling schools.

A public relations disaster for all of us, teachers involved rolled their eyes, then, shrugging their shoulders impotently, sank into further demoralization behind their scarlet letters. If we posted a child's failing grade on the bulletin board we would be accused of corporal punishment, abuse which could end up costing us our job; as teachers we had no such protection. But though the tabloids highlighted the outrage of uninformed parents who thought the data meant something, better-educated parents were not having any of the lynching spree. After all, even the best schools in the city were getting some low rankings, and smart parents saw the idiocy of reducing a teacher's effectiveness to a number.

At least the *New York Times* and most education bloggers made an effort to place the reports in context, echoing Chancellor Walcott's view that no reliable conclusions could be drawn from the data. But his words were just lip service: the DOE had not headed off the devastation treacherous Klein had orchestrated after promising not to. Besides, at a press conference subsequent to the data release, Bloomberg excoriated the teachers union, snarling that the "arrogance of some people" against publicizing the discredited reports was "astounding." "Parents have a right to know every bit of information we can possibly collect about the teacher who is in front of their kids. This is about our kids' lives."[27]

But it seemed to be more about Bloomberg's neurotic compulsion to wreak vengeance on the UFT, and for a short time, his mission was fulfilled: the absence of control over their public degradation proved traumatic for many teachers, adding another gratuitous stress to the already horrific job. You could not help but wonder, what would the attrition rates be like going forward? How much training and expertise would be sacrificed to the whims of a mayor whose sadistic buffeting had reached the point of emotional vivisection?

As it turned out, a majority of New Yorkers were with us, a subsequent poll showing only twenty percent of city respondents trusted the DOE's Teacher Data Reports as a valid measure for gauging teacher effectiveness; just thirteen percent of New Yorkers said the next mayor should retain complete control of the schools; people disapproved sixty-one percent to twenty-six percent of

Bloomberg's handling of the public schools; most believed his control of the public schools has been a failure, by fifty-seven percent to twenty-four percent; and the numbers that were music to our teachers' ears: by sixty-nine percent to twenty-two percent, New York City parents of public school kids trusted the teachers union more than the mayor.[28] At least the civilians were on our side.

Still, even though it was short-lived, the viciousness of the TDR debacle had a profound effect on thousands of city teachers. The revisit of the McCarthy era was the last straw in a decade of them. In a perpetual state of exhaustion, the never-good-enough teachers were at the nadir of morale I had seen in my ten years, which was to say, Death Valley-low. Everyone was playing Lotto religiously, the idea of gutting it out for the pension, at this rate of self-destruction, inconceivable. Numbed staff straggled in at dawn, their souls splintering in a progressive fragmentation of defeat. It was just a matter of time before we would be reduced to pixellations.

Rosemary's Baby launched a new offensive, employing the unguents she relied on as her goons to check teachers' notes in the conference records and new "chalk talk" logs. Adding to the minutiae that already consumed them, teachers were being asked to conference, as confirmed by written notes, with each student for reading, writing, math, science and social studies, in a class of twenty-five students, then, one hundred twenty-five times weekly. With this latest demand in a continuous, merciless squeeze, the school building itself seemed to be in a steady grip of contraction.

In the meantime, without any irony whatsoever, Rosemary's Baby had begun using a new catch phrase on school communications, a saccharin line from a poem: "Where hope grows miracles blossom!" Like other of her messages best endured with an insulin injection, this schmalz graced directives Rosemary's Baby sent out to the staff she had rendered, yes, hopeless. Our despondency was in line with a study detailing the demise of teacher morale: far fewer teachers felt job satisfaction, while the number likely to leave teaching had surged.[29]

We were living in a demoralizing era when teachers could get fired at the drop of a hat, conveying contempt not only for teachers but the families who relied on them. Arne Duncan did not merely champion these initiatives, his silence signaled tacit approval when governors attacked teachers and their collective bargaining rights. Even in New York, in a successful assault on organized labor and middle class families, Democrat Governor Cuomo rammed through a new pension plan for future teachers and other state employees requiring more be paid into the plan, while benefits would be reduced.

Apparently, the powers that be were not paying attention to the attrition statistics: just in the city more than sixty-six thousand teachers had resigned or retired since Bloomberg took control of the schools, the most common single reason for leaving the lack of support from supervisors and the DOE. Unless those underlying working conditions are improved and teachers are respected in the hierarchy, the revolving door will continue to spin. Indeed, nearly one third of teachers hired in the 2008-2009 school year had left even before they were eligible for tenure, a mere three year commitment.[30]

In the last couple years so many more reasons for turnover had been added: the threat of termination with the mayor pressuring principals to fire teachers; a loss of job security from principals unfairly extending probation before tenure, as well as a constant potential for lay-offs; the release of Teacher Data Reports to humiliate teachers; and now new teachers will receive acutely reduced benefits, making even beginning a career in education far less attractive.

According to the Quality Review rubric, if "the tone of the school is not respectful or orderly" that condition incurred the worst grade. Certainly the dictatorial rule and treatment of specific teachers, as well as the often slapdash organization of the administration, met this low-scoring criteria. Now the hypocrisy was really driven home with Respect For All Week, the formal national initiative against bullying. Slogans defining respect confettied the entrance hall: "treating others the way you want to be treated;" "showing kindness and consideration;" and "accepting others for who they are." In fact, on Valentine's Day Rosemary's Baby announced over the PA system, "Not only because it's Valentine's Day...we're people, we're human...we have to love each other every day." Then, after announcing a schoolwide poster contest concerning respect, Rosemary's Baby proceeded to Pallas's room to continue the love, sitting for hours taking negative notes designed to harass and terminate the teacher.

In the meantime, scandals over fraud and incompetence continued to rock City Hall. The city comptroller was launching an inquiry into the mismanaged 911 project begun in 2004 to upgrade the city's emergency response system; the initiative kept getting delayed while costs ballooned, from one billion to now over two billion dollars. Despite his purported interest in transparency, Bloomberg was obstructing the release of a report on that fiasco, while the teachers union was suing him for his two-year refusal to release DOE email correspondence concerning charter schools.

In line with mismanagement in the other city departments, the DOE's negligence was put on trial again when the City Council held hearings on gigantic federal Medicaid funding the DOE missed filing for, reimbursements for many services required by the city's one hundred sixty-eight thousand special needs students. Due to the ineptitude of the DOE, just a fraction of as much as five hundred million dollars that is available per year had been claimed, grossly negligent given the budget cuts we had endured. How many school aides laid off the previous spring could still be working, helping manage the chaos during lunch time and recess? The chairperson of the city council's education committee thrashed the DOE representatives, pointing out that were this a private industry they would be fired. Yet soon after, it was discovered a company with a three-year, forty million dollar contract to provide afterschool tutoring had bilked the city out of eight hundred thousand dollars in sessions that never happened.

Once again the ELA and math simulations of the state tests reared their ugly heads; again the kids did horribly. A fourth grade teacher, one whose class sported the same accessory, a blank stare, everyday, mourned sarcastically, "And it's all my fault!" Indeed, the pressure was pervasive and inescapable. In the kindergarten, a place which used to be a happy combination of creative play and learning, a defeated teacher who had just gotten five new kids while three others had moved away agonized, "Now what's going to happen to my scores?"

That same teacher struggled to teach her huge class when one student, a severely backward wisp of a boy, Marquis, monopolized her attention with his constant acting out. The kid's mother was schizophrenic, and the father, with whom he lived, refused to put Marquis in special ed. Because the parents, like customers, were always right, Marquis turned the teacher's hair white, while perpetually robbing learning from the rest of the class.

Similarly, another child in the class, Jahdon, required an extra service, speech therapy, though his clueless mother had told the teacher he stuttered because "he's thinking about what he's going to say." The mother's denial, but in fact, cruelty, given how the world treats impediments, exasperated us to the point I felt compelled to write her a letter. I spoke in glowing terms of Jahdon's intelligence and extreme frustration with his stutter, a temporary speech issue for which we had teachers eager to help. Desperate to save the boy, I even referenced *The King's Speech*. The parent ignored our pleas and continued to keep her bright little stuttering boy out of school half the time.

Hallelujah! All of a sudden, some light at the end of the tunnel arrived in the form of a resolution opposing high-stakes testing from, of all places—the birthplace of NCLB—Texas.   Written by the Texas Association of School Administrators (superintendents, principals and assistant principals), the declaration was a revolutionary call-to-arms against the farcical policy prevailing for the previous decade, excoriating an accountability system which has been "strangling our public schools and undermining any chance that educators have to transform a traditional system of schooling into a broad range of learning experiences that better prepares our students to live successfully and be competitive on a global stage." The manifesto demanded not only a halt to testing, but the creation of a public school system which "encompasses multiple assessments; reflects greater validity, uses more cost efficient sampling techniques and other external evaluation arrangements, and more accurately reflects what students know, appreciate and can do in terms of the rigorous standards essential to their success, enhances the role of teachers as designers, guides to instruction and leaders, and nurtures the sense of inquiry and love of learning in all students."[31] The stream of verbosity was never more welcome to the ears of millions of equally indignant teachers, fed up with the inane prescriptives of the last decade; hopefully the movement would gain enough traction nationwide to end the lunacy. By early 2013 the number of Texan school boards signing the manifesto would climb to eighty-six percent, and still growing.

The prior June, when Pallas had received a "U" for the year from Rosemary's Baby, she had filed an appeal of the rating. Now for the hearing Pallas had a new asymmetrical punk haircut; channelling her inner Lisbeth Salander signaled a feisty change from mild-mannered school marm. Rosemary's Baby weighed in via video conference, while Pallas presented parent testimonials from that year as well as an actual parent in the flesh to support her case. It turned out Rosemary's Baby had not followed correct procedure when giving Pallas the "U," so it looked hopeful for the long-suffering teacher. Undeterred, the day after the hearing Rosemary's Baby and Moore ensconced themselves in Pallas's room taking copious notes. The petty dictators were in too deep for their egos to retreat, gifting the teacher with an eight-page Letter to File for their hours of trouble. Really.

The persecution had already been wrong on so many levels; now it was the extraordinary waste, in time the administrators were spending in her room, as well as dispatching lengthy incriminatory letters, that was doubly offensive. Were there not bigger fish to fry than typing up vicious diatribes and other acts of manic indulgence? Pallas asked the UFT district rep to file formal harassment charges.

Meanwhile, at a panel on urban school reform in Washington, D.C., Bloomberg trotted out the spurious claim he had been making for years, that he had cut the achievement gap in half. But his pronouncement was no truer now than it had been before. Indeed, it was hard to figure whether Bloomberg was deluded or had simply stayed true to his CEO roots, endlessly pep talking his investors no matter what. After a decade in charge of the schools, unable to square his goals or his ego with reality, Bloomberg's blinders were as fortified as ever. In fact, between 2003 and 2011, the achievement gap on the New York state tests had shrunk by a one percent pittance, and actually increased by three percent on the superior NAEP measure.[32]

Though Obama had voiced his opposition to the emphasis on it, his Race to the Top program was actually expanding testing. In partnership with other states, New York went ahead with preparing a national Core Curriculum (standards) and assessments, to begin as early as the age of five (later expanded to even pre-k). In 2014, students in grades three through eleven will take four tests in math and five in reading annually. Moreover, since test scores will be used to determine teacher effectiveness, several tests per year in science, social studies and all other subjects will be added in order to evaluate those teachers. Since someone will have to grade them, the rumor was we would be having many half-days of school, even less instruction time for kids, so afternoons would be dedicated to scoring. Apparently in the future going to school will involve very little learning, just endless test-taking. You can't make this stuff up.

Rosemary's Baby had ambushed me a couple weeks before in a second grade, where she watched me teach a lesson while she scribbled notes for the informal observation. When I went to her office to pick up my copy of her report, I asked what the relationship was between the Quality Review and our school Progress Report. She said the reviewer will follow up on issues which scored low, like communication, determining how those areas were being addressed. I was surprised Rosemary's Baby highlighted the poor grade we teachers had given her on communication—it was out of character for her to expose her vulnerability. She went on to say going forward we cluster teachers would have to conference with our students every week (six hundred fifty times). Moreover, I would be required to record the conferences, as well as individual goals, with notes in a log. In terms of instruction, I should differentiate the work for all levels of students, providing them with separate materials prepared in advance to tweak the general lesson. Whichever kids did not understand, I would reteach the lesson to in a small group during every class. Those students who still did not get it were to be taught a quick mini-lesson the next week. And what was I to do with the rest of the class during this? I asked. I was to give them something else to do. Then the next time, how would I catch up the laggard group with the rest of the class?

I could feel my eyes growing wider with each absurd directive. It was clear Rosemary's Baby was just blurting out reformspeak; little had been thought through, but she was not about to backtrack and admit her improvisation. After a couple more nonsensical ideas, a teacher came and interrupted us, Rosemary's Baby visibly grateful to be off the hook. Deftly referring back to the bad communication grade on our Progress Report she finished with, "It was good communicating with you, Ms. Sturt."

When I told Rosemary's Baby I would have to be out for six weeks for shoulder surgery, she was floored: there were teachers out on maternity leave. I asked if she had money for a substitute teacher and she said she did not. In fact, all year we had not had subs from outside because Rosemary's Baby had spent that money on other things, like the fifteen hundred dollar per day professional developers, and, less wastefully, a new math program to replace the progressive Everyday Math the teachers had hated for years (now the DOE let schools discard it though they would not foot the bill for a new one). I left the office feeling her anger zapping me, yet I had had perfect attendance the year before.

I resented her resentment: it was not my fault she had mismanaged the school budget. In fact, all sorts of illegal stuff involving special ed staffing had been going on all year since she had spent all the money. Federally-mandated staff were pulled from special ed inclusion classrooms to sub in others, while on half-days some temporary paras were told to stay at home so the principal could save money, a violation of one-to-one services for the kids involved. Students who were pulled out for mandated small group remediation sometimes lost that, too, as their teacher was required to sub in a special ed class for the day. Later in the year more special ed violations emerged: many kids mandated to be in self-contained classes of twelve had been put in inclusion classes instead. These were serious infractions, since they involved federal laws mandating services to disabled kids.

One late afternoon a high-maintenance fifth grade girl, Tyshemia, who always rushed through her work, interrupted me five minutes into my lesson.

"Can we start now?" she asked loudly.

I ignored her. Then two minutes later she asked again, almost yelling, "Can we start now?"

I said, "I heard you the first time—you're being very rude. You need to shut your mouth." Not the most polite riposte, but it had been a long day faced with similar boorish behavior.

The next day I was charged with "verbal abuse:" Rosemary's Baby and Moore showed me statements several kids had written. They were all different. One said I called Tyshemia "stupid," one said I called her an "idiot." One said I had called Tyshemia's work "ugly." Some were embellished to the point of creative writing. Moore noted that no matter how they all differed, they all said I had told Tyshemia to "shut up." I told Rosemary's Baby and Moore how much this reminded me of eight years before when a girl I had not allowed to print had lied and said I had called her an "idiot;" she had gotten her friends to back her up, resulting in a letter in my file. Amazingly, just like before when Marielly accused me of calling her an "idiot," it was Sanchez who had egged Tyshemia and friends on with the current allegation.

My conviction prompted me to recall two wondrously perverted Pennsylvania court rulings the previous summer, decided in favor of students. Both had victimized adults in their schools in cyberspace, then beaten lawsuits against them using freedom of speech as their defense. One, an eighth grade girl who had been punished twice for violating the dress code, created a fake profile of the principal and posted it on MySpace. The phony page insulted the principal and his family members, including portraying him as a sex pervert. The mean girl ended up getting suspended for ten days, then without missing a beat, sued the principal and the school district, and won.

Another high school senior did pretty much the same thing to his principal, using the Internet for contemptuous mockery and lies, such

LAUREL M. STURT

as the man's drug and alcohol use. That kid, after being suspended, transferred to another high school and was forbidden to participate in his graduation ceremony. Unchastened, the student and his parents sued the school district, asserting the cyber-scorn was not libel but free speech. They also won. Since neither threatening teachers or students, nor causing a disruption to school, like calling for a walk-out, had been part of the postings, incredibly, nothing illegal had transpired. The kids had all the rights.

Bloomberg slashed afterschool and day care funding again, the programs by now decreased by sixty-one percent in the last five years.[33] In return for hurting poor families already smarting from the economic crisis, Bloomberg saved only fifty million dollars, less than what he had paid the four hundred fifty dollars-an-hour consultant clowns who had screwed up the school bus routes five years before. I could not understand Bloomberg's priorities, shafting kids and parents, while wasting millions on DOE and other department no-bid contracts and consultants, many exorbitant, incompetent and ultimately, fraudulent. Then there was Bloomberg's sacrosanct welfare for corporations, even as he denied it to the neediest citizens. Half the corporations doing business in the city were not paying real estate taxes; their fair share would support the afterschool programs that keep my students, at least for awhile, from the clutches of the Cartoon Network.

Back at school after surgery, I found I lost my voice the first day. The kids were wild from spring fever as well as the fact the state tests had transpired while I was out. This year the tests had been worse than ever: three days instead of two, each day, ninety minutes a pop. For special ed kids who had double time that meant three hours in a chair for three consecutive days, and for teachers proctoring the test, the same grueling time on their feet since sitting was not allowed. Because those kids usually finished fast despite their extra time allotment, there were dozens of eight to eleven-year-olds nailed to chairs for hours with nothing to do.

As controversial as the tests had always been, this year's—the first of a five-year, thirty-two million dollar contract to a new testing company, Pearson,—hit a new low. The questions were plagued by mistakes, with incorrect answers, two correct answers or deceptive typos. Others were ambiguous or not relevant to the curriculum or grade level. On translated versions of the exams, there were over twenty language errors resulting in nonsensical questions. The tests even got media attention over the fourth graders' struggle with an adapted story about an anthropomorphic pineapple and a hare having a race: the answers were so twisted to the already beyond-weird tale that the author of the original passage declared he himself could not answer the six questions correctly. Parents organized protests against high-stakes testing, their children carrying placards, "I AM NOT A TEST SCORE," a contention which applied to infuriated teachers as well.

While I had been out, Rosemary's Baby had continued persecuting several regulars, including the school nurse, whom she had complained to her supervisor to be "disheveled and breathless;" this impossibly shallow critique was sufficient to launch a campaign of harassment. The nurse ended up transferring out at the end of the year.

Rosemary's Baby had begun hounding a new victim, veteran teacher Ms. Murphy, seizing on her with her perverse obduracy. In mid school year a new kid, K-von, had been placed in her class. Though much older than the rest of the kids, K-von was so backward, he did not even know the alphabet. In fact, from my brief exposure to him (he was usually absent for Friday's art class since, like many of the struggling kids, he enjoyed three to four-day weekends), like other teachers, I felt he might be retarded. To add to the difficulty of teaching him, K-von's behavior was off-the-charts insane, creating daily havoc and even running out of the room. That Murphy, a tough teacher whose stern attitude was conveyed in a sullen expression and frequent, high-decibel yelling, could not subdue the child, spoke volumes about the extreme case.

The situation reached a head when the kid's mother complained to the city emergency system 311 that Murphy was verbally abusing the child. Since this involved official, outside criticism of Rosemary's Baby as the principal, now it was on: she embarked on a campaign of terror, ambushing the teacher frequently with long, menacing classroom visits, much like the strategy against Pallas. At the same time, Rosemary's Baby reportedly did not cooperate even when the district union rep got involved, refusing to talk the situation out in meetings. By the week before the QR, Murphy's anxiety issues were such that she took a couple weeks of leave. Murphy was one of the no-nonsense, hard-as-nails teachers, yet not quite a match for malevolent Rosemary's Baby's pit bull obsession.

Considering the months of frantic build-up to it, the week before the QR, Rosemary's Baby was more hysterical than ever. Teachers were given a final checklist of things the reviewer might grade for, items from complete conference logs to tiny arrows on wall charts, then the APs went from room to room to follow up. When he came back empty-handed, Rosemary's Baby sent Rodriguez back a second time to collect scalps for her delectation: some teachers had not addressed specific issues on the checklist and they were now in the hot seat.

With just a few days to go, the frenzied last-minute directives to staff continued. My attendance board came down and the musty mission statement from Principal Dearest went up, surrounded by cartoon faces of children of different races: "Through equity, respect and empowerment we will create a community of learners both big and small."

That the staff *still* could not agree they had received this treatment was immaterial. The tenets were not for them, after all, but the quality reviewer. So were the convivial photos of teachers collaborating that suddenly appeared on the hallway walls. At last the marker graffiti in the stairwell, "Fuck this school"—more likely to have been scrawled by a teacher than a student at this point—had been painted over. Then two days in a row on the white board outside the office, where daily announcements were posted, "Questions the reviewer might ask your students:" appeared. The lists of potential queries, provided so teachers could coach the kids with correct, faked responses, were the last touches in an extravaganza of smoke and mirrors that had consumed virtually the entire school year.

Regrettably, I was to miss the QR. In exchange, I got exposure to another facet of the state tests when I was assigned with two other teachers from my school to grade district math results at a middle school uptown. Part of a large group, we were trained on three questions at a time, then graded them in assembly line fashion. The five-day experience was interesting; what impressed me most was the number of safeguards in place to make sure the tests were fairly and accurately scored, a positive even though clearly just another exorbitant component in the testing gravy train.

We returned the day after the Quality Review to a triumphant message on the white board: "We scored a 'proficient' on the Quality Review! Wow!" The staff was invited to a celebration in the library that afternoon of the decent, "B" equivalent grade.

The school was buzzing about the previous two days. The first day the reviewer had gone into classrooms of her choice, the next day into ones picked by Rosemary's Baby. The specter of each visit, whether random or planned, prompted every emotion from the hapless teachers involved—from garden-variety stage fright to screaming, cursing, full-on freakout. The reviewer had also interviewed teachers in grade groups to ascertain their level of collaboration, then brought up Rosemary's Baby's bad grade in communication on the school's Progress Report—had it improved? A flagrant toady spoke up in Rosemary's Baby's favor, while others were loathe to speak their mind in front of the suck-ups, who would surely report back to her.

Unbelievably, the day after the successful *denouement,* Rosemary's Baby was seen popping in and out of classrooms to make sure nobody was "relaxing." Later that afternoon at the celebration, Rosemary's Baby made a speech detailing our success as well as places where improvement could be made. At one point she spoke of a parent who had been interviewed as part of the QR. When the reviewer asked if the parent had been informed about a specific curriculum issue, the parent answered "no." Yet that same parent had been at a discussion of that very subject at the Curriculum Night the previous fall! Many of us laughed out loud: the parent was, after all, exactly like most of our students. Since she had not been endlessly coached prior to the QR, she could not answer correctly. Though pre-selected, nobody had thought to build the parent a hut in our Potemkin Village.

After Rosemary's Baby spoke we had cake. Several teachers standing around, however, were far from festive. They had received threatening letters that day for not having everything on the checklist from the week before. Even though the QR had passed, Rosemary's Baby was badgering teachers who had worked their asses off the previous nine months in service to her keeping her job. They were given just three days to address any essential missing criteria, like tiny arrows on bulletin boards.

I had returned from scoring the tests with some interesting information: other schools had voted to keep students home for two days the last week of June, that way teachers could get necessary professional development regarding upcoming Common Core curriculum changes New York state was making. Yet we had not been offered that possibility at my school. Now, in a cluster meeting I brought up the issue with Rosemary's Baby; she smacked her forehead with a gasp, saying she had forgotten to arrange the vote because she had been so involved with the QR. Out of hundreds of schools, professional development, really important for a change, because teachers would need the new information to plan over the summer for next year, was denied our staff alone, because of Rosemary's Baby's selfish, single-minded concentration on the Quality Review.

By this point we had gone two and a half years without a contract, four years without a pay raise. Had the four percent now, four percent later raise accorded other unions in 2009 been given teachers as promised, at least we would have been able to *almost* keep up with four years of inflation. Since Bloomberg had screwed us upon his re-election, now we were that much poorer. Though the contract negotiations had long before gone into arbitration, the union would just wait out Bloomberg's tenure as mayor, ending a year and a half down the road. Bloomberg had mentioned recently that he did not think his successor should give retroactive pay to unions whose contracts had expired—another volley, as ever, at us.

In a morning's blitz, Rosemary's Baby visited the teachers who had gotten letters detailing their missing checklist items. After sitting in their classrooms writing massive notes on stunning trivialities, Rosemary's Baby raked the teachers over the coals in her office the next day, prompting one to sob inconsolably through the entire meeting; Rosemary's Baby ignored the literal *cri de coeur*. In a curious display of gratitude for their months of effort, as part of the group shaming Rosemary's Baby promised to visit their classrooms every day from now on.

Two weeks later a police officer with a child in our school hosted an assembly on the subject of bullying (we could never get enough of that) and its consequences; at one point in the discussion Rosemary's Baby loudly interjected the beyond-ironical observation, "Making someone feel bad about themselves is bullying."

As long as I had been there, we had never had a strong union rep in the school. The current one, Pereira, had tried somewhat to organize the teachers the year before, but like Graham before her, did not attend meetings downtown, almost never held them for the staff, and did not publish a newsletter nor publicize, nor usually attend, rallies. Given the apathy in the school—there was not even pseudo psolidarity—I had relinquished my position as delegate, and nobody else wanted it, so we had none.

Now, at the end of my tenth year, though I was planning to leave teaching, the dismal performance of our union reps, enabling of despotic principals, so infuriated me, I decided I would stay if I could organize the teachers and give the school a union presence it had never known. As it was supposed to be done it would be a big job. However, I was willing to make the sacrifice just to get some justice for the downtrodden teachers. Yet, throwing my hat into the ring against the standing rep, Pereira, and Graham, who wanted the job again, who should win but the latter, who had been driven out three years before. Graham barely edged Pereira—the votes were virtually split between the two.

The only proponent of change, I received just a quarter of the teachers' votes. The truth was, most of the staff was unaware of their lackadaisical performance; notwithstanding their ignorance, the sad fact was militancy was nonexistent in a place where Stockholm Syndrome had become the default emotional setting. As an activist and a vociferous advocate of the Fredrick Douglass motto, "Power concedes nothing without a demand," I had been stoked to put on the gloves and get into the ring with Rosemary's Baby for these craven people. Yet again, the masochistic teachers had chosen a union rep with no glimmer of the gumption our school so desperately needed. Well, I tried.

A recent spate of depraved teachers, such as ones having affairs with their high school students, was a news bonanza for the exultant *New York Post*. Shamelessly politicizing the moment, Bloomberg seized the diem to attack the UFT anew, now for "defending" teacher sex offenders—as if. In fact the UFT had more stringent provisions in our contract than even state law, instantly removing the accused from the classroom and, if there is probable cause, the payroll while an investigation is conducted. The union also supported a teacher's entitlement to due process, a constitutional right the last time I looked; Bloomberg insisted an accused teacher be fired on the spot. A couple weeks later the state legislature came through to protect teachers' privacy, voting to keep future teacher evaluations for parents' eyes only. Bloomberg had wanted their humiliating public disclosure, like the mortification of February's media *auto-da-fe*, to continue going forward. Now our long overdue raise seemed further afield than ever.

In the meantime, the UFT had won the lawsuit against the DOE, forcing its release of years of emails relating to charter schools. Because of the heavy redactions on many of the emails, a lawsuit was later filed; when it came to its corporate agenda, the DOE's vaunted transparency and accountability apparently didn't require all public information be made public. The disquieting findings detailed Bloomberg and Klein's cozy relationship with charter school advocates, including a determination to raise money for charter lobbying efforts, increase charter schools and keep them from being unionized, while encouraging for-profit charter management. Using their city positions to promote privatization, the mayor and former chancellor had *actively campaigned against* the very public schools they had been entrusted to uphold.

This was hardly a news flash, however, as for several years the DOE had been pushing charter schools into already overcrowded school buildings, the ruse of sharing space in actuality a destablilizing ploy to undermine the existing school. Once the public school had been destroyed and closed through the siege strategy, then naturally, the occupying charter school could simply expand. At least, outraged communities had begun to organize in opposition to these tactics, backed by two bills proposed by the UFT, one requiring parent/teacher consensus when co-locating charter schools in public school buildings, the other demanding an immediate moratorium on closing schools.

The end of school came and with it, our silly graduations. The five-year-old kindergarten girls, some teetering on high heels long before it seemed right, belted out Katy Perry's "Firework" in their Chipmunks voices, the auditorium typically airless as the heat index topped one hundred degrees outside. Nearby school systems had issued a heat advisory and closed that day; as long as Bloomberg sat in air conditioning himself, we would never get that. The parents, meanwhile, got a taste of our water fountains. If the grudging trickle made an appearance at all, the frustrating attempt at ingesting the tiny arc yielded no satisfaction. The pipes, as I had learned long before from the custodians, had been in need of wholesale replacement for decades.

Months before, after Pallas had a miscarriage she connected to the ongoing abuse, Rosemary's Baby had dropped her persecution of another victim, Casares, after she had become pregnant. Besides, the test scores for her class had risen. Once again, Pallas got an unsatisfactory "U" rating for the year, which she would duly appeal at the union district office the day after school ended. Despite her spectacular presentation at the appeal hearing of the "U" rating she had received the year before, the DOE had found against Pallas, as it did in these cases ninety-seven percent of the time—less an appeals process than a cruel farce. Indeed, so biased were the hearing officers, there were fifty cases of "U" ratings that had been sustained as valid despite the lack of a single supporting document in the teacher's file; teachers' careers had been destroyed with a mere rating sheet scrawled with a "U" by a principal.

Pallas was interviewing at other schools, with difficulty: they all wanted a copy of a successful observation or a reference from the principal. She could only attempt to explain her situation, pointing out her thirteen unimpeachable years before the onslaught of Rosemary's Baby. When classes were formed for the next year, Rosemary's Baby deemed three of Pallas's criminal boys necessary to split up, even as she had tortured Pallas for the past year over her inability to manage them. Indeed, the most difficult of the three, Davaughn, was slated for a special trip the next year up the river to District Seventy-Five. When Pallas's class went on a field trip in the last weeks of school and Davaughn was not allowed to attend, Rosemary's Baby huffed that she was not going to "babysit him" if he were left behind, giving the lie to the raft of letters she had put in Pallas's file condemning the teacher's powerlessness over the child.

The annual Balloon Dance was a kind of prom for the fifth graders around graduation, really just an occasion to get dressed up. As our security guard DJed rap music from a corner of the stifling cafeteria, boys in suits and girls in elaborate sequined gowns mainly rocked self-consciously from one foot to another. A couple crack dancers who had been studying Michael Jackson videos soaked up the limelight, while several girls in the Bronx version of Herve Leger rocked their vpl sausage-casings in sky-high platforms and makeup.

In that interlude between the *Mad Men* era and the Summer of Love when *I* was in fifth grade, we still wore white gloves to church; the most risque we risked was an impromptu miniskirt, rolling up our waistband a block from home. Now, a group of horrified teachers watched these little girls we had known since kindergarten spill out of their dresses as they shimmied and ground to the beat; a bowl of condoms between the Capri Suns and chips would not have been out of line. Despite the unsettling, incipient sophistication that had already spirited some miles away, seeing these kids for the last time never failed to bring a lump to my throat. I had spent six years with them and like any mom, still saw them as babies.

The last day saw the worst disorganization we had ever experienced as regular closing-up procedures devolved into chaos. Many teachers, including myself, had no position posted for the next year. It seemed an omen. After all, I had finally made my goal of ten years—time to plan my exit.

As I walked to the train, seagulls swooped and called to each other overhead. My first year, I had been astonished to see them so far inland, but now I was used to their occasional visits. When the pickings were slim in their aquatic habitat, they could always count on the smorgasbord of garbage arrayed on these streets, the sensory attributes played up now in the sizzling heat. I had always gazed at the birds, envious that they could just fly away. Now it would finally be my turn.

12

Three and a quarter million incompetent teachers are responsible for wrecking the futures of America's kids, as well as the nation's retreat from global greatness. Roving bands of educators—flush with job protections and inflated pensions—have been mugging Girl Scouts, defrauding old ladies and pushing the blind into traffic. These evildoers, indeed, have caused the current economic crisis! We live in an era of teacher-bashing, and it is stunningly unfair.

From my first week in a New York City school, I have felt strongly impelled to share the realities of teaching with a society oblivious to its challenges. Of the nagging concerns obliging me finally to write, the unjustified *fatwa* against teachers has inspired the greatest urgency. Even as I have seen around me dedicated saints in a thankless endeavor redeemed only by their devotion to kids, instead of celebration, teachers have sustained condemnation.

Moreover, my sense of outrage at what I have discovered, aspects unimaginable to civilians, has prompted me to describe the quotidian truth of life inside, hopefully shedding light on the daunting demands inherent in educating dysfunctional students in a dysfunctional system. Among the laundry list of appalling features, the most profound have been the dearth of moral leadership as well as the staggering expense of the widespread fakery standing in for authentic education. The ever-present, hulking shadow of high-stakes testing completes the tragic triptych, destructive in itself even as it enables and exacerbates the other two negatives.

Googling the search term "teacher-bashing" these days yields a whopping seven million plus results; the woeful global academic rankings of our kids have only stoked the national obsession with our decline in the world. The apocalyptic hysteria—concretized federally with the No Child Left Behind Act and in the cities, with mayoral control of the schools—has inevitably seized on a scapegoat: teachers. The facile, Manichean education reform movement parallels the magnified zeal of religious fundamentalists in recent times, simplistic attempts to muster a semblance of control in an era defined by complexity and uncertainty.

But the premise that "accountability," the darling buzzword of the educational *Zeitgeist*, is in and of itself the cure-all for public education is disastrously unsophisticated: with lives of children and teachers ravaged in service to its oppressive directives and high-stakes testing, accountability has proven less a panacea than a scourge. A political and media blitzkrieg shrill with vilification has kept the dedication of suffering, micromanaged teachers off the radar, obscuring their commitment and sacrifice, while they suffocate from the chokehold of national and local mandates; in the past twenty years the government has decided it can no longer trust them to do their job.

Teachers question how they ever became the villains in this cockeyed scenario, taking the blame in a system they have had no role in creating. In fact, test scores reveal nothing of a teacher's instructional practice. Moreover, unlike other professions, teachers have been held accountable for the performance of their students, as if they are definitively responsible. If a patient did not take their medicine, a doctor would not be faulted for their health failing—yet calumny routinely stalks teachers culpable for the test scores of students who do not take their medicine, either.

Furthermore, how can a teacher be held accountable for the performance of a psychologically-disturbed, learning-disabled kid living in a homeless shelter with her ex-con, drug-addled grandmother, out of school for half the year? Reformers do not care, viewing students as faceless widgets assembled with teacher machinery, pressed out through the assembly-line gears of "education" factories more evocative of *Modern Times* than scholastic centers of intellectual cultivation: the success or failure of the product, notwithstanding the raw materials, rests on the machinery. Yet the incontrovertible fact is, the most accomplished teacher cannot force students to learn.

Charitably, the mass denunciation of teachers is a distraction to deflect attention from the true systemic problems lodged deep in the strata, issues not capable of being addressed with a Bandaid. The signs, however, point to a more pernicious perspective—an agenda to privatize the over six hundred billion dollar per year public school system, best expedited by destroying its biggest obstacle, unionized teachers.

After all, education is the new Gold Rush, with private equity and hedge funds fiercely competing to stake their claims. It bears repeating: between 2005 and 2011, venture capital investments in the K-12 education sector skyrocketed from thirteen to three hundred eighty-nine million dollars.[1] The possibilities are limitless, given the fevered reforms at local levels driving panicked districts and administrators to scramble on board with the latest gewgaw: curriculum, test prep, technology, professional development et al, that will save their schools from being closed. The feeding frenzy continues as those nevertheless closed schools, their buildings replaced with privately-run entities, supply additional profits.

Every impossible mandate that comes down from the state or federal government represents another "Eureka!" of nuggets to the profiteers, who grease the wheels with money to local pols, amassing contacts and contracts to assure their increasing share of tax dollars. We're the only nation in the world that is privatizing education, flagrantly undermining an institution essential to the public good, now reduced to just another—in the American style, Supersize— business opportunity for the mercenary. Indeed, considering what we've become as a nation, pawns of a venal agenda, the quaint values of our Stars and Stripes have been rendered obsolete: a mighty dollar sign would better telegraph our true special interests, these days.

In fact, for all the delirium over the alarming statistics for American kids, for example, most recently, among the top thirty-four countries fourteenth in reading, seventeenth in science and twenty-fifth in math, rarely publicized is the fact that American students make up the largest portion, twenty-five percent, of high scoring science students in the world. In second place is Japan, with a distant thirteen percent slice of the global high achievers.[2] This under-reported phenomenon is the result of the stellar contribution of U.S. schools specific to wealthy areas.

In fact, when American schools are separated out in terms of poverty level, our kids rank first in the world in reading and science, and third in math, in schools with a poverty rate of less than ten percent. Even where the poverty level goes up to twenty-five percent of a school's students, American kids maintain their first place in reading and science. Inevitably, as the poverty rate rises the rankings drop in equal proportion, to the point where our national averages, then, doom our global position.[3]

Given this analysis, the enemy to our collective success is not teachers, but poverty. Of the top twenty-five industrialized nations, the U.S. ranks embarrassingly at the very bottom in terms of the number of children in poverty.[4] These stats put the emphasis on teachers' responsibility for our educational outcomes in perspective; despite the "no excuses" mantra of reform proponents, the evidence is unequivocal: poverty impacts...and how.

In the competitive interviews to become a Teaching Fellow, the most decisive crucible of all had been our response to one simple question: do you believe as a teacher you should have lower expectations for any students? I had answered correctly—no. Indeed, I argued, maintaining a high bar for everyone was obviously necessary to propel performance upward. Now, a decade later, I have not renounced my belief in the utility of a lofty target, notwithstanding my adjusted pragmatism regarding expectations. My idealism, though battle-scarred, cloaks me like a carapace, stubbornly protecting my vision of quality in a sea of mediocrity; whether starry-eyed or dimmed with cataracts of denial, my outlook persists in the face of sobering reality.

The fact is, for all my frustration, my idealism vis a vis the kids themselves remains in tact: I still believe they are innately capable of educating themselves out of poverty. My pessimism, though, resides in my discouragement with an education system in crisis, starved of sense as much as money; given this, I have not lost faith in the kids so much as in their potential to progress in the absence of intensive, expensive intervention. Ours is a society in which the best resourced public schools have ten times the funds of the least resourced ones. Over time, with the concentration of power into fewer and fewer hands, light years away from the inner city, my diminished outlook has been abetted by America's increasing inequality and shrinking capacity for upward mobility.

The crippled state of something as basic as my school's water fountains seems an apt metaphor for the impoverished system: sustenance merely *appears* to be there when in actuality, there is just the faintest dribble. What better analogy for education than water, life force, and we are party only to the *pretense* of supplying it. The school system is a faked world all its own, mandates raining down without any understanding of what is or is not feasible, much less concern over that shortcoming. Indeed, over time I have developed the suspicion that the directors and their directives are no more rooted in reality than the mirage that is my school.

It is as if Michael Crichton had designed a *Schoolworld* in which everyone from Arne Duncan down to the lunch ladies merely goes through the motions, while poor kids continue to drown in the barrage of phony life preservers. The whole performance depends on a cherished idea rooted in the most fortressed denial: despite decades of research determining socioeconomic status to be the most important indicator of a child's academic performance, education reformers insist poverty has nothing to do with students' low achievement. Until the formidable task of educating children in poverty is fully comprehended, let alone embraced, there can be no change. In this regard the impediments consistent with a poor child's upbringing bear renewed examination, for those who would truly reform rather than revile.

By age four, the average child in an upper-middle class home has heard forty-five million words, while their counterpart in poverty has only been exposed to thirteen million. But it is not just the quantity of words a child hears that is important, it is the quality: children of professionals on average hear thirty-two affirmatives (encouragements) and five prohibitions(discouragements) per hour, while a child on welfare hears, on average, just five affirmations and eleven prohibitions per hour. Affirmations have a positive effect on a child, giving them self-esteem and the character traits important to learning, like motivation and persistence. Prohibitions do the opposite, contributing to feelings of low self-worth and helplessness. Therefore, since later literacy is predicated on listening, speaking, vocabulary and knowing information during the years prior to school—all supported by an environment full of words—the achievement gap begins even before a child enters school.[5]

Oral language tests administered before first grade predict children's later reading ability in fourth through eighth grades, those measured with low skills ending up as strugglers, while the early higher performers become excellent readers. Moreover, the achievement gap cannot simply be erased in the first years of school, not only because of the huge variance of prior exposure to words, but because kids spend more time at home than school. Thus, the low-level ones arrive in school at that level and never catch up. Children in professional homes also have less exposure to television and more to books read aloud to them, enhancing the experience of advanced vocabulary and grammar, since written texts are more complex than spoken language. Further, reading aloud to children supports their ability to orally comprehend, a skill required when listening to a teacher.[6]

Parents with high socioeconomic status have more resources than low-SES parents, and not just financial. Of course, money provides more books, computers, greater intellectual opportunities, enrichment, and extra educational tools, like tutoring. Better housing, less anxiety about finances, and a calm environment in a safe neighborhood, among other beneficial attributes, impact wealthy children's learning positively. Daycare providers tend to be warm, their influence leading to higher reading and math scores in elementary school. Then, also, the drive to place their children in superior schools, even if it means moving to a better school district, characterizes wealthy parents.

But the primary resources high-SES parents may share with their children are their own knowledge and skills—education which they impart naturally or by design. They understand child development and as discussed, speak frequently to their children, and mainly in affirmatives. Read to frequently, the children of well-educated parents benefit, moreover, from more quality time spent with them. High-SES parents are also involved in their children's schools, a factor in their children's high achievement.[7]

By contrast, low-SES children are often born to parents with poor lifestyle choices—smoking, drugging and drinking—and a general lack of healthcare, so they are frequently born prematurely, at a low birth weight or with fetal alcohol syndrome, conditions which induce cognitive deficits in the infant. A large percentage of special ed classes are students born under these circumstances, so no wonder many of ours were stunted intellectually as well as physically. After birth, the children lack access to good health care and nutrition, many developing chronic health problems like asthma which prevent them from attending school and so result in negative academic outcomes (the Bronx has the highest asthma rate in the nation).

Low-SES children benefit more from attending more days of school than do their wealthy counterparts, because they then get at school what the other kids are getting at home. Exposure to lead in substandard housing can affect their cognitive abilities, while crowded housing can create chaos and noise which again negatively impact cognition. Poor kids tend to get harsh, insensitive daycare providers and later in their inferior schools, are likely to be given inexperienced, minimally qualified teachers. Their parents speak to them less, with a simpler vocabulary and mainly in directives, considering the home situation is often crowded. Lower SES children are read to less frequently, while they watch far more television than their higher SES counterparts. Parents are less connected to their children's schools, a situation that predicts low achievement from their children.

Further, there is a connection between stressed-out, depressed parents and their kids' behavioral problems. Living with cold, inconsistent parenting in this environment of chronic stress, children's psychological pain ends up manifesting physically: they suffer actual brain damage.[8]

I had often felt exasperation when working with kids who, no matter how many times they see a word, cannot remember it when it reappears in the text. The difficulty comes from a lack of "working memory," a mental capacity crucial to learning. Children living in poverty have disrupted brain circuitry, sustained from the time of conception through early childhood, due to "toxic stress." This psychological/physiological phenomenon stems from chronic stressors in the family environment, pre- and post-natal: abandonment; parents hooked on drugs or alcohol; violence; emotional, physical and sexual abuse; neglect; crowding; criminal activity; and myriad other detriments.

The hostile situation triggers stress hormones which interfere with brain development, the toxic stress creating permanent harm since it is rooted biologically—for life. Not only is academic performance doomed, but without concerted efforts at behavior modification, the self-destructive behaviors initiated by the damaged brain lead to the maddening cyclical visitation of poverty on generation after generation, as survivors of a traumatic childhood raise their own children in the same stressful chaos.[9] The saving grace in this scenario is the power of affection: love and hugs have been found to temper toxic stress, heading off later low achievement at school, drug abuse, criminality, and even physical ailments like heart disease and diabetes.[10] Thank God for William's mom.

Many of the kids in my school, then, trudge to school every day from their houses of horror, laden with baggage; the malevolent influences they have to endure at home are hard to fully reckon. Along with their cognitive issues, the anger, depression and anxiety engendered by their sad lives at home clearly fuel their tendency to impulsively act out. Indeed, though their slow-motion processing of new information can be irksome, their lack of "self-regulation" (as self-control is called in psychology) is most annoying as that behavior prevents the entire class from learning. Clearly, positive educational achievement and later success in life is predicated on good self-regulation, just as poor self-regulation is tied to outcomes like low scholastic achievement, welfare and prison. Once again, hugs every day keep the police/repo-man away: it is parental affection expressed in a predictable, organized home that fosters self-control in a child.[11]

Given these considerations, education reformers at every level need to change it up. After all, a decade of expensive reforms has yielded no improvement, notwithstanding Bloomberg's annual bragfest over climbing graduation rates. While the DOE's four hundred fifty-five percent increase in spending on consultants (two hundred sixty accountability experts alone) since 2004 did not go to desperately needed staff in schools, apparently the largesse has not been for naught: in 2011 a Bronx high school posted a ninety-five percent graduation rate! Yet fewer than eleven percent of those students proved college-ready, an eighty-four point difference.[12]

We need to stop investing in educational theatre and truly commit to tackling the elephant in the room, poverty, providing prenatal care and ongoing healthcare and nutrition for kids; increasing the minimum wage and expanding job training, afterschool and child care; supplying basic education and parenting classes to poor adults; and increasing school-to-parent outreach and cooperation. Instead of starving inner city schools, we need to bring them up to par with their magnificently-resourced upscale counterparts, building shining new schools with a respectful, positive vibe kids and parents entrain with, raising their own game.[13] As much lip service as the suits downtown pay the business model, how can they expect profit/improvement with so little investment?

Now is the moment to wheel out the industrial-strength poverty-buster par excellence: universal early childhood education.[14] With their obsession to close the achievement gap, the educational reformers have been focused on remediation of the existing problem rather than preventing it in the first place, a strategy ineffective in cost and efficiency. School resources, class size, teacher quality and all the other variables pale in comparison to the impact of early childhood education prior to kindergarten, pre-k. As discussed, early negative experiences for disadvantaged children result in impaired cognitive abilities and a dearth of social skills. These, including the ability to focus, persevere, control impulses and get along with others, are just as essential as cognition in determining academic and future success in life. Prenatal care as well as quality early childhood education from birth to age five develop both sets of skills, erasing the luckless slate typically condemning an impoverished child.

The final ingredient in the success equation, character—self-esteem, self-control, determination, motivation, responsibility and positivity—is mainly contributed by good parenting. Though early childhood education can offset a deficit in parenting to a degree, supports to parents—home visits, parenting classes and childcare—further enhance character in disadvantaged kids.[15] These crucial investments head off later social costs like special education, welfare, illness, and crime; instead of burdens to society, early interventions foster well-adjusted, productive children, then adults.[16] Moreover, they produce exponential payoffs as improved parenting extends to succeeding siblings and ultimately becomes passed down generationally.

As such, early childhood supports to the poor constitute not only a humane, even moral imperative, but ultimately benefit all of us in a win/win better world. Instead of blank stares, the kids in our kindergarten would come equipped with a foundation of knowledge and social skills, ready to learn, not to be babysat through the years. It will be challenging and it will be expensive, but will it cost more than the testing leviathan in all of its incarnations? More than the latest educational trend to come down the pike? More than the colossal social cost of lives given over to welfare or prison sentences?

Even where the need to fund famished schools *is* conceded, that rare but politically-safe, quick-fix standby of simply throwing money (yet still insufficient amounts) at high-poverty schools to address inequality hasn't been effective, nor has forced racial integration been successful. Indeed, the low performance of desegregated schools, nevertheless populated with impoverished students of different races, pegs homogenous SES as the major obstacle to success. Of any current strategy, then, it is not surprising recent research indicates socioeconomic integration of schools to be highly effective at increasing the achievement of high-needs kids.[17] When middle class schools (where less then fifty percent receive free or reduced price lunch) take in populations of lower income students, those kids are immersed in enhanced, more stable surroundings. Naturally they thrive, surrounded by peers who not only tend to be more academically motivated and engaged, but have less behavior issues.

Moreover, lower SES kids brought into the middle class mix benefit from a committed parent constituency involved with school concerns, while the higher expectations of strong teachers can only lift their achievement accordingly. Even the improved physical environment and resources—a nicer school in a better, safer neighborhood—obviously inspires resonance with the more upbeat tone.

Unfortunately, the remedy of choice, literally, these days, charter schools, with their high concentration in poor neighborhoods, are vastly more segregated in terms of SES than regular public schools. Given the effects of poverty, no wonder charter school results have been dismal and woefully cost-ineffective, albeit brilliantly cost-effective for the bottom line of the privateers legislating/operating them.

I saw the benefits of mixing SES, and its natural, concomitant promotion of diversity, in my son's elementary school in midtown Manhattan, where kids from the projects thrived in a mix inclusive of all rungs of the middle class. My personal experience has been echoed in the beneficent results of a large-scale application of the theory, blending lower and higher SES groups, in eighty school districts serving four million kids (ten percent of the nation's students). To sum up, I need only invoke the imprimatur of education diva par excellence, Finland: of fifty-seven of the most advanced nations, high-achieving Finland has the lowest level of socioeconomic segregation in its schools.[18]

So far the national program to eliminate the achievement gap has not worked any better than Bloomberg's local experiment. As long as educational policy is designed by a distant elite immune to the effects of its mandates, the dysfunctional loop will continue with continued underinvestment and its corollary, underachievement. A prerequisite for policymakers entrusted with the fates of millions must be mandatory, in-your-face experience *teaching* (how bold of me) in a high-needs school for a minimum of ten years. Only those who have been there, neither bureaucrats nor businessmen, have the knowledge, or the heart, to tackle a mission of this magnitude. The clueless politicians, pundits and wonks have had their turn, not just failing but worsening a grave situation with a generation lost to high-stakes testing. Imagine the returns if the prodigious, profligate investment in that—fifty billion dollars per year by estimates—went instead to hiring an additional one million teachers.

It is high time we drove a stake through the education/resource vampire that is high-stakes testing. The era of the All-Mighty Test has reduced learning to the regurgitation of some math and reading skills bubbled on a scantron answer sheet, the empty ritual determining a kid's promotion to the next grade, a high school student's diploma, which teachers are rewarded or fired, which schools are privatized and which schools, no matter their history in the community, are closed. Across the country traditionally successful, innovative schools are now deemed failing and subjected to test prep and mandated curriculum. Testing and pedagogical directives have crowded out actual education, wasting hours of valuable learning time while having no proven impact on student achievement. At the same time, the misadventure has birthed expensive departments within all levels of government, charged with overseeing the gargantuan machine. As testing mandates have burgeoned, these entities have multiplied to Kafkaesque bureaucracies-within-bureaucracies, gobbling up education budgets just as the tests themselves have devoured precious learning time.

For the majority of America's children there has been no escaping it: *The Test that Ate America* has been an equal opportunity plunderer, cheating youth and taxpayers alike (and in future, all Americans). To pay for them, schools have gone without teachers, supplies or decent infrastructure just to appease the testing gods; the necessity for actual test administrators on staff, too, cannibalizes school budgets that much further. The casualties have been students (resentment is high, while motivation is at an all-time low, along with college readiness), teachers (highest attrition rates ever), and schools: tests have not only changed their mission, but since the spotlight is constantly on testing, entire public systems have morphed into Kaplan dispensaries.

Moreover, as seen on the New York versions, tests, full of errors and ambiguities, are not even valid measurements: heinous mistakes have occurred, yet scores still stand. Immigrant kids simply cannot pass the exam, while, equally ridiculous, a gifted child and a struggling child in special ed are held to the same standard. Yet choruses of protest draw the assertion there are neither mitigating circumstances nor excuses; oh, the joy of the no-brainer, one-size-fits-all blanket solution to a complex problem. No wonder high-stakes testing is the legacy of George W. Bush.

As exemplified by the Texas Miracle, moreover, the iron-fisted culture of testing intrinsically assures a parallel culture of cheating. States and localities manipulate test scores through crude or elaborate contrivance, while the ruse continues after the results come in, numbers crunched every which way until pass rates...pass. As long as the appearance of success is valued over true education, passing as panacea will persist. As President Bush pointed out in 2001, "You teach a child to read, and he or she will be able to pass a literacy test." It is that simple.

Despite the bluster of support from reformers, there are so few positives to high-stakes testing, it is brazenly clear the practice is not, in fact, primarily a tool of accountability but one of entrapment, to measure/fire teachers and close schools. But even well-meaning reformers innocent of an insidious agenda could benefit from the wisdom of Albert Einstein, member of the American Federation of

Teachers, who said, "Everything that can be counted does not necessarily count. Everything that counts cannot necessarily be counted." Fortunately, notwithstanding the strident demagoguery from politicians and pundits, communities and parents have overwhelmingly embraced their children's teachers.[19] Nevertheless, terrorized and demoralized teachers cannot possibly function optimally, and their students suffer as well.

Given the underpaid, joyless pressure cooker teaching has become in today's negative environment, an already severe attrition problem (twenty percent vs. Finland's two percent per year) will reach crisis proportions. With nearly half of teachers quitting before their fifth year, the turnover already costs taxpayers almost seven and a half billion dollars a year in lost investment. Moreover, we are not creating the optimal framework for teachers to become experts: in order to get teachers to the ten thousandth hour threshold, and more importantly, beyond, Malcolm Gladwell would agree teachers need to be respected, supported and well paid.

The transformation we require bears looking, once again, at the almost hackneyed example of Finland, the go-to country for educational inspiration. Over decades Finland has evolved into a leader in world education, the effort founded on cultural traits of community, shared responsibility and social justice, while valuing education as elemental to the nation's future. Expert teachers are created by culling the best candidates in a competitive field (ours traditionally have come from the bottom third of their noncompetitive college class)—teaching is the most admired profession—then submitting them to rigorous preparation. Finland values and empowers teachers, trusting them with the autonomy appropriate to a professional. As such they are free to design and personalize their teaching practice, never forced to deliver prescribed curriculum in a specific fashion. There is neither high-stakes testing for students (nor even grades in the first five years, since they can promote patterns of failure), nor formal evaluations for teachers; like the old days in America, a good teacher is simply one who helps students progress. Teachers generally stay at a school for life, while only between ten and fifteen percent ever leave the profession altogether. Finland's child poverty rate is a fraction of ours, less than three percent compared with our over twenty-three percent (of thirty-four advanced countries, only Rumania's poverty rate is higher than ours), and there is intensive investment in special education and ongoing remediation to mitigate its effects, even as the general population enjoys small class sizes. Outside of education, the welfare state levels the playing field with free supports like early childhood education and childcare, even preventive procedures to head off learning and developmental deficits before children enter school.[20]

In the next decade, more than half of America's teachers will be up for retirement. It is critical to end the politicization as well as the pretense of education and, like the best-performing countries in the world, invest in rich, authentic public education delivered by empowered, fulfilled teachers. Crucial to the excellence of our students is a holistic approach, addressing poverty while resourcing schools in all neighborhoods equally and balancing schools with an equitable SES mix. As for high-stakes testing, all of that paper will make festive confetti in the ticker tape parades honoring its demise, while the money saved will fund endless educational purposes. The lobbyists, profiteers and other parasites will have to find another carcass to scavenge: led by teachers as nation-builders, a renaissance in our schools will signal the resurgence of America. An educated population is, without question, a nation's most precious resource.

The "critical thinking" skills those in power contend essential in our twenty-first century students have been ironically lacking in these very leaders. As we embark on this adventure in integrity, we must approach education reform with the utmost gravitas, never again eschewing serious reflection in favor of the expedience of denial. Glib titles can no longer stand in for resolute policy. There is no silver bullet, no matter how catchy the catch phrases of our government-cum-Madison Avenue campaigns. After all, the quick fix of No Child Left Behind— the Tang of educational reform—was given us by the same administration that foolishly "Mission Accomplished" the war in Iraq; we cannot afford any more magical thinking.

We will need to lose our sophomoric predilection for instant gratification, as well, considering it took the Finns decades to build their education system and we have many times their poverty rate. Ultimately, we will have to be the adults in the room, rolling up our sleeves for perhaps an even tougher, longer slog. At this point, with a generation lost, we have no choice but to change.

The public has long been aware of a teacher's plight in the slums; less well known is today's equal uphill battle, but with enemies all around, and no sign of the cavalry coming any time soon. For years, as much as I had yearned to tell my story, not only was I loathe to revisit the experience, but I sheerly lacked the energy to write a book. Vacations, the only possible time, were interludes of balance and sanity I used to fortify myself for the next round of depletion. Ultimately, my chagrin compelled me to the *Sitzfleisch* requisite to the task; now more than ever the stupidity, corruption and injustice I have seen demand illumination and redress.

I hope I have succeeded in limning the angst and pressure of trench warfare in a high-needs school in this fraught era. Though this was no invitation to a pity party, but an honest observation of life on the inside at a time of upheaval, it is telling that in the telling, I was hard put to come up with synonyms for "desperate," "exhausted," "pointless" and "bizarre." After a decade I am heading for the exit: life's too short to chase a pension, especially if you are crawling through a desert in a *New Yorker* cartoon to get there. Burned out and demoralized, I will soon be reduced to a statistical cliche, just another digit in the attrition data. I had sought to make a hands-on contribution to social justice, yet if it brings truth to bear on the present crisis in education, perhaps this book has the greater significance. Notwithstanding my *Weltschmerz* (nor the fact that I am suddenly favoring German words), whatever else I am doing in life, I will return to the high-needs kids to volunteer as a tutor—I never could get that gum from the first day completely off my shoe. Through it all my love for the kids has remained constant, in fact my longevity, such as it was, depended on that. In future I trust their value will finally be affirmed with righteous education, bountiful water fountains and—dare we hope?—an air conditioner or two.

POSTSCRIPT

Though I had not expected to, in September 2012 I went back for one final round. I was looking to challenge Rosemary's Baby on behalf of the chronically complaining staff, and resuming the union delegate position, one which nobody else wanted, I would do just that. As it turned out, as challenging as we had ever known the kids or administration to be, all would pale in comparison with a sadistic principal emboldened by two years of acquiescence and apathy—we were now in the clutches of a consummate, card-carrying psychopath. No amateur, this one would not be dismembering insects, but the lives and futures of teachers.

Rosemary's Baby had volunteered our school to pilot a teacher evaluation program called the Danielson Framework, her shiny new toy to make teachers twist in the wind.[1] Actually supposed to be a means of improving teacher performance, Rosemary's Baby had obviously seized upon the program as an undisguised opportunity to terrorize teachers anew; though it was neither mandated nor approved yet for future use, she forced it on us, like every other oppression, simply because she could.

In our introduction to the evaluation the first day of school, Rosemary's Baby's Powerpoint presentation began with the outrageously misleading, out-of-context quote from research which Joel Klein & Co. had doctored to vilify teachers in their propaganda: "A teacher is the most important factor in a student's achievement." The transparent ploy to pressure further, already-decimated teachers was unquestioned by staff unfamiliar with the truth. Infuriated, I confronted the crafty use of the phrase and launched into a defense of teachers. Rosemary's Baby and her new sidekick—the resented crony Gonzalez who had now brown-nosed her way into becoming an expensive third assistant principal—caught red-handed, visibly squirmed during my discourse, then predictably, attacked me defensively.

Later, I viewed the official Danielson presentation on the DOE website: Rosemary's Baby and Gonzalez had added in the deceptive quote themselves. Taking a page from Nixon's playbook, this augured a year in which dirty tricks, stalking, spying and downright lies would characterize a despotic administration brazen in its ruthless strong-arming and paranoia. Rosemary's Baby, ever nonchalant about her conspicuous motivation, left little to our imagination—in emailed memos she would literally quote the Wicked Witch of the West, "All in good time, all in good time." That Rosemary's Baby self-identified with an iconic chartreuse serial killer was not lost on "my pretties," her victims mounting as the school year went on.

Now the psychological warfare of as many as seven administrators, not just from our school, swooping drone-like into our classrooms in ambush "informal" Danielson observations, proved an added pressure and indignity even as the bursting work load persisted. In the kindergarten alone, teachers were required to individually assess their students twelve times in math, nine times in reading and five times in writing: twenty-six times per year per child; classes were so large, this took place several times per day. This begged the question, when would there be time to teach? Since by now we knew the majority of paperwork data was not meant primarily to assess/support students, but used by the DOE to evaluate principals, hours of effort (and loss of instruction) would end up, just lifeless digits on spreadsheets downtown. Indeed, by this point the mayor's accountability division had attained such exaggerated proportions, I envisioned it as one of Albert Speer's monolithic, fascist flights of fantasy.

Since this year's fresh crop of micromanaging directives now combined with the constant threat of impromptu, "gotcha" evaluations, as brutal as the job already was, given the lack of engagement, low caliber and poor behavior of a preponderance of the kids, now it incredibly became worse, crossing the boundary of bearable. Moreover, the principal was on a tear, going after teachers for their senior salaries, their tenure or because they simply had the temerity to challenge her. Like frogs brought to a boil gradually, Rosemary's Baby had pushed our tolerance for abuse over the previous two years; now she put the lid on the pot.

Mental health leaves ramped up while many planned their permanent escape, still others facing the inevitability of an involuntary departure at the principal's hands. Rosemary's Baby's menacing tactics were no better exemplified than with the hapless guidance counselor she had illegally excessed the year before, in a bid to keep the obsequious one with less seniority. Having won her position back through her justified union grievance, the senior counselor returned to immediate harassment beginning with the very first period of the first day, Rosemary's Baby stalking her with her camera in the auditorium prior to giving a welcome back (irony not intended) speech. The weird bullying continued daily, Rosemary's Baby calling desperately on every power she had, including repeated hounding with rigged observations, even casually mentioning the counselor's child was in an honors program supervised by a friend of hers—at this point the appearance of a severed horse head would not have been shocking.

The persecution culminated in tragic circumstances which Rosemary's Baby shamelessly provoked and then exploited, reportedly coming in the next day wearing a hospital bracelet; lives (because we have families) had been ruined because an abused staff member had had the gall to win her job back, fair and square. Another competent teacher, hired as a temp just for that school year, had the nerve to be out sick with the flu and pneumonia; terrorized systematically and punished with unmerited "U"s to the point of a mental health breakdown, Rosemary's Baby's vicious destruction of that teacher's career was even more gratuitously evil, given the teacher was a temp and not coming back. Since at this juncture Rosemary's Baby had provoked several lawsuits, planned or in progress, when a photo of her victim mysteriously appeared in a newspaper article about teachers with past misconduct, theories abounded: given Rosemary's Baby's penchant for maleficence, the sudden exposure was beyond suspicious.

Even those known for a fact to be retiring—early, and forced— were gifted their last day with an observation rating them "Unsatisfactory." With this bon voyage "U" for the road, Rosemary's Baby extended her cold dead fingers far into their futures so they could never teach again, indeed, not even substitute teach as a back-up in uncertain economic times, such was the power of a "U."

In this sense, Rosemary's Baby had much in common with her role model and enabler, dictatorial Bloomberg, on his way out yet fast-tracking charter school co-locations, usually planned six to eight months in advance, as far ahead as fall of 2015, nearly two years after he leaves office. He had also been busy negotiating contracts with vendors and consultants which extend as much as nine years into the future! This typical domination from a mayor who had consistently overreached—like when he pushed his way into a third term in office—illuminated the arrogance that only he can capably govern the city, and will continue to do so regardless of the rights of city voters to another mayor's approach. Worse, he will go on to bully and manipulate policy in countless areas because of his prodigious fortune, one which has grown by leaps and bounds during his tenure as mayor. Friend to Michelle Rhee, Bloomberg has donated money to organizations that promote his reform attitude such as Students First, while even seeking to influence local elections, for instance giving one million dollars to a Los Angeles coalition to help elect candidates towing his education reform party line.

Indeed, so difficult does Bloomberg find it to let go, in this year's ongoing teacher evaluation battle with the UFT, at the last minute he torpedoed a final plan agreed to by his negotiators: like most other city laws, the framework provided for a "sunset," and Bloomberg's sanctimonious mindset could not fathom a sunset on his enduring quest to fire teachers. Later, when the evaluation issue was submitted to binding arbitration and resolved by the state in June, State Education Commissioner John King dissed Bloomberg at its release when he declared, "New York City is not going to fire its way to academic success."[2] Bloomberg, who spun the new evaluation system as a victory for education reform, had insisted on a framework with greater emphasis on student test scores, as well as empowering the DOE to fire teachers at will; the new plan, instead, has multiple factors designed to support and improve teachers throughout their career. That was the UFT spin, at least. In practice, a malevolent principal could still twist the formula to condemn, and terminate, a teacher, while low test scores could, it turns out, in and of themselves, determine a teacher to be "ineffective."

Even as Bloomberg's considerable resources will afford him the pleasure of muscling policy long after he's gone as mayor, he had steadfastly refused to give us city workers our due. For the first time in New York history, the entire three hundred, fifty thousand people who keep the city running were without contracts, some since 2007. Since ours had expired in 2009, days prior to our enabling Bloomberg's third term, in one of the most expensive cities in the world, a Metrocard alone had risen thirty-eight percent.

As the year progressed and Rosemary's Baby ratcheted up the tyranny, we never knew which of her picayune peccadillos would flavor that day's hormonal soup. To merely ask her a question she proved unable to answer, in a meeting, in front of other people, could predict, even months later, the loss of a job. As it turned out, Rosemary's Baby would set her cap for me, too, and not in a lacy Louisa May Alcott way.

Because Rosemary's Baby had formed several inclusion classes with special ed students combined into mainstream ones (extra credit for principals), classrooms were empty, so Sanchez and I each got our own art room. Since the beginning of each year was always fraught with changes, Sanchez amusingly sported, walking perfectly, her filthy rehabilitation boot for the entire month, invoking the injury she'd milked a whole two years before: if an art room were to be taken back it would be mine, not hers. By October the boot was magically retired, but clearly at the ready in case the violins were called up to play again.

But though I finally had my own room, I got a pittance of supplies, about one hundred dollars worth for one thousand class periods a year, working out to ten cents a class, about one third of a penny per student! My requests for supplies went unheeded, while Rosemary's Baby repeatedly also refused to provide a laptop so I could use the Smartboard, which did not have a bulb anyway. There ended up being no advantage to having a room, save the fact that I could play music while the kids (ideally) worked; a fistfight accompanied by the soothing strains of Satie's "Gymnopedies" was, without a doubt, among the most novel experiences of my life.

In October I did well when ambushed with an informal observation, then in November Rosemary's Baby gave me a formal one, which was rated the best possible "highly effective" and inspired much bizarre, overkill unction on her part. I could not pass her in the hall without her exuding over my lesson, gushing how great I was and how she had told everyone she knew. These diabetic inductions, moreover, were accompanied by disturbing squeals and winks. A couple weeks later, though, I would be wondering, "Where's the love?"

In the meantime, we had been grappling with the arrival of the Common Core State Standards (CCSS) New York had agreed to in 2010 in exchange for Race to the Top money, even as research by the Brookings Institute determined, "The empirical evidence suggests that the Common Core will have little effect on American students' achievement. The nation will have to look elsewhere for ways to improve its schools."[3] Moreover, because the standards and tests based on them had never been field tested, henceforth our nation's children were to be exploited as guinea pigs in a massive and cruel education experiment.

Despite the lack of evidence to support them, the federal government had forced the untried CCSS on forty-five cash-starved states, the District of Columbia and territories in return for more than four billion dollars, even as Obama and Arne Duncan asserted they were created by states and were adopted on a voluntary basis (in fact the federal government is forbidden to mandate a national curriculum, but the carrot of money to the recession-famished states assured compliance).[4] Massachusetts, a state with better, tested standards than the new ones proposed, junked its own, simply to get the federal cash.

In recent years, of course, Bill Gates, a self-proclaimed education czar—neither elected nor appointed by voters, legislators or officials—had been using his colossal fortune to unilaterally determine the course of American education, a public system he had written off as "obsolete."[5] With what would come to nearly two hundred million dollars from the Gates Foundation, by the end of 2013, an organization named Achieve, the National Governors Association, and the Council of Chief State School Officers developed the new standards; still other organizations got the lion's share in payouts simply to endorse the standards. Among other disastrous fallout, the mad rush to reverse policy would end up conferring an obscene amount of power on one person: David Coleman, the new president of the College Board, was behind their design, so now the SATs would be based on them. As such they will influence the educations of public *and* private students—millions of kids, the nation's future. Outrageous.

Among the Common Core's justifications, neocon proponents exploited the purported emergency our international test scores represent, to inspire fear and acquiescence, promoting the new standards as a tool to compete globally in a threatening world. The transparently jingoistic, as well as opportunistic call-to-arms was hurled by frantic Joel Klein (who, sly as ever, stands to make millions from the changes) and Condoleeza Rice in their 2012 gonzo book *U.S. Education Reform and National Security,* warning that along with the Common Core a periodic "National Security Audit" is necessary since public schools "constitute a very grave national security threat facing this nation."[6]

The new approach *seemed* reasonable enough, but then again, so had the feel-good righteousness of No Child Left Behind. The new standards were presented as grade-level concepts and skills requiring instructional changes including a focus on vocabulary, more nonfiction text, the ability to make arguments based on evidence, and strengthening essential math concepts. The new Common Core tests, then, would emphasize the higher-level cognitive abilities the standards seeks to instill in curriculum nationwide. For example, kids are expected to analyze, critique and create, with the capacity to develop evidence-based theses and solve unusual problems. Ultimately, multiple choice questions will be completely eliminated.

The previous June we'd missed two vital days of Common Core professional development in the last week of school, because Rosemary's Baby had been too obsessed with the Quality Review to schedule them. This instance of mismanagement, more than any other, would represent the nadir of Rosemary's Baby's typical solipsism and callousness; now the over-riding compunction to save her own skin that had fixated her on the QR, while failing to support the teachers and students, was more glaringly incompetent than ever. Teachers' jobs and kids' educations depended on mastering this new, complex approach, while for both groups, futures lay in the balance. Ultimately, throughout the year classroom teachers ended up being given scant, rudimentary professional development concerning the Common Core, while only after half the year was over did we clusters finally get a *soupcon* of professional development, fifteen minutes of a state video briefly explaining the standards.

Back in early 2010, the state Department of Education had mandated the new Common Core standards would be used in the 2013 state ELA and Math exams. Yet for three years the DOE had dithered, not developing the unified, systematized curriculum that would prepare our kids for the tests, but instead telling principals like Rosemary's Baby to make teachers untrained in such a crucial endeavor to write it on their own—ludicrous moreover because there was no time already, given the blizzard of paperwork. Undoubtedly the DOE's lack of support was to save money: between the army of consultants and three hundred lawyers charged with firing teachers (versus the UFT's legal staff of three) there were so many mercenary mouthes to be fed. Yet results of a UFT survey sent out to teachers indicated half had not received any professional development on how to teach to the new standards, while they had also not been supplied with the requisite time, resources like textbooks and software, and support to satisfy the new mandates.

Alarmingly, over eighty percent of new and untenured respondents said their principals had ordered *them* to write Common Core curriculum themselves, even as such a task was out of their field of expertise, not to mention their job description. Also, despite the fact that the Common Core's assessments would be computer-based, many complained few working computers were available in their schools, the situation in mine. Indeed, the astounding lack of preparation was nationwide: an AFT poll in May found even as seventy-five percent of teachers approved of the Common Core, less then one third had been provided with training or resources to teach to it. As Randi Weingarten, president of the AFT put it, "Though nothing has been spent to prepare teachers the government is spending three hundred, fifty million dollars on new tests aligned with the CCSS."[7]

In December we finally had a long overdue staff union meeting. Newly made the delegate, to the lackluster UFT chapter leader's consternation I announced, "The UFT's *now* in the building!" Like the other disgusted people in the room, I was fed up with the administration. When one person proposed we boycott the phony Christmas staff events like the potluck lunch, and another noted a sign should be put up to make the administration aware, I volunteered to write the declaration; forty-two of us voted in favor of the sign. Later that morning I posted a forceful message, citing demoralization and stress as our reasons for not participating in a pretentious, hypocritical ritual of "family" that could never stand in for respect and appreciation conveyed on a daily basis; I was simply resonating with the imprisoned Chinese poet Liao Yiwu, "I never intended to be a hero, but in a country where insanity ruled I had to take a stand."[8]

Within an hour, not only had the sign been ripped down by one of Rosemary's Baby's goons, the principal herself was in my room observing me informally, giving me the first of countless "U"s and letters to my file that would pile up the rest of the year. My impeccable ten-year history of "Satisfactory" "S" ratings, and recent high grades on observations, indeed, my teaching career itself, was stopped dead in its tracks by Rosemary's Baby's insecure caprice—in a matter of minutes I rocketed to Number One on the Hit Parade. In a flash, her winking effervescence vanished, a crusade beginning to assure me a "U" rating at the end of the year: multiple observations, formal and informal, pre-cooked in a microwave designed to nuke my future and me to oblivion.

Any pretext to attack was greedily seized upon, my overheard, playful comment to the first grade boys who were my best friends—they were "under arrest" when I lined them up—sickly twisted to indict me. The dozen delighted boys were conscripted to write obviously coerced statements uniformly stating they felt "sad," while Rosemary's Baby charged me with "traumatizing" them. Why, then, were they all laughing—one told a staff member "it was funny"—and indeed begged me every time I saw them again, to be "arrested" anew?

When I subbed all day in a fourth grade class, a seven-hour donnybrook marathon which occasionally broke into a class, with *eight* behaviors in it and half of the rest, marginals (with zero help, as ever, from administration) and I told them having to babysit their class made me not want to teach anymore, I got a letter for that. (Meanwhile crony teachers were busy shaming their kids literally to tears, without consequence.)

I was accused of sleeping, though having just thrown up, I had merely put my head down in my empty classroom (Rosemary's Baby indicated she was concerned about my health—I might fall asleep during a class!).

Falling on ice on the way to school gave me a severe limp and an emergency doctor's appointment for a knee injection I was lucky to get before he went on vacation. Rosemary's Baby would not allow me to leave twenty minutes early for it, though another teacher was permitted to leave more than an hour early for her doctor's appointment.

An innocent comment that "soccer is very popular in Africa" was recast as "ethnic discrimination," the student, according to Rosemary's Baby, "devastated." Sent to the DOE in Brooklyn to a hearing over it, the principal vowed to dock my pay, though I had been told to take the day for "official business." The DOE ended up convicting me of the ethnic discrimination charge, the official report incredibly showing that instigator Sanchez, once again, had been behind the kids making statements against me. You can't make this stuff up!

Out having surgery to get my shoulder replaced, from years of carrying heavy art materials up and down stairs, Rosemary's Baby demanded I be examined by a DOE doctor to force me to return to school sooner than my own doctor decreed. The DOE doctor, however, concurred with mine. Rosemary's Baby was insatiable, at this point, she had become mythic: to me she was the Minotaur. Others saw her as a more modern monster, Hannibal Lecter.

In the meantime, you could not help but wonder who was minding the store. Along with the usual chaos of slapdash administration, illegal situations abounded. Disabled students legally necessitating particular classroom setting placements were incorrectly assigned, expediency evidently superseding the letter of the law. When a teacher was absent, inclusion classes required at all times to have both a special ed and general ed teacher were not provided a substitute. At times, students mandated to have one-on-one paras went without them, while teachers reported students with disabilities meant to receive federally-funded services were not necessarily getting them, though the money had been provided; the UFT official in charge said Rosemary's Baby would be named to a union Principals in Need of Improvement list, though that inconsequential label could never make up for a child's loss of education.

Later in the year, the annual legally mandated HIV/AIDS lessons were skipped while Rosemary's Baby did everything but call on David Copperfield to conjure the illusion of "quality" for the network Quality Review. Naturally, we received a crash course in all the things we were supposed to be doing all year, most of which was news to us, in order to save *her* job.

Rosemary's Baby showed unremitting incompetence in budgeting, organization and staffing decisions, while there was

virtually no student discipline (we would suffer from that, not her—
the low suspension stats would make her look good to the DOE) and
scant infrastructure: no librarian, no qualified computer teacher,
insufficient functional computers. Rosemary's Baby was too busy to
manage the school, investing every moment instead in the far more
amusing pursuit of oppressing teachers. This she did in the company
of her henchmen, Gonzalez and Moore, armed with Danielson
checklists of things they could never themselves do; most teachers
were getting "U"s left and right (though naturally and ultimately, the
favored ones did better).

Indeed, Rosemary's Baby, offering to teach a fifth grade whose
teachers were owed a preparation period, famously bombed: when
she failed to instruct the kids on the meaning of idioms, she resorted
to singing/writing a rap song with them, then when that was a bust
she auditioned them for a school talent show which never happened.
It was unclear to us how Rosemary's Baby's instruction contributed
to the catch phrase of the moment, "career and college readiness."
We were not surprised that even as she labeled us "ineffective" she
embodied that principle in spades herself: at a meeting about the new
Common Core curriculum a page had to be explained to her, after
which she exclaimed heartlessly to the worked-to-death teachers,
"That's why *I'm* not a *teacher*!"

Pallas had been taken out of the classroom and put in the office
where she not only made a fine example, in Dracula style, for the rest
of us, but very expensive Xerox copies at eighty thousand dollars a
year, her teacher's salary. Instead of being used to teach, she was
awaiting the trial Rosemary's Baby had initiated to take away her
teaching license, it could take years. Driving others out into early
retirement and pushing several to the brink—they escaped on mental
health leaves—among other consequential mayhem, Rosemary's
Baby destroyed the science program so that expert instruction was
lost and the important state tests were not given by a certified
administrator. Justifying her persecution of our dedicated, veteran
science teacher, the only staff member who spent every vacation in
voluntary professional development, Rosemary's Baby had
exclaimed to another teacher, "Old people can't change!," as blatant

an instance of age discrimination as any prosecutor has had the fortune to possess.

Despite that prejudice, Rosemary's Baby offered equal opportunity suffering to all, the forced absence of so many teachers resulting in the kids being warehoused for hours in mass preps in the auditorium. The students had spent more time than ever this year in that Pixar Purgatory: since Rosemary's Baby had put Gonzalez and another flunky in charge of recess, this year the unhappy kids were only going outside for fresh air, if they were lucky, every other day. As ever, the unmistakable impression given by the principal was of a "leader" not invested in service to the kids as the teachers were, but to herself and the perpetuation of her power: virtually absolute power, in fact, with absolutely no accountability. Our school would make a riveting television reality show, if it were not a tragic farce— one produced by taxpayers.

Systemwide, we had the highest class sizes in fourteen years. Bill Gates, at least, would approve. Like other reformers, he encourages large class sizes as a cost-saving tool, though conveniently not, himself, attempting to do this at home. When we clusters taught the huge two-teacher inclusion classes, Rosemary's Baby used a bureaucratic loophole to deny us a second teacher, and it was excruciating. Normally managed with difficulty even by their own *two* classroom teachers, now their challenging behavior, and far more of it, only magnified once the kids were out of their home territory.

At the same time, Rosemary's Baby had imposed the straitjacket of her one-size-fits-all template on me, requiring art take a back seat to math and ELA: art for its own sake was now dead, and the creativity, spontaneity and joy had been squeezed from my passion. Every art class was to be linked to whatever that grade was doing in those two tested subjects; since this required unprovided time to meet with classroom teachers, this articulation was apparently to be magical. The fairytale theme continued with the endless list of trivial, downright crazy pursuits now forced on us, among them, yet again: differentiation of lessons for different groups of learners, within which each lesson was supposed to be individually crafted for a particular child! The micromanaged, intensive directives for each lesson were so numerous, it would only be possible to fulfill them teaching robotically with a script, while the minutiae required was so byzantine and nonsensical—so many details not having anything to do with art—I was hard pressed to remember them, let alone teach them. Even the forced note-taking in conferencing, data suddenly necessary to prove I was conferencing, something I did naturally as a teacher, proved untenable for me: whenever I attempted it, after a couple minutes I would end up putting my clipboard down, lean over and teach. Oops!

By January, the idea of a petition to get Rosemary's Baby removed was gaining traction among us. Most of us agreed our unbearable working conditions afforded us at best a miserable security, or secure misery. A union official had confirmed rumors Rosemary's Baby had been kicked out of her previous school a few years before, all traces of which had been mysteriously scrubbed from the Internet, yet she had reincarnated, unscathed, as a principal in the system again...hmm. Now, many of us having reached critical mass, in the absence of union leadership, I jumped in to fill the vacuum.

Though the idea of signing was highly controversial considering the guaranteed retaliation, understandable given what had happened to me after Potluckgate, by spring I had written a declaration and hosted a meeting for staff to sign, complete with Rosemary's Baby's secret police attending (all of them in fact known to us, but as union members, the rats had to be invited), one ostensibly recording the entire proceeding. It was a commonplace that virtually all of the staff despised Rosemary's Baby; had they not been afraid to lose their jobs, a certitude given her vengeance, the outcome would be a landslide in our favor. I actually used that pervasive terror as my main argument in exhorting them to sign: the fact you are afraid to sign is why you *must* sign.

But misinformation, drama and intrigue fostered by the resident sycophants conspired to undermine the petition, destroying the momentum and delaying it until the next month. Ultimately, forty-one percent signed. Just six more people would have brought the number to a majority, and the UFT bringing its big guns: officials, speakers, organizers, community outreach experts for parent support, to bear on the situation. As it was, nearly June, the initiative was halted, at least until the next school year. Although the integrity of the brave participants had been inspiring, the hypocrisy the issue exposed in the two-faced invertebrate contingent was shocking, the polarity between good and evil, palpable. When the O'Jays "Back Stabbers" blasted from a car outside, it seemed even the universe was weighing in.

It was beginning to be clear, the only sure result the rigorous new Common Core standards would have would be the increased failure rate on state tests so tough they guaranteed an avalanche of low scores, especially from high-poverty students, those with disabilities and ELLs—our kids. Bloomberg, whose DOE was responsible for not having supplied schools curriculum on which the tests would be based, chose to fault the state education commissioner: "Please don't blame the children," Bloomberg magnanimously declared.[9]

Indeed, by February the DOE had determined because of the difficulty, the bottom ten percent of those failing would be required to attend summer school. But summer school was easier work than the regular year, plus unlike the new tough Common Core test, the summer school test would be multiple choice: the upshot, more promoted Unready into the next grade. But worse, far more than ten percent were forecast to fail, so this signaled a new, unapologetic, unabashed version of social promotion: below grade level, failing kids would be promoted as usual to the next grade, but even more confounded to do the harder Common Core work the next year.

Judging by the simulation administered in early February, the difficulty of the tests had been upped plenty—our kids were at a loss. According to most of us, the fifth grade questions could only be conceivably answered by ninth graders, and even then, only those in higher socioeconomic schools. Of an inclusion class of twenty-eight, only one scored a 2, below grade level (a kid from Bangladesh), while the rest failed with a score of 1. In the class with the highest performers only two kids scored a 3, at grade level, while half a dozen scored a 2—the remaining majority failed. As ever, our students lacked the basic prior knowledge and vocabulary that higher SES kids come to school with every day. Responding to a question asking fourth graders to compare the attitudes of two different authors, one student detailed his mother's negative view of kids with an "attitude."

Another, when confronted with *The Secret Garden*, an arcane 1911 text featuring a dialect with instances of "ere," tha'," and "an'," answered a question with an utterly random commentary on the character's apparent speech problem. A question about the Civil War was a bust as well because it required prior knowledge the kids were supposed to have gotten in fifth grade, but had never been taught. Because the state mandated only one hundred, twenty minutes of social studies a week—and only half of that at best was provided because it was not a tested subject like reading, writing and math—the kids had a paltry dose of it. (Science, another subject supposed to be taught by the classroom teacher as well as the cluster science teacher, was getting the shaft as well, because it did not figure into the "important" tests.)

All this was exacerbated by the fact that kids are still, eleven years after I started, regularly promoted to the next grade while reading a full year below grade level; now the previous low bar for promotion, a 2 on state tests—at its lowest point the equivalent of a D-, F+ grade—had been decreased to accommodate the masses that would score a failing 1. How could this insanity ever foster the latest darling goal of the reform movement, "college/career readiness?"

Meanwhile, the school's totalitarian construct had become almost comically cliched, given the stock fixtures of fascism in force: secret police, false accusations, trumped up charges, arrests, kangaroo courts, mysterious disappearances, and banishments to Siberia (the Rubber Room proved yet alive and well, for some). Indeed, the installation in the office of a giant cult portrait of Rosemary's Baby appeared imminent. It seemed only a matter of time before Orwellian cameras would accessorize a scene replete with inculcation, the kids robotically pledging daily "...I'm smart and uniquely beautiful..." and other affirmatives along with the bizarrely negative, "...I made it through yesterday, I know I can make it through today." The next phase might well be our coerced public confessions in the school yard, genuflecting in dunce caps while loudspeakers blast propaganda.

To complete the oppression, staff members were encouraged to report on each other, at times writing denunciatory statements. According to one source, Rosemary's Baby even had the brass to broadcast loudly she knew who had signed the petition to get her removed. Notwithstanding everything else she had done, this chilled us to the bone, Rosemary's Baby surpassing our quaint, unsophisticated notions of evil: though Rosemary's Baby had embraced *her* inner Joe McCarthy, *we* were not about to name names.

In March, a mere six weeks before the tests, the DOE finally announced new curricula aligned with the new standards. In the absence of leadership from the DOE, the UFT had stepped in with a website "Share My Lesson" where teachers contribute lessons they've aligned to the Common Core.[10] Even with a curriculum finally provided, though, next year's tests would hardly be that much more fair, given the absurdly steep increase in difficulty.

In the meantime, in April our kids went on to take the high-stakes Common Core math and ELA tests they would be unlikely to pass, the stress prompting instances of stomach ache, vomiting, even pooping in their pants. (Seventy percent of city kids would end up failing the Math test, while seventy-four percent failed the ELA.) The situation was simply surreal: that familiar student nightmare which still plagues us decades out of school—of being tested on new material, in a class you did not know you were in—was now the real horror facing millions of kids. Equally grotesque was the fact that teachers ratings, and destinies, would be tied to those farcical scores, in the evaluations Race to the Top had forced on states.

All that had changed since NCLB's mandated "proficiency" was the requirements had been upped, and dizzyingly so. Moreover, in this most recent costly iteration of throwing the education baby out with the bathwater, established investments were to be summarily shown the door. For example, the decades-old mandate from

Teachers College that students read "just right" books would now be anathema, only impossible, inflated texts will be allowed.[11] The constraints of teaching with the Workshop Model, another gift from Teachers College, forced on me even as it did not always apply to my subject (Rosemary's Baby used it to ply me with "U"s), would be jettisoned like so many equally "best practices," into the reform dustbin in the sky. But these mere tips would be nothing relative to the iceberg itself, the sea change impacting all facets of education, including the grievous loss of expertise. As one overwhelmed teacher put it, "They're making us learn completely new content and new teaching strategies. Everyone feels like it's their first year teaching."

Obviously, authentic educational reform is like turning around an aircraft carrier: painstaking, fraught with effort, and delicately incremental; half-baked as it is, the Common Core is at best just another reform shot in the dark, more catchy soundbite than actual progress. This pattern in education policy had struck me initially as well-meaning but stupid; during the course of writing this book, however, I had come to comprehend the paradigm not so much as ridiculous but insidious and destructive, an impression only fortified by the recent mandate. Because the inescapable conclusion is, in fact, the rushed, untested, impossibly rigorous Common Core is just the latest strategy to undermine education, eliminate unions and expose an institution dedicated to the public interest to the pillage of privatization. Belying its beneficent pretense of improving education, the Common Core's hyperfocus on high-stakes testing alone, one that pales next to the NCLB torture, exposes its aim to rigidly determine, through test scores, the fates of students, teachers, schools and districts.

This forced, all-encompassing reversal of the previous decade's pedagogical approach means, of course, an unprecedented bonanza to the predators swooping in with the latest education bibelot—be it curriculum, iPads or online learning—the new standards call for. Notably, the Common Core's nationwide mandate of virtually continuous assessments guarantees an even greater windfall to the senior vulture at the education carcass, a testing industry already bursting at the seams with profits. Not for nothing were the new standards developed with the explicit involvement of corporate testing honchos.

The bungling, monopolistic Pearson test publishing company, of the bizarre pineapple questions in 2012, is not only supplying the expanded official tests but diagnostic tests, pretests, interim tests and simulation tests. As the largest education company in the world, moreover, Pearson's political lobbying has assured its market domination of every school necessity, including test preparation booklets, remediation materials, textbooks, online courses, and every other conceivable education moneymaker, to the tune of billions in annual sales. Never content to leave a profitable stone unturned, Pearson has even taken over the formerly nonprofit-run GED test, as well as teacher licensing tests, charging whatever it likes.

Given the political climate these days, the Common Core's draconian rigor and warp speed implementation is dazzlingly accommodating: the new approach just sets up a cherished neocon and neoliberal target, public schools, for further failure.[12] As the latest malevolent rendition of a specious, pernicious reform designed purposely to enable the mercenary privatization driving every education initiative these days; "college and career readiness" is the operative cover this time around, much as NCLB had touted the elimination of the achievement gap.

Reformers do not even pretend to disguise their glee: at a conclave of business leaders Jeb Bush exuded the increased failure rates would precipitate "a rude awakening" to the nation's schools.[13] I imagine he was rubbing his hands together when he said that—the sweeping changes the Common Core requires represent a renewed extravaganza of exploitation, with stunning business opportunities for him and his fellow reform scavengers.

With its severe ramifications and agreeable alignment with reform ideas, the Common Core blitz coincided this year with an acceleration to breakneck speed of the outsourcing of education to profit-driven corporations. Most state education legislation now is formulated by out-of-state corporations which stand to profit from such wondrously appellated "reform" (reforming their bottom line, that is).[14] Jeb Bush's Foundation for Excellence in Education (FEE), much like ALEC, lobbies governments and districts while raking in dollars from companies such as K12 Inc and Connections Education, pushing for-profit virtual education sans the pesky presence of actual (unionized) teachers. As such, the Common Core presents a no holds barred, one-stop shopping opportunity for the right, the bonus: dismantling the teachers unions.

An entire generation has been lost to NCLB. Now the next would be lost to the suspiciously, senselessly Olympian goals of the Common Core. Incredibly, education is being shaped not by what is best for our kids or the nation, but what returns dividends and profits to investors. To turn venal Joel Klein and Condoleezza Rice's assertion on its head, doesn't this rape of our resources—intellectual, financial, and so much more—in fact, "constitute a very grave national security threat facing this nation?"

That the needs of those serving our children can trump the needs of the children themselves is an indictment, in a nutshell, of the exaltation of greed and its destructive cost to society, a culture reigning supreme since the eighties. Till now, on-board big city mayors have used these reform tactics against the low hanging fruit of high-poverty, low-scoring schools; yet middle class, suburban schools, buttressed with satisfied parents, have proven impervious to the siren of privatization. Add the abrupt, seismic shift of Common Core difficulty, stir in the waste of valuable learning time through constant testing and voilà, down topple the test scores and the last schools to stand in the way of wholesale privatization. As Rome burns, then, at least one of the Bushes may finally justifiably declare "Mission Accomplished."

In the process, the socioeconomic status quo stands firm, the privileged at the top maintaining *their* position: the schools their children attend have a rich curriculum with minimal or no testing, quality teachers, small class sizes and other important resources. Wonder, inquiry and joy pervade this true learning. By contrast, the schools of the rest suffer education malnutrition: relentless, eye-glazing test prep and testing; principals pressured over test scores; narrowed, threadbare curriculum and less well-trained, demoralized teachers scrambling for their job security.

This amounts to a shocking educational inequality, only aggravated by the concurrent decimation of the teaching profession, in which the ever-decreasing few willing to enter the field are being trained differently. One candidate racks up years of excellent training in a traditional university preparation program, while the other is subjected to baptism by fire—thrown into high-needs classrooms unprepared, most destined to leave, like the majority of Teach For America conscripts, within two years.[15]

Thanks to NCLB and the Common Core, in this officially-sanctioned, bifurcated system, rich kids get to enjoy a real education which benefits them now and in the future, while poor kids are simply trained to cough up correct test answers. Moreover, since those tests have been made impossibly difficult to pass, millions will no longer be able to even attain a high school diploma, a scenario which guarantees legions of minimum-wage workers whose numbers will keep that pittance down at slave-wage status. The achievement gap between rich and poor students, then, alarmingly up by fifty percent since 1980 (just as income inequality in general has widened), will be that much more gaping a chasm.[16]

By the end of May, Rosemary's Baby had cooked my inevitable year-end "U" rating to a charred well-done. Called to the office so many times to sign incriminating letters for my file, I proposed erecting a crucifix there for the convenience of all concerned. In the spring I had filed a Special Complaint of Harassment with the union, adding supporting documentation to it up until the end of the year—the issue would be reviewed in the next school year. Of course, given Bloomberg's empowerment of principals, Rosemary's Baby would likely escape any consequence. In the meantime, despite my degrees in art history, design and illustration and professional art experience in and out of the classroom, because of the "U" I would be forbidden an art position next year: kindergarten was to be my next assignment (had I stayed).

Because of her "U," the experienced science teacher had also been placed in a classroom, undoubtedly stocked with difficult kids: the principal's classic James Bond ejector seat for a tenacious teacher. Rosemary's Baby had no qualms about denying the kids the expert science experience the teacher had accrued over years, and in a subject arguably more crucial than any other to our "global competitiveness." As ever, there was no accountability for principals.

Just like the science teacher, notwithstanding my decade of "S" ratings, the one, final scarlet "U" meant transfer impossible—I would never again be allowed to teach in the city system, not even as a substitute. Going to another school district would be virtually impossible, too, with such a bad rating. In its humble history, has a potluck ever had such destructive power?

Meanwhile, for a guy who said at the beginning of his tenure, "You will judge me on education," Bloomberg was not talking at all about education these days, apparently not wanting to remind the public of his hubris.[17] Despite the glory he had hoped to capture as the "Education Mayor," Bloomberg's legacy never got a foothold on that longed-for pedestal. The school system had not been run professionally; in another job he would have been fired.

Among countless other negatives, Bloomberg blew hundreds of millions on consultants and contracts, many of which were at best, wasteful, and at worst, fraudulent; closed one hundred forty-nine schools; gave unbridled encouragement and support to charter schools, at the expense of the rest; ignored community needs and views by co-locating many of them in existing schools, dramatically decreasing the quality of education in the host school; emphasized tests and test scores to the detriment of every worthy facet of education; and arrogantly dismissed parent and teacher input. Yet in a spring press conference, citing the mayoral candidates' collective agreement they would change course on education if elected, Bloomberg asserted "the city has no future" if the next mayor agrees with the UFT on changes.[18]

The good news is, informed, angry people are increasingly choosing to stand up, and in numbers.[19] This year there have been fantastic breakthroughs on the grassroots mobilizing front, tens of thousands coming together on social media as well as the streets. The anti-testing movement has taken off across Texas as well as the country, while specific actions, like teachers in Seattle refusing to administer a test, have received colossal national backing from all manner of professionals and concerned parents.[20] Nationwide, parents are coming together to opt their children out of the state tests, as well as protest the tyranny of the developmentally inappropriate Common Core curriculum.

In Chicago, where teachers successfully struck last fall, and Philadelphia, massive coalitions of teachers, parents, students and community members have solidified to challenge all manner of reform outrage including budget cuts, staff layoffs, school closings and other threats to thriving schools and communities. Those pheisty Philadelphians even launched a hunger strike! Going forward, these two fierce cities provide a brilliant example for the rest of us, uniting and organizing at the grassroots level to fight for this, truly, *human* rights issue of our time, the right to a decent education. We need to coalesce around proven non-negotiables including sufficient funding, universal pre-kindergarten, community schools with wraparound services, quality teacher preparation, a rich curriculum free of high-stakes testing, and the socioeconomic integration of schools. By refusing an apartheid in which the one percent and the ninety-nine percent receive vastly different educations, community by community we will drive back the privatizers, restoring the "public" to a system committed to all.

Hell, yeah.

NOTES

CHAPTER ONE

1. US Government, *No Child Left Behind, Elementary and Secondary Education Act (ESEA)*, Public Law 107-110, Jan. 8, 2002, Washington, D.C., http://www2.ed.gov/policy/elsec/leg/esea02/107-110.pdf.

CHAPTER TWO

1. Moises Velasquez-Manoff, "The Great Divide: Status and Stress," Opinionator blog, July 27, 2013, http://opinionator.blogs.nytimes.com/2013/07/27/status- and-stress/.
2. New York State Department of Education, *New York State Safe Schools Against Violence in Education (SAVE)*, July 24, 2000, Albany, http://www.p12.nysed.gov/sss/ssae/schoolsafety/save/.
3. Michael Bloomberg, *Remarks by Mayor Michael R. Bloomberg Major Address on Education at New York Urban League's Dr. Martin Luther King, Jr. Symposium, January 15th, 2003.*
4. Sarah Garland, "Bloomberg Moves Schools Toward Corporate Model," *New York Sun*, January 19, 2007.
5. Sol Stern, "A Negative Assessment," *Education Next,* Fall, 2005.
6. Paul Kischner et al., "Putting Students on the Path to Learning: The Case For Fully Guided Instruction," *American Educator,* Spring 2012
7. Barbara Feinberg, "The Lucy Caulkins Project: Parsing a Self-Proclaimed Literacy Guru," *Education Next*, Summer, 2007.

8. E. Duursma, et al., "Reading Aloud to Children: The Evidence," *Archives of Disease From Childhood*, July, 2008.

9. National Education Association, "Research Spotlight on Parental Involvement in Education." Patte Barth, "Most Effective Parental Involvement," *American School Board Journal*, Fall, 2011.

10. Angeline Lillard, Jennifer Peterson, *The Immediate Impact of Television on Young Children's Executive Function, Pediatrics,* September, 12, 2011.

CHAPTER THREE

1. Brian Cambourne, "Seven Conditions of Learning" (Video no longer posted.)

2. Paul Kirschner et al., "The Case For Fully Guided Instruction," *American Educator,* Spring, 2012.

3. Sol Stern, "A Negative Assessment," *Education Next*, Fall, 2005.

4. Jonathan Alter, "Howard Dean, Destiny or Disaster?," *Newsweek*, August 11, 2003.

5. Matthew Clavel, "How Not To Teach Math," *City Journal,* March 7, 2003.

6. Raymond Domanico, "Ending Social Promotion, Once Again," *Gotham Gazette*, February 5, 2004.

7. According to UFT President Michael Mulgrew, in comments to a UFT Delegate Assembly, New York, Spring, 2013. See: Diane Ravitch, "Newsflash: Bloomberg Backs Down on Social Promotion," dianeravitch.net, June 3, 2012.

8. Jim Trelease, "Texas Education Miracle: If Money Talks, Is It a Miracle?," trelease-on-reading.com, 2002-2005.

9. Rebecca Leung, "The Texas Miracle," CBSnews.com, February 11, 2009.

CHAPTER FOUR

1. Milton Friedman, "Public Schools: Make Them Private," Cato Institute Briefing Papers, No. 23, June 23, 1995.

2. Robert Greenwald, "Want to See How the Kochs Are Ending Public Education?," MichaelMoore.com, August 15, 2011. See also:

Joanne Barkan, "Got Dough? How Billionaires Rule Our Schools," *Dissent*, Winter, 2011.
3. Diane Ravitch, "What You Need to Know About ALEC," Bridging Differences blog, Alternet.org, May 3, 2012.

CHAPTER FIVE
1. "Hurricane Katrina Kid," posted by MrDelvinj, YouTube, April 16, 2007.
2. David Herszenhorn, "4th Grade Reading Scores in City Schools and Statewide," *New York Times*, May 19, 2005.
3. Matthew Clavel, "Against Everyday Math," *City Journal*, March 7, 2003.
4. National Council of Teachers of Mathematics, *Math Standards and Expectations*.
5. "Teacher Quality," *Education Week*, July 8, 2011. 6. Pasi Sahlberg, "Lessons From Finland," *American Educator*, Summer, 2011.

CHAPTER SIX
1. Daniel T. Willingham, "Can Teachers Increase Students' Self-Control?,"*American Educator*, Summer, 2011.
2. Elissa Gootman and David M. Herszenhorn, "Consultants Draw Fire in Bus Woes," *New York Times*, February 3, 2007.
3. Danny Hakim, "Group May Sue Over Money Owed to Poor New York School Districts," *New York Times,* November 28, 2012.

CHAPTER SEVEN
1. New York City Department of Education, *Progress Reports*, updated June 12, 2013.
2. New York City Department of Education, *School Survey*.
3. New York City Department of Education, *Quality Review*.
4. Bill Tucker, "Smarter Data Systems: The New York City Experience," The Quick and the Ed, March 15, 2010
5. Barack Obama, Father's Day Speech, Apostolic Church of Chicago, June 15, 2008, YouTube, June 15, 2008.
6. Big Brothers Big Sisters Organization.

CHAPTER EIGHT
1. Jennifer Median, "Standards Raised, More Students Fail Tests," *New York Times*, July 28, 2010.
2. National Center For Education Statistics, *NAEP: National Assessment of Educational Progress*.
3. Esme E. Deprez, "Mayoral Control Alone Doesn't Fix Schools, Rutgers Institute Study Finds," October 12, 2010.
4. Diane Ravitch, guest of Valerie Strauss, "Mayoral Control Means Zero Accountability," The Answer Sheet, *Washington Post*, August 4, 2010.
5. Lisa Featherstone, "Report Card: Ending Mayoral Control," *Brooklyn Rail*, April 21, 2012.
6. Steven Greenhouse, "Share of the Work Force in a Union Falls to a 97-Year Low," New York Times, January 23, 2013.
7. Dave Eggers and Ninive Clements Calegari, "The High Cost of Low Teacher Salaries," *New York Times*, Op-Ed page, April 30, 2011.
8. United States Department of Education, Race to the Top Fund.
9. William Mathis, "Research-Based Options for Education Policy Making," National Education Policy Center, September, 2012.
10. Stephanie Simon, "Private Firms Eyeing Profits From U. S. Public Schools," *Reuters,* August 2, 2012.
11. Jim Horn, "The Nation Exposes Obama's Cynical Education Gambit," Schools Matter, May 30, 2009.
 See also: Marion Brady, guest of Valerie Strauss, "Educator: Race to the Top's False Assumptions," The Answer Sheet, *Washington Post*, October 23, 2009.
12. Richard Rothstein,"How To Fix Our Schools," Economic Policy Institute, October 14, 2010. 13. Center for Research on Education Outcomes (CREDO), *Multiple Choice: Charter School Outcomes in 16 States*, June, 2009.
13. Diane Ravitch, "The Myth of Charter Schools," *New York Review of Books*, November 11, 2010.
14. Leonie Haimson, "An Afternoon at Princeton With Arne Duncan," Parents Across America, April 21, 2011.

15. Harold L. Scott, "High Stakes Tests and Student Achievement." National Research Council, Incentives and Test-Based Accountability in Education, National Academy of Sciences, 2011; Valerie Strauss, "Report: Test-Based Incentives Don't Produce Real Student Achievement," The Answer Sheet, *Washington Post,* May 28, 2011.

16. Adam Taylor, "26 Amazing Facts About Finland's Unorthodox Education System," December 14, 2011, *Business Insider.*

17. Michael Honda, "Preserving the American Dream: A Teacher-Turned- Congressman Starts a National Dialogue on Equity," *American Educator*, Spring, 2011.

CHAPTER NINE

1. Diane Ravitch, "Bloomberg's Bogus School Report Cards Destroy Real Progress," *New York Daily News*, Opinion, Sept. 8, 2009.

2. Michael Barbaro, "In a Term Limits Question, Bloomberg Sees 'Disgrace,'" City Room blog, *New York Times*, May 28, 2009; see also Michael Barbaro and David Chen, "Bloomberg's Latest on Terms: 3 For Him, But Only 2 For Everyone Else," *New York Times*, October 25, 2010.

3. Fred Siegel and Sol Stern, "The Bloomberg Bubble Bursts." *Commentary*, March, 2011.

4. Sol Stern, "Can New York Clean Up the Testing Mess?," *City Journal,* Spring, 2010.

5. Jennifer Medina, "Standards Raised, More Students Fail Tests," *New York Times*, July 28, 2010.

6. Educators 4 Excellence, *Principals Matter,* March, 2012.

7. Karin Chenoweth, "Leading For Learning," *American Educator*, Fall, 2012.

8. T. Walker, "Bullying of Teachers Pervasive in Many Schools," *NEA Today*, May 16, 2012. (Check out the hundreds of teacher testimonials in "Comments.")

9. Solution Tree features titles like *Working With Difficult and Resistant Staff* by John and Sheila Eller, February, 2011.

10. Todd Whitaker, *Dealing With Difficult Teachers, Second Edition (Larchmont, New York: Eye on Education, 2002).*

11. Robert Kolker, "A Bronx Science Experiment," *New York,* December 4, 2011.

12. Educators 4 Excellence, *Principals Matter*, March, 2012.

13. Jennifer Medina, "Standards Raised, More Students Fail Tests," *New York Times*, July 28, 2010.

14. Sol Stern, "Bloomberg's Kids Just Aren't Learning: What the Grim NAEP Results Are Telling Us—The Great School Reform That Never Came To Pass," *New York Daily News*, December 9, 2011.

15. Michael Goodwin, "Teachers Hostage To 'Success,'" *New York Post*, May 28, 2011.

16. Fernanda Santos, "College Readiness Is Lacking, City Reports Show," *New York Times,* October 24, 2011.

17. Annenberg Institute, *Is Demography Still Destiny? Neighborhood Demographics and Public High School Students' Readiness for College in New York City*, October, 2012.

18. Harry Siegel, "Citizen Bloomberg - How Our New York Mayor Has Given Us the Business," New Geography, July 22, 2011.

CHAPTER TEN

1. Steven Sawchuk, "Teacher Turnover Affects All Students' Achievement, Study Indicates," Teacher Beat blog, *Education Week*, March 21, 2012.

2. Richard D. Kahlenberg, "Bipartisan, But Unfounded: The Assault on Teachers' Unions, *American Educator*, Winter, 2012. Diane Ravitch, "The Myth of Charter Schools," *New York Review of Books*, November 11, 2010.

3. David A. Stuit, Thomas M. Smith, *Teacher Turnover in Charter Schools*, National Center on School Choice, 2009.

4. Pasi Sahlberg, "Lessons From Finland," The Professional Educator, *American Educator*, Summer, 2011.

5. New York State Department of Education, *Dignity for all Students Act*, July 1, 2012.

6. Joel Klein et al., "How To Fix Our Schools: A Manifesto," *Washington Post*, October 10, 2010.

7. "Teacher Quality," *Education Week*, August 4, 2004, updated July 8, 2011.

8. James S. Coleman, E*quality of Educational Opportunity*, Johns Hopkins University, 1966.

9. Esme E. Deprez, "Mayoral Control Alone Doesn't Fix Schools, Rutgers Institute Finds," October 12, 2010.

10. Sol Stern, "Bloomberg's Kids Just Aren't Learning: What the Grim NAEP Results Are Telling Us—The Great School Reform That Never Came To Pass," *New York Daily News,* December 9, 2011.

11. Fernanda Santos, "News Corp., After Hiring Klein, Buys Technology Partner in a City Schools Project," *New York Times,* November 23, 2010.

12. Leonie Haimson, "The Widening Murdoch Scandal and the Wireless No- Bid Contracts," *Huffington Post,* July 14, 2011.

13. "Michelle Rhee's Big Annoucement," O Network, December 06, 2010.

14. Jack Gillum and Marisol Bello, "When Standardized Test Scores Soared In D.C., Were the Gains Real?," *USA Today*, March 30, 2011.

15. John Thompson, guest of Anthony Cody, "Did Duncan Load the Bullets into Michelle Rhee's Smoking Gun?," Living in Dialogue Blog, *Education Week,* April 16, 2013.

16. John Kugler, "Rhee Bragged About Taping Students' Mouths Shut While She Was a Teach for America 'Teacher,'" *Substance News,* September 22, 2010.

17. Diane Ravitch, "The Cathie Black Emails," DianeRavitch.net, May 2, 2013.

18. NEA Reviews of the Research on Best Practices in Education, *Research Spotlight on Parental Involvement in Education,* National Education Association.

19. New York State Department of Education, *Educational Neglect.*

20. Reality-Based Educator,"Fraud At DOE Involving Outside Consultant, I.B.M. And Verizon," Perdido Street School blog, April 28, 2011. There are so many other examples, they can not be listed

here; a book could be written just about DOE corruption under Bloomberg.

21. Henry Goldman, "Bloomberg Gets Bad Grades From 78% of School Parents, Poll Says," *Bloomberg*, May 11, 2011.

22. Jersey Jazz Man, "Rhee Lawyers Up," Jersey Jazzman blog, January 18, 2013.

23. "The Education of Michelle Rhee," *Frontline*, PBS, January 8, 2013. 24. Michael Winerip, "Amid a Federal Education Inquiry, An Unsettling Sight," *New York Times*, February 26, 2012.

CHAPTER ELEVEN

1. Maisie McAdoo, "The City Can't Get Rid of Teachers?," *UFT New York Teacher,* P. 9, February 2, 2012.

2. Melanie Moran, "Teacher Performance Pay Alone Does Not Raise Student Test Scores," September 21, 2010.

3. Scott Emerick, Erick Hirsch and Barnett Berry, "Conditions For Learning:Teacher Working Conditions as Catalysts For Student Learning," infobrief, ASCD.org, October, 2005.

4. "Did the CFE Lawsuit Fail?," NYC Public School Parents blog, January 28, 2009.

5. Adam Taylor, "26 Amazing Facts About Finland's Unorthodox Education System," *Business Insider,* December 14, 2011.

6. Richard D. Kahlenberg, "High-Flying, High-Poverty Schools,"*American Educator,* Winter, 2012-2013.

7. European Commission, *Education At A Glance 2013*, June, 2013.

8. Sol Stern, "A Negative Assessment," *Education Next*, Fall, 2005.

9. Yoav Gonen, "Special Ed Kids Changing Class," *New York Post,* May 2, 2012.

10. New York City Department of Education, *What Is SESIS?*

11. New York City Department of Education, *Response to Intervention.*

12. "Cheating Allegations on the Rise in New York City Public Schools," School Choice International, August 23, 2011.

13. "Absenteeism Epidemic Hinders Academic Achievement," *American Educator*, September/October 2012.

14. National Education Association, "Research Spotlight on Parental Involvement in Education."

15. Mary Ann Giordano and Anna M. Phillips, "Mayor Hits Nerve in Remarks on Class Sizes and Teachers," December 2, 2011.

16. "The Terminator: PIP+ Observer," New York City Rubber Room Reporter, October 10, 2010.

17. Yoav Gonen, "80% at CUNY Need Remedial Courses," *New York Post*.

18. Philip Nobile, "The Dirty Secret of Regents Cheating Exposed, Part 1," February 7, 2011.

19. "*State of the Union 2012*: Staying in School," President Barack Obama, posted by BarackObama.com, YouTube, January 25, 2012.

20. T. Walker, "How Do High-Performing Nations Evaluate Teachers?," *NEA Today*, March 25, 2013.

21. Andy Waddell, "I'll Never Forget Mr. White: A Teacher's Legacy," *American Educator,* Spring, 2012.

22. Leo Casey, "Teacher Evaluation: Principals, Principles And Power," Edwize.org, March 12, 2012.

23. Megan Slack, "Everything You Need to Know: Waivers, Flexibility, and Reforming No Child Left Behind," remarks by President Barack Obama, February 9, 2012.

24. Philissa Cramer, "City Releases Teacher Data Reports - and a Slew of Caveats," GothamSchools.org, February 24, 2012.

25. Christina Hoag, "Rigoberto Ruelas' Suicide Raises Questions About LA Times Teacher Rankings," *Huffington Post,* September 28, 2010.

26. Diane Ravitch, "How to Demoralize Teachers," Bridging Differences blog, February 28, 2012.

27. Dana Rubinstein, "Bloomberg on public teacher evaluations: Parents Have the Right to Know, and Anyway You Asked For It," *Capital New York*, February 28, 2012.

28. "Poll March 14 2012," Quinnipiac University; "Poll February 8 2012," Quinnipiac University.

29. Joy Resmovits, "Teacher Survey Shows Record Low Job Satisfaction In 2012," *Huffington Post*, February 21, 2013.

30. United Federation of Teachers, *Attrition and Experience of NYC Teachers and Pedagogues*, February, 2010.

31. Valerie Strauss, "In Texas, A Revolt Brews Against Standardized Testing," The Answer Sheet, *Washington Post*, March 23, 2012.

32. Leonie Haimson and Diane Ravitch , "The Education of Michael Bloomberg," *The Nation*, April 17, 2013.

33. Campaign For Children NYC, *Impact Brief: New York City's Diminishing Investment in NYC Children and Working Families*, March 5, 2012.

CHAPTER TWELVE

1. Stephanie Simon, "Private Firms Eyeing Profits From U. S. Public Schools," *Reuters*, August 2, 2012.

2. Organization for Economic Cooperation and Development, *Programme for International Student Assessment* (PISA) 2009 Key Findings.

3. International Study Center, *Progress in International Reading Literacy Study and the Trends in International Math and Science Study*, Lynch School of Education, Boston College.

4. Elise Gould and Hilary Wething, "U.S. Poverty Rates Higher, Safety Net Weaker Than In Peer Countries," Economic Policy Institute, July 24, 2012.

5. Betty Hart and Todd Risley, *The Thirty Million Word Gap*, Rice University, 2004.

6. James J. Heckman, "Schools, Skills and Synapses," Working Paper 14064, National Bureau of Economic Research, June, 2008.

7. Daniel T. Willingham, "Why Does Family Wealth Affect Learning?" *American Educator*, Spring, 2012.

8. Ibid.

9. Center on the Developing Child, "Toxic Stress: The Facts," Harvard University.

10. Nicholas D. Kristof, "A Poverty Solution That Starts With a Hug," *New York Times*, January 7, 2012.

11. Jack P. Shonkoff, M.D., *The Lifelong Effects of Early Childhood Adversity and Toxic Stress, The American Academy of Pediatrics*.

12. Yoav Gonen and David Seifman, "City Glad, State Sad Over HS Grad Rates,"*New York Post*, June 12, 2012.

13. Michael Honda, "Preserving the American Dream: A Teacher-Turned- Congressman Starts a National Dialogue on Equity," *American Educator,* Spring, 2011.

14. James J. Heckman, "Schools, Skills and Synapses," Working Paper 14064, National Bureau of Economic Research, June, 2008.

15. Thomas Sticht, "Getting It Right from the Start: The Case for Early Parenthood Education," *American Educator*, Fall, 2011.

16. James J. Heckman, "The Economics of Inequality: The Value of Early Childhood Education," *American Educator,* Spring, 2011.

17. Richard Kahlenberg, "From All Walks of Life: New Hope for School Integration," *American Educator*, Winter, 2012/2013.

18. Ibid.

19. Tim Walker, "Gallup Poll: Americans Support Teachers, Favor More Education Funding," *NEA Today*, August 22, 2012.

20. Pasi Sahlberg, "Lessons From Finland," The Professional Educator, *American Educator*, Summer, 2011; Pasi Sahlberg, "A Model Lesson: Finland Shows Us What Equal Opportunity Looks Like," *American Educator,* Spring, 2012.

POSTSCRIPT

1. Charlotte Danielson, *The Framework For Teaching Evaluation Instrument, 2013 Edition*, The Danielson Group, Princeton.

2. New York State Education Department, "Commissioner King Releases NYC Teacher and Principal Evaluation Plan," press release, June 1, 2013.

3. Tom Loveless, "The 2012 Brown Center Report on American Education: How Well are Students Learning?" Brookings Institution, February 2012.

4. The National Governors Association, *Implementing the Common Core Standards,* Common Core State Standards Initiative, Washington D.C.

5. Bill Gates, *Prepared Remarks for the National Education Summit on High Schools*, Bill & Melinda Gates Foundation, February 26, 2005.

6. Joel Klein, Condoleezza Rice and Julia Levy, *U.S. Education Reform and* National Security: Independent Task Force Report (New York: The Council on Foreign Relations, 2012)

7. American Federation of Teachers, "AFT's Weingarten Calls for Moratorium on High-Stakes Consequences of Common Core Tests," press release, April 30, 2013.

8. Liao Yiwu and Wenguang Huang, *For a Song and a Hundred Songs: A Poet's Journey through a Chinese Prison* (New York: Houghton Mifflin Harcourt, 2013)

9. As per remarks made by UFT president Michael Mulgrew at a UFT Delegate Assembly, New York, early 2013.

10. http://www.sharemylesson.com/

11. New York State Department of Education, *Grade 1 ELA Domain 4: Early World Civilizations*, EngageNY.org

12. Diane Ravitch, "Why I Cannot Support the Common Core Standards," dianeravitch.net, February 26, 2013.

13. Terry Ryan, "Business Leaders Rally Around Common Core," EdExcellence.net, July 19, 2012.

14. Robert Greenwald, "Want to See How the Kochs Are Ending Public Education?," MichaelMoore.com, August 15, 2011. See also: Joanne Barkan, "Got Dough? How Billionaires Rule Our Schools," *Dissent*, Winter, 2011.

15. Diane Ravitch, as posted by Valerie Strauss, "The Problem With Teach For America," The Answer Sheet, *Washington Post,* February 15, 2011.

16. Sabrina Tavernise, "Education Gap Grows Between Rich and Poor, Studies Say," *New York Times*, February 9, 2012.

17. Lisa Featherstone, "Report Card: Ending Mayoral Control," Brooklyn Rail, April 21, 2012; Fred Siegel and Sol Stern, "The Bloomberg Bubble Bursts," *Commentary*, March, 2011.

18. United Federation of Teachers, "Our Sensitive Mayor," *New York Teacher*, May 30, 2013.

19. Valerie Strauss, "The Revolution is Here," The Answer Sheet, *Washington Post,* May 17, 2013.

20. Sign the *National Resolution on High-Stakes Testing* at TimeOutFromTesting.org.

ADDITIONAL READING

Darling-Hammond, Linda. *The Flat World and Education: How America's Commitment to Equity Will Determine Our Future.* New York: Teachers College Press, 2010.

Kotlowitz, Alex. *There are No Children Here: The Story of Two Boys Growing Up In the Other America.* New York: Anchor Books, 1992.

Kozol, Jonathan. *Fire In the Ashes: Twenty-Five Years Among the Poorest Children in America.* New York: Broadway Books, 2012.

Kozol, Jonathan. *Savage Inequalities: Children in America's Schools.* New York: Broadway Paperbacks, 1991.

Meier, Deborah and George Wood. *Many Children Left Behind: How the No Child Left Behind Act is Damaging Our Children and Our Schools* Boston: Beacon Press, 2004.

Meier, Deborah. *In Schools We Trust: Creating Communities of Learning in an Era of Testing and Standardization.* Boston: Beacon Press, 2002.

Noguera, Pedro. *The Trouble With Black Boys...and Other Reflections on Race, Equity, and the Future of Public Education.* San Francisco: John Wiley & Sons, 2008.

Nogueira, Pedro and Jean Yonemura Wing. *Unfinished Business: Closing the Racial Achievement Gap In Our Schools.* San Francisco: John Wiley & Sons, 2006.

Ravitch, Diane. *Reign of Error: The Hoax of the Privatization Movement and the Danger to America's Public Schools.* New York: Random House, 2013.

Ravitch, Diane. *The Death and Life of the Great American School System.* New York: Basic Books, 2010.

Tough, Paul. *How Children Succeed: Grit, Curiosity, and the Hidden Power of Character.* New York: Houghton Mifflin Harcourt, 2012.

Tough, Paul. *Whatever It Takes: Geoffrey Canada's Quest to Change Harlem and America.* New York: Houghton Mifflin, 2008.

LET YOUR VOICE BE HEARD
JOIN THE GRASSROOTS MOVEMENT TODAY!

SIGN the *National Resolution on High-Stakes Testing* at
TimeOutFromTesting.org/nationalresolution.

JOIN groups, among the many:

BADASS TEACHERS ASSOCIATION
https://www.facebook.com/groups/BadAssTeachers/

BADASS PARENTS ASSOCIATION
https://www.facebook.com/groups/BadassParentsAssociation/

OPT OUT OF THE STATE TEST: The National Movement (local
groups as well)
https://www.facebook.com/groups/unitedoptout

DUMP DUNCAN
https://www.facebook.com/groups/dumpduncan

LACE TO THE TOP
https://www.facebook.com/groups/362783697181185/

PARENTS & TEACHERS AGAINST COMMON CORE
STANDARDS
https://www.facebook.com/groups/PEACCS/

Network For Public Education.org

Parents Across America.org

Class Size Matters.org

Viva Teachers.org

Teachers Plus.org

Educators 4 Excellence.org

Empathy Educates.org

Teachers Letters to Bill Gates.com

Go Public School.com

There are also Facebook and other organizations addressing local education issues, such as Grassroots Education Movement NYC—Google to connect with your local group.

ABOUT THE AUTHOR

A long-time social activist, in 2002 Laurel M. Sturt left a career in fashion design to become an elementary school teacher in a high-poverty community of the Bronx. Laurel is a graduate of The Madeira School and received her Bachelor of Arts in Art History from Vassar College. Subsequently she received an Associate degree from the Fashion Institute of Technology in Design and Illustration, as well as a Master of Arts in Education from City College, New York.

Laurel has a son, with whom she lives in Manhattan.

Davonte's Inferno is her first book.